REDEFINING ROLES

REDEFINING ROLES

The Professional, Faculty, and Graduate Consultant's Guide to Writing Centers

EDITED BY
MEGAN SWIHART JEWELL
JOSEPH CHEATLE

UTAH STATE UNIVERSITY PRESS
Logan

© 2021 by University Press of Colorado

Published by Utah State University Press
An imprint of University Press of Colorado
245 Century Circle, Suite 202
Louisville, Colorado 80027

All rights reserved

 The University Press of Colorado is a proud member of the Association of University Presses.

The University Press of Colorado is a cooperative publishing enterprise supported, in part, by Adams State University, Colorado State University, Fort Lewis College, Metropolitan State University of Denver, Regis University, University of Colorado, University of Northern Colorado, University of Wyoming, Utah State University, and Western Colorado University.

ISBN: 978-1-64642-084-1 (paperback)
ISBN: 978-1-64642-085-8 (ebook)
https://doi.org/10.7330/9781646420858

Library of Congress Cataloging-in-Publication Data

Names: Jewell, Megan Swihart, editor. | Cheatle, Joseph, editor.
Title: Redefining roles : the professional, faculty, and graduate consultant's guide to writing centers / edited by Megan Swihart Jewell, Joseph Cheatle.
Description: Logan : Utah State University Press, [2020] | Includes bibliographical references and index.
Identifiers: LCCN 2021003982 (print) | LCCN 2021003983 (ebook) |
  ISBN 9781646420841 (paperback) | ISBN 9781646420858 (ebook)
Subjects: LCSH: Writing centers. | English language—Rhetoric—Study and teaching (Higher) | Academic writing—Study and teaching (Higher) | Tutors and tutoring—Vocational guidance. | Graduate teaching assistants—Vocational guidance. | English teachers—Vocational guidance.
Classification: LCC PE1404 .R3823 2020 (print) | LCC PE1404 (ebook) | DDC 808/.0420711—dc23
LC record available at https://lccn.loc.gov/2021003982
LC ebook record available at https://lccn.loc.gov/2021003983

The University Press of Colorado gratefully acknowledges the support of Iowa State University toward the publication of this volume.

Cover illustrations by Cat_arch_angel/Shutterstock.

This book is dedicated to the writing center consultants with whom I have worked over the years. This book would not have been possible without their insights.
—Megan

This book is dedicated to the many consultants I have worked with over the years, and to my supportive wife Barbara and son Conor.—Joseph

CONTENTS

Foreword

    Elizabeth H. Boquet   xi

Introduction

    Joseph Cheatle and Megan Swihart Jewell   3

PART 1: FACULTY AND PROFESSIONAL CONSULTANTS

1. Redefining Training for Faculty Tutors: Practical Strategies for Creating Sustainable Professional Development
   Miriam E. Laufer   17

2. Modular Training for Professional Writing Center Consultants
   Fallon N. Allison   31

3. Examining Assumptions about Training and Development for Writing Center Professional Consultants
   Anne Shiell   44

4. Reading between the Lines: Professional Tutor Training with the Stanislavski System for Actors
   Irina Ruppo   58

5. Professional Tutors, Shifting Identities: Narratives from the Center
   Kimberly Fahle Peck, Lisa Nicole Tyson, Amanda Gomez, and Steffani Dambruch   71

6. Teachers versus Tutors: Is There a Place for Faculty Tutors in a University Writing Center?
   Arundhati Sanyal and Kelly A. Shea   86

7. Between Definitions: Negotiating the Role of Professional Writing Consultants Online
   Matthew Sharkey-Smith   101

8. Faculty and Professional Consultants, the Writing Center, and STEM
   Catherine Siemann   111

PART 2: GRADUATE STUDENT CONSULTANTS

9. When Is a Peer Not a Peer? Negotiating Authority and Expertise in Graduate Student Writing Consultations
   Marcus Weakley and Mark Pedretti   125

10. Integrating Graduate Student Consultants: Community Building in Writing Centers through Onboarding and Mentorship
    Genie Giaimo and Joseph Cheatle   139

11. Critical Mentorship in the Writing Center: Teaching Intentional Kindness and Rhetoric of Respect in Staff Education
    Anna Sicari   152

12. Graduate Tutor Professional Development—and Collaborative Leadership—in an Undergraduate Writing Center
    Rebecca Nowacek, Matt Burchanoski, Danielle Clapham, Will Fitzsimmons, Alex Frissell, Lisa Lamson, and Anna Scanlon   165

13. (Graduate) Friends with Benefits: Writing Relationships into the Center
    Elise Dixon and Cassie J. Brownell   179

14. Making the Invisible Visible: Valuing Labor in the Design of an Observation-Based Mentor Program for Graduate Student Writing Tutors
    Alex Wulff   192

15. Investing in Graduate Tutor Training: A Sustained Approach
    Vicki Behrens and Alex Funt   204

16. Disciplinary Ambassadors in the Graduate Writing Center: A Professional Development Framework for Graduate Consultants from Diverse Fields
    Kristin Messuri   216

17. Genre Knowledge and (Cross)Disciplinary Awareness: Preparing Graduate Consultants to Support Proposals
    Elizabeth Festa   229

18. An Inquiry-Based Approach for Customizing Training for Graduate Student Tutors
    Megan Boeshart Burelle and Meagan Thompson   241

Index   253
About the Editors   263
About the Authors   265

FOREWORD

Elizabeth H. Boquet

Writing center scholarship is filled with tiny stories about when and how people found their way to writing center work: Were you an undergraduate whose professor recommended that you become a tutor? Were you a faculty member who had the chance to pick up additional hours in your college's academic resource center? Were you a graduate assistant who was assigned to be a Writing Across the Curriculum (WAC) fellow for reasons that were never entirely clear to you? Or do you consider yourself, as I consider myself, to have many starting points in your history with writing centers, moments when you connected again and reconnected, in new and different ways, to this important work. For me, one starting point involves my work as an undergraduate peer tutor; another, as a professional staff member in a college access program; still another as a graduate assistant who committed once and for all (by way of a dissertation topic that made pretty much any other academic path unlikely) to a career in writing centers.

In this collection, Megan and Joseph, along with their contributors, make the case that our field is limited by the overrepresentation of staff education resources and conversations focused on undergraduate peer consultants and, correspondingly, that we have not paid sufficient attention to the staff development needs of professional, faculty, and graduate consultants in writing centers. They make a solid case. In my own writing center work, I know how much I rely on the professional and graduate consultants and how little I prepare them for those essential roles. In my own scholarship on writing centers, I have been relatively quiet on the importance of our professional and graduate consultants to our various operations. I have elided my own histories as a graduate and professional consultant in favor of an origin story that highlights my undergraduate peer tutor identity.

As I read the chapters in this collection, I am increasingly conscious of the degree to which my own research has contributed to the positioning of undergraduate peer consultants as the primary beneficiaries of staff education or at least to the presumption that graduate students and professional consultants do not have sufficiently distinct needs to warrant their own consideration in staff development materials. I am grateful to have an opportunity to revisit the full sweep of my personal history in writing centers and pleased to play a small part in the broadening of the scholarship on staff education and professional development, writ large.

If the history of writing centers began and ended with undergraduate peer consultants working with undergraduate writers, it would be a short history indeed. Faculty, professional consultants, and graduate assistants provided the vast majority of instructional support in writing labs and clinics from their very beginnings, and (spoiler alert) they never went away. While the rise of undergraduate peer consultants (beginning in the 1970s) enlarged the pool of potential writing assistants and changed the dynamics of writing assistance available at colleges and universities, writing centers have remained places where writers are met at their points of need by networks of support. Those writers have come from all corners of their communities, their schools, their colleges, and their universities. Professional, faculty, and graduate consultants have always been and continue to be central figures in writing center work, and resource guides such as this one are an important element of the history, the present, and the future of this field.

Writing center resources for staff development have often been at-the-point-of-need documents. When I began researching writing center history for the dissertation that planted my feet firmly in writing center soil, I tracked down mimeographed sheets of staff-meeting agendas, photocopies of early *Writing Lab Newsletter*, still stapled together in the upper left-hand corner, business-meeting minutes from national meetings and proceedings from regional conferences, accessed on nearly obsolete microfiche machines. The field's early publishing was driven by what writing center staff needed to know to work with writers, by what writing centers needed to do and be to fulfill their promise. Resource development pushed the field forward. It still does.

Resource manuals for staff education, then, are important artifacts: they identify gaps, tell us something about where the field has been, and shape where the field is going. Megan, Joseph, and this collection's contributors continue in that tradition, addressing a critical gap in the field's resources and one that will advance the scholarship in this area. I thank them for connecting and reconnecting me to this work and for including me in this pedagogical turn.

REDEFINING ROLES

INTRODUCTION

Joseph Cheatle and Megan Swihart Jewell

The essays in this collection address the complexities involved in tutoring arrangements that do not fit neatly into the traditional undergraduate peer-to-peer model, which has been the primary focus in most training literature for writing center consultants. While building upon this established body of undergraduate consultant training resources, we hope to incorporate within the conversation training issues involving professional, faculty, and graduate consultants. We use the term "professional" to refer to writing center consultants who are not primarily teaching and who are not enrolled as graduate or undergraduate students; we consider professional consultants, as opposed to faculty, as those hired to work exclusively (or near exclusively) in the writing center. We use the term "faculty" to describe consultants whose primary responsibility is teaching and only work in writing centers as a secondary responsibility. And we use the term "graduate" consultants to refer to both those that are normally graduate assistants whose main instructional responsibility is to work in writing centers and those whose wages are not necessarily attached to an academic stipend, but who are enrolled in a graduate program. For our purposes, we have grouped the chapters on faculty and professional consultants together because, for the most part, they encounter similar dynamics in writing centers.

Our title, "Redefining Roles," is intended to open up a dialogue that accounts for and involves all levels of writing consultant training while more accurately reflecting the long-standing realities of center staffing. As Elizabeth Boquet notes in the foreword, many writing centers started out as faculty- or graduate-staffed centers. And, according to the 2016–17 report of the Writing Center Research Project at Purdue University, writing centers continue to be staffed by these populations in significant numbers. Of the 270 writing centers polled, 129 writing centers (47.8%), indicated that they employed graduate consultants, while 17.4 percent indicated they employed faculty consultants, and 29.3 percent indicated they employed professional consultants (Writing Centers Research Project Survey n.d.). These numbers not only show that writing center consultants are composed of graduate, faculty, and other professionals, but they also reveal that nonundergraduate consultants make up a significant percentage of those who work in writing centers. The assumption in the lack of published training materials specifically written for nonundergraduate consultants is that this population, particularly those experienced in classroom teaching, do not need writing center–specific training: after all, they've instructed in classrooms, hold degrees, and therefore implicitly know how to consult. Yet, the essays in this collection illustrate the various ways that not only do such assumptions fail to account for the complex demands of individualized writing center instruction, but they also serve to weaken the strides taken over the past forty or more years to validate the intellectual work we undertake as writing center professionals working in challenging academic contexts. Our collection serves to make visible these consultants' efforts, to continue rescuing writing centers from the scholarly and institutional obscurity of error correction, itself a myth built upon a faulty and elitist premise, and to recognize the higher-order intellectual labor that we have long performed.

While we address how institutional status mediates one's writing center practices, the roles that consultants adopt from session to session are continually being redefined as part of the very nature of the position. In writing centers in particular, the roles continuously shift—and, indeed, institutional status adds another layer to an already complex instructional environment. Jackie Grutsch McKinney's (2013) book, *Peripheral Visions for Writing Centers*, is instructive here: McKinney charts the complex demands of writing center positions in terms of intellectual and emotional labor, noting the ever-changing higher-order, lower-order, intellectual, and emotional work required of consultants and directors (2013). On any given day, for example, she points out, an administrator or consultant may need to switch gears between answering questions about commas for a novice writer, to delivering instructional content to a large classroom of students, to tackling a higher-level organizational issue in a graduate-level thesis. In addition, writing center administrators and consultants, often composed of contingent faculty, must more than many other university employees deal with fluctuating work conditions, such as changes in offices and other scheduling or teaching demands unique to a more institutionally vulnerable staff. The importance of our collection lies in the fact that we are addressing and—most important—validating the complex and nuanced work that a significant number of writing center consultants perform while also acknowledging the ways in which institutional status mediates one's responses to the challenges of writing center positions.

The impetus for this collection began more than fourteen years ago, when Megan began directing a writing center staffed mainly by writing faculty who were teaching first- and second-year writing courses across the university while working in the center as part of their overall instructional load. Early on, she began searching for resources on how to negotiate the complex interactions regarding teaching versus tutoring roles that accompanied this staffing arrangement. While the writing center that Megan directed was also staffed by humanities graduate students, mostly from the English Department, and while it later grew to include undergraduate peer consultants from all campus majors, most of its staff included PhD-holding instructors with years of classroom experience. Yet, as would be expected, even though many of the faculty had years of experience with the tutorial model of meeting one-on-one with students, a startling number of them had no formal writing center experience. At first, this lack of writing center experience among faculty consultants did not seem like a major area of concern: After all, these were well-credentialed scholars that the university was fortunate to have staffing its writing centers. Yet, while they proved to be skilled consultants, Megan found that addressing the complex needs of faculty in the specific context of a writing center was a challenge that required many forms of impromptu problem-solving and de facto policy-making. In terms of problem-solving, Megan, along with the faculty consultants, had to negotiate additional issues that, more or less, had to do with both a consultant's institutional status as well as the expectation that only undergraduates (primarily eighteen- to twenty-two-year-olds) staff centers. Some examples include

- What to do when a student comes in with a poorly written writing prompt written by a faculty colleague
- What to do when your own student books multiple appointments with you regarding your paper assignment
- What to do when more of your students have access to your writing center hours than others
- How to put students at ease who arrive at the writing center expecting a (younger) peer consultant and not a faculty member
- What to do when you see an undergraduate tutor being overly directive while working with a student
- What to do when you see a graduate student tutor incorrectly describing the role of the writing center to a student

These are only a few of the issues that are faced in many writing centers composed of a diverse body of consultants working in diverse fields in a challenging academic job market context; and center practices certainly have evolved thanks to the willingness of staff to engage in a collaborative approach to thoughtfully considering these issues. They have, over the years, worked through the tangled issues and ever-present specter of institutional authority, administrative demands, curriculum changes, and varying forms of oversight and assessment that are often, for faculty, at the center of such complex dynamics. They have learned to negotiate within the various level of student-teacher authority accompanying *all* levels of consultants, from professionals and faculty to graduate and undergraduate students. And, finally, they have learned through trial and error the various ways in which they can use the multiple roles to best work with our campus writers—they have learned, and continue to learn, how to best redefine their roles.

Early on, Megan also discovered that training new consultants was a process of trial and error and thus began to see the need for writing center resources geared specifically toward such a mixed population of consultants. There are several reasons for this gap in the training literature. As mentioned, primary is the assumption that professional, faculty, and graduate student consultants are more experienced and need less training in their one-on-one work with students. Yet, our research and experiences as mentioned above—as well as the accounts from several of the authors included in this collection—show that this could not be further from the truth. Further, most writing center training manuals are rhetorically cast toward undergraduate peer consultants and do not necessarily address the particular dynamics of other types of consultants. Indeed, the emphasis on undergraduate peer tutoring in training manuals, including the challenges undergraduate peer consultants face and the reciprocal benefits they receive, has served to elide the presence of a distinctly different instructional dynamic encountered by professional, faculty, and graduate student consultants. At the time, in order to compose training materials that acknowledged such authority issues in her writing center, Megan gathered together materials that offered context-specific advice in the Case Western Reserve University Writing Resource Center while simultaneously drawing from the well-established and incredibly useful handbooks already on the market, such as Leigh Ryan and Lisa Zimmerelli's (2016) *Bedford Guide for Writing Tutors*; Christina Murphy and Steve Sherwood's (2011) *The St. Martin's Sourcebook for Writing Tutors*; Shanti Bruce and Ben Rafoth's (2009) *ESL Writers: A Guide for Writing Center Tutors*; and various foundational essays by writing center scholars such as Muriel Harris on recognizing the various roles a tutor plays, and by Andrea Lunsford on negotiating a writing center session.

While Megan still employs these materials, she also had to compose supplemental training materials for faculty and graduate consultants that address frequent nonundergraduate peer topics, like the fact that they are often older, teach their own classes, and occupy institutional leadership roles. Additionally, she queried and drew from The WCenter listerv, seeing it as an important "go-to" resource, making use of the collective knowledge of other writing center practitioners.

Joseph joined this project when he was hired to teach at Megan's institution while also serving as a faculty consultant in the writing center. During his two years working in the center, he became increasingly interested in how professional consultants occupy a unique institutional space on campus as well as a unique space in the field of writing center studies. He also noticed many of the same complex interactions between various groups of consultants that Megan experienced. Together, we published an article in *WLN: A Journal of Writing Center Scholarship* titled "Toward a Professional Consultant's Handbook: Researching Support and Training Methods" (Jewell and Cheatle 2016). In this work, we argue that professional consultants (in this case defined as nonundergraduate and graduate consultants) are often overlooked in training manuals because there is an assumption that they need less training than do undergraduate and graduate consultants. We identified a few key areas for professional consultants that need to be examined, including the tension of collaborator versus teacher, working with current and former students, maintaining professional boundaries with faculty in other disciplines, working with graduate students, working with faculty in a formal session, and professional development. We ended by citing the need for a guidebook, such as this, for consultants that are not necessarily undergraduate students.

While completing this initial study and publication for *WLN*, we also became interested in other consultants with unique situations, for example, faculty and graduate student consultants, that are not explicitly addressed in the peer tutor-training manuals that are most frequently directed toward undergraduate students. We see differences in these populations (professional, faculty, and graduate consultants) from undergraduate consultants in the areas of training, authority during consultations, mentoring, and professional development. Because of these issues, we believe that the time has come for a guide that not only draws upon these foundational texts but also recognizes the complex dynamics of nonpeer writing tutoring. The chapters we present here illustrate a fundamental first step in that process, and we are confident that they will generate even more conversations regarding writing centers in the coming years. In addition, our collection may be useful for centers employing undergraduate consultants because it attends to the important dynamics between different types of consultants. We have included eighteen chapters representing public and private, large and small, and four- and two-year US and one international institution; furthermore, authors include administrators, faculty consultants, professional consultants, and graduate consultants.

FACULTY AND PROFESSIONAL CONSULTANTS

As was previously noted, chapters on faculty and professional consultants have been combined in this part because of the significant overlap regarding issues encountered between these two populations. Chapters in this part were written by a diverse group of authors representing large and small institutions, public and private schools, four-year institutions and community colleges, online and in-person centers; chapters also cover a wide variety of subjects relevant to professional and faculty consultants. And while the chapters cover a wide range of topics, they broadly encompass training and the unique issues facing professional and faculty consultants.

Faculty and Professional Consultant Training

Four chapters provide training ideas and plans for faculty and professional consultants. In "Redefining Training for Faculty Tutors," chapter 1, Miriam E. Laufer explores the common misconception that faculty tutors need less training than peer tutors or even no training at all, an idea that is emphasized throughout chapters in this essay regarding nonpeer consultants. Drawing on her experience training faculty consultants at a community college, Laufer points out the areas of peer tutoring that may be applicable for faculty members while noting that specialized training for faculty consultants can leverage the existing knowledge of faculty consultants to create a professional learning community. In "Modular Training for Professional Writing Center Consultants," chapter 2, Fallon N. Allison uses her experience as a director of a community college writing center to design a series of online modules for training professional consultants. Because time and resources are an issue for professional consultant training, Allison uses online training to deploy and organize training modules based on the needs of the consultants. Through this process, Allison helps professional consultants enter the discourse community of the writing center while navigating the logistical hurdles that face administrators who want to provide training for professional consultants. Anne Shiell, in chapter 3, "Examining Assumptions about Training and Development for Writing Center Professional Consultants," challenges the assumption that professional consultants don't need training. Like Allison, she created modular trainings that are flexible and address the changing needs of professional consultants at her online writing center. As she notes, institutional human resources onboarding is often insufficient for writing centers; therefore, her additional training focuses on helping introduce professional consultants to the institutional knowledge of the center. This training, according to Shiell, results in increased staff engagement and retention. Chapter 4, Irina Ruppo's "Reading between the Lines: Professional Tutor Training with the Stanislavski System for Actors," provides an international perspective on writing centers. Managing a center in Ireland, Ruppo draws on the work of Constantin Stanislavski (the renowned theater practitioner) to create a series of training exercises for consultants designed to encourage empathetic engagement with texts and negotiating graduate/undergraduate authority issues during consultations; her essay engages current theories on directive tutoring and can be used in various training situations. Together, these four chapters provide a number of approaches to training professional and faculty consultants that can be used by other centers or can be used to inform other writing centers' practices. And while specific chapters may focus on faculty or professional consultants, we believe that the training models and ideas function for both groups of consultants and represent worthwhile avenues for exploration.

Faculty and Professional Consultant Identities, Roles, and Authority

Four chapters address the identities, roles, and authority of faculty and professional consultants in writing centers and within institutional contexts. Chapter 5, Kimberly Fahle Peck et al.'s "Professional Tutors, Shifting Identities: Narratives from the Center," provides first-person narrative accounts of the personal lives of professional tutors. Fahle Peck et al. focus on the plural careerist identities of professional consultants and how those careers inform each other; they look at what skills each bring from previous (or other) careers as well as how these other careers inform their identities as professional consultants. Arundhati Sanyal and Kelly A. Shea, in chapter 6, "Teachers vs. Tutors: Is There a Place for Faculty Tutors in a University Writing Center," examine the difficulties faculty face when taking on the persona of a tutor. Through a survey of faculty consultants representing a range of academic ranks and disciplines, Sanyal and Shea determined that faculty consultants view themselves as distinct and different from peer consultants. Drawing on these surveys, Sanyal and Shea found that faculty consultants must negotiate their role with students during consultations while resisting the expectation of authority. Matthew Sharkey-Smith's chapter 7, "Between Definitions: Negotiating the Role of Professional Writing Consultants Online," provides valuable insight into what he depicts as the liminal institutional status of professional consultants who are, indeed, inseparable from their status. He discusses his own experiences and advocates a perspective whereby professional consultants' dual statuses are "sites of opportunities" while sharing his experiences in an online consulting model. Finally, Catherine Siemann's "Faculty and Professional Tutors, the Writing Center, and STEM," chapter 8, addresses professional and faculty consultants working at primarily science, technology, engineering, and mathematics (STEM) institutions. Siemann advocates that professional and faculty consultants serve as "expert outsiders" during consultations in order to leverage their extensive—often classroom—experience. She further draws on Andrea Lunsford's notion of the Burkean Parlor to emphasize shared power and control as well as collaboration. As Siemann notes, this model functions particularly well at STEM institutions because it is difficult to recruit peer tutors. By addressing different identities, roles, and authority for professional and faculty consultants, these chapters are relevant to administrators and other consultants alike because they underscore the lived experiences of professional and faculty consultants performing labor in writing centers; furthermore, the voices of such consultants strongly illuminate the critical issues regarding the writing center work that they address.

GRADUATE STUDENT CONSULTANTS

In the part on graduate consultants, there are ten chapters by both current graduate consultants, former graduate consultants, and administrators who work with graduate consultants. These chapters fall into four broad categories: training, authority during consultations, mentoring, and professional development. While the topics could apply to undergraduate, professional, or faculty consultants, they are geared specifically to graduate consultants and, as such, represent concerns that may be unique for them.

Authority

Two chapters focus primarily on graduate consultant authority during consultations. Marcus Weakley and Mark Pedretti's chapter, "When Is a Peer Not a Peer? Negotiating Authority and Expertise in Graduate Student Writing Consultations," chapter 9, examines the power dynamics that occur between graduate consultants and graduate clients. While looking at a writing center at a graduate-only university, Claremont, in Southern California, the authors focus on the importance of content knowledge, versus general knowledge, in consultations between graduate students. They also discuss different types of trainings and strategies to address this issue of content disparity. Another work that focuses on authority between graduate consultants and graduate clients is Elise Dixon and Cassie Brownell's work "(Graduate) Friends with Benefits: Writing Relationships into the Center," chapter 13. Their work examines standing appointments, specifically the experiences of standing appointments between Dixon (the consultant) and Cassie (the client). As Dixon and Brownell point out, there are some in writing center studies who believe standing appointments run counterintuitively to the grand narrative that writing centers are there to help the writer, not just the writing; and, as such, there is a concern that standing appointments could become a crutch for clients who rely too much on one specific tutor. The authors argue that these standing appointments, rather than function as something negative, can help support a sustainable relationship and promote growth for graduate clients working with graduate consultants. In tracing their own unique experiences, Dixon and Brownell argue that standing appointments can result in co-mentoring, networking, and a sustained relationship that goes beyond the center.

Training

Four works included in this collection focus on training for graduate consultants. Elizabeth Festa, in "Genre Knowledge and (Cross)Disciplinary Awareness: Preparing Graduate Consultants to Support Proposals," chapter 17, explores how to best support graduate students writing proposals across a wide variety of disciplines at Rice University's writing center. Festa engages in the specialist-versus-generalist consultant debate, advocating for teaching graduate consultants the specific genre of proposal writing. In order to develop training modules for the National Science Foundation (NSF) Graduate Fellowship program, they collaborated with the institution's Graduate and Postdoctoral Studies Office. This training ensured that all graduate consultants could work on proposals, specifically those from the NSF Graduate Fellowship program. Megan Boeshart Burelle and Meagan Thompson, in "An Inquiry-Based Approach for Customizing Training for Graduate Student Tutors," chapter 18, reimagine graduate consultant training at their writing center that is staffed only by graduate consultants. Using an inquiry-based approach, they developed a set of heuristic questions that help position administrators to prepare graduate consultants to negotiate their role as consultants in the center, teach consulting practices, and encourage collaboration. Vicki Behrens and Alex Funt, in "Investing in Graduate Tutor Training: A Sustained Approach," chapter 15, trace the development of a training plan for graduate consultants at the University of North Carolina at Chapel Hill Writing Center. Because it is more comprehensive than an orientation or a workshop, and continues throughout the academic year, they term this training "onboarding." This onboarding focuses on feedback and reflection, graduate consultant involvement in administration, and building community to create a more engaged staff. Graduate consultants, termed "coaches," have a wide array of activities (e.g., peer coaching, feedback, and reflection) to help integrate them into the center and create a sense of community. Similar to Behrens and Funt, Joseph Cheatle and Genie Giaimo view training as onboarding because it is ongoing throughout the academic year. Their work, "Integrating Graduate Student Consultants: Community Building in Writing Centers through Onboarding and Mentorship," find that brief presemester orientations are not sufficient to create a positive and effective workplace culture. Rather, through a yearlong onboarding process, they examine how onboarding can be more engaging while welcoming graduate consultants into the professional writing center community.

Professional Development

Two works focus on professional development for graduate consultants. Kristin Messuri, in "Graduate Writing Center: A Professional Development Framework for Graduate Consultants from Diverse Fields," chapter 16, reconceptualizes the generalist-versus-specialist debate for graduate consultants at the Texas Tech University Writing Center to promote professional development. Messuri positions the specialist knowledge of individual graduate students as a benefit for the center; graduate consultants leverage their home disciplines to explain disciplinary conventions to other graduate consultants as well as create rhetorical reading guides for training. Establishing graduate students as "experts" in their own discourses provides them professionalization opportunities as they introduce their discipline's values, writing, and pedagogy. This work also serves to introduce graduate consultants to the field of writing center studies as they become disciplinary ambassadors for the center. Meanwhile, Rebecca Nowacek, Matt Burchanoski, Danielle Clapham, Will Fitzsimmons, Alex Frissell, Lisa Lamson, and Anna Scanlon's work "Graduate Tutor Professional Development—and Leadership—in an Undergraduate Writing Center," chapter 12, provides a program for professional development drawn from Marquette University's Ott Memorial Writing Center. The authors highlight the importance of introducing graduate students to the center and collaborative project opportunities. The result of their program is that graduate consultants feel welcomed into the community of writing center practice while helping to sustain the culture of the center.

Mentoring

Three works explore mentoring, a high-impact practice in higher education, for graduate consultants in writing centers. Joseph Cheatle and Genie Giaimo, in "Integrating Graduate Student Consultants: Community Building in Writing Centers through Onboarding and Mentorship," chapter 10, examine a peer-mentoring program for graduate consultants. This mentoring model is needed, they argue, because graduate students have different training than undergraduate students; undergraduate students often take a required course or extended training that is not always required of graduate students. As Cheatle and Giaimo demonstrate, there are positive outcomes for both mentors and mentees, and because graduate students come from various disciplines and departments, a mentoring program can be an effective way to create an inclusive environment and community. Anna Sicari, in chapter 11, "Critical Mentorship in the Writing Center: Teaching Intentional Kindness and Rhetoric of Respect in Staff Education," argues for the important role writing centers play in the academic experience of graduate consultants. Sicari writes that administrators should be mentoring graduate consultants in intentional kindness and the rhetoric of respect. Through this type of mentoring, modeling, and teaching, Sicari focuses on the human aspect of the center and the people working in it. Last, Alex Wulff's "Making the Invisible Visible: Valuing Labor in the Design of an Observation-Based Mentor Program for Graduate Student Writing Tutors," chapter 14, discusses the creation of a mentoring program, including observations and assessment rubrics for that program. He also argues for the importance of making labor visible in writing centers, specifically for graduate consultants, that compensates them for the work they provide through activities like mentoring.

Taken together, the two parts of our handbook addressing nonpeer consultants work not only to identify various groups of consultants, but to illustrate the rich interactions happening every day in US writing centers and abroad. Indeed, we hope that by sharing the voices of those involved in professional, faculty, and graduate staffed centers, we can both (a) broaden the idea of a writing center as an undergraduate-for-undergraduate center and (b) underscore the critical problem-solving that takes place, often "on-the-spot," among staff in any given session. Further, we hope to shed light on the many situations encountered daily by writing center administrators working in multistaffed centers, from assisting consultants navigating interpersonal dynamics in sessions, to conducting staff meetings and trainings to address all staffing concerns, to representing the expertise of *all* consultants to their campus communities, including to those responsible for funding. Our collection makes clear how many writing center professionals engage daily in complex, critical work and, we hope, opens the door to more dialogue on the roles our consultants play. We see our Redefining of the roles as the first important step in acknowledging the dynamics of nonpeer tutoring, and we certainly hope that it is not the last.

REFERENCES

Bruce, Shanti, and Ben Rafoth, eds. 2009. *ESL Writers: A Guide for Writing Center Tutors.* Plymouth, NH: Boynton/Cook Publishers.

Jewell, Megan, and Joseph Cheatle. 2016. "Toward a Professional Consultant's Handbook: Researching Support and Training Methods." *WLN: A Journal of Writing Center Scholarship* 41 (3–4): 10–17.

McKinney, Jackie Grutsch. 2013. *Peripheral Visions for Writing Centers.* Logan: Utah State University Press.

Murphy, Christina, and Steve Sherwood. 2011. *The St. Martin's Sourcebook for Writing Tutors.* Boston, MA: Bedford / St. Martin's.

Ryan, Leigh, and Lisa Zimmerelli. 2016. *Bedford Guide for Writing Tutors.* Boston: Bedford / St. Martin's.

"Writing Centers Research Project Survey." n.d. Purdue Online Writing Lab. https://owl.purdue.edu/research/usability/owl_uxd_research.html.

PART 1

Faculty and Professional Consultants

1
REDEFINING TRAINING FOR FACULTY TUTORS
Practical Strategies for Creating Sustainable Professional Development

Miriam E. Laufer

The comparative lack of available materials for faculty tutor training in the writing center field suggests that faculty are less in need of such training. Steven Strang brought the dearth of training materials to the writing center community's attention in 2006, as did Megan Jewell and Joseph Cheatle when they put out their call for a professional and faculty consultant's handbook in 2016 (Jewell and Cheatle 2016; Strang 2006). Throughout the intervening ten years and currently as noted by subsequent authors in this collection, there has remained an impression in the field, and among the wider higher education community, that faculty tutors need less training than peer tutors or even none at all (Jewell and Cheatle 2016; McKinney 2013; Sanyal and Shea, chapter 6; Shiell, chapter 3). Jill Gladstein and Brandon Fralix's "National Census of Writing" in 2014 supports this widespread impression, revealing that though 99.9 percent of peer tutors in writing centers across the nation received training, 32 percent of writing faculty tutors did not receive any training at all (Gladstein and Fralix 2013). However, the long-standing presence of faculty tutors at several institutions, including mine and many of the authors in this book, requires training materials suited for them. Although, as Jewell and Cheatle discovered, faculty do not have the same training needs as peer tutors, I have found that faculty tutors have different gaps in tutoring pedagogy and, furthermore, different and even more compelling motivations to participate in a professional learning community. The objective of this chapter is to share sustainable professional development strategies for the many institutions that have faculty tutors, but either, like Seton Hall University, as noted in chapter 6 by Arundhati Sanyal and Kelly A. Shea in this collection, do not yet have trainings in place, or who are looking for additional professional development content.

DOI: 10.7330/9781646420858.c001

As noted by Sanyal and Shea, as well as Anne Shiell (chapter 3), the primary differences between peer and faculty tutors arise in terms of education, professionalism, time constraints, and funding. Faculty tutors are experts in their field who may have decades of experience in teaching, tutoring, or both. For example, at the community college writing center I managed, we had faculty who had tutored for five, ten, or fifteen years, in addition to teaching classes. We also had faculty who were brand new to tutoring but had taught classes for decades. The professional development training I created had to take all these variations and considerations into account.

Furthermore, a significant difference between faculty and peer tutors is that the tutors were not my students, but my professional peers. I had just as much to learn from them as they did from me. Therefore, over the past four years of trainings, several faculty tutors have suggested or led training, and I've adjusted the structure of trainings based on their feedback. Our collective efforts, somewhat intentionally, somewhat accidentally, resulted in an ongoing professional learning community, exemplifying Kenneth Burke's "unending conversation," which has been enriching for me personally, and according to their comments, for at least some of our ten to fifteen faculty tutors (Burke 1973). Conversations during training on linguistic diversity, pronoun usage, working with students with disabilities or anxiety and English language learners, continued in person during tutor downtime and via our tutor Blackboard community. These conversations empowered us as a group to become more thoughtful and intentional with effective tutoring practices appropriate to the professional level of faculty.

I would like to share how and why I created our training for faculty tutors and, consequentially, our professional learning community, which has benefited us so much, so that other centers can replicate or adjust some or all of these concepts and strategies for their own benefit in the particular context of their own centers and tutors.

FACULTY TUTOR TRAINING IS NOT PEER TUTOR TRAINING

Due to their educational credentials and professional experience, faculty tutors do not require the same training as peer tutors. However, teaching and tutoring are distinct roles (Harris 1995; Moneyhun and Hanlon-Baker 2012). As was the case at our center, some faculty have been tutoring for many years while others are newer, and everyone's awareness of writing center pedagogy is different. The faculty tutors' primary position was as faculty members and few spent more than, say, two hours a week in the center while classes were in session. Even English department faculty are not necessarily familiar with writing center or tutoring pedagogies, which emphasize different goals and outcomes from classroom teaching or professor feedback to students (Shiell, chapter 3). Into this gap, existing writing center literature and tutor guides, though primarily structured for peer tutors, became useful for us.

Two mainstays of writing center pedagogy, Stephen North's "The Idea of the Writing Center" and Leigh Ryan and Lisa Zimmerelli's *The Bedford Guide for Writing Tutors*, served us well in introducing or emphasizing the concept of "giving the writer control of the paper" (North 1984; Ryan and Zimmerelli 2016). Although this is a basic concept taught as gospel to peer tutors, it requires a different approach with faculty tutors. For faculty members who have been teaching, but not tutoring, for years, "giving the writer control of the paper," as traditionally practiced in North's model and outlined in Ryan and Zimmerelli, can be a foreign idea. Faculty members are used to grading papers silently by hand or on their computers, and directly showing their students where and what the mistakes are. It may seem natural to faculty, when presented with a paper from a tutee, to read the paper silently, mark the mistakes, and then proceed to explain them to the student. It is not enough, nor is it appropriate, therefore, simply to instruct faculty not to write on the paper or tell them to ask questions to draw out the student's meaning. Faculty tutors want and deserve to know the pedagogical reasons behind these practices. Using sources that I could show them was helpful, as was respecting the value of their experiences. As a group, we read Steven J. Corbett's (2008) "Tutoring Style, Tutoring Ethics" and debated the merits of direct versus indirect tutoring. In the course of that discussion, we came up with guidelines that we collectively agreed on in terms of a reasonable balance between directive and non-directive pedagogy that we felt would be most helpful for our students. One of our guidelines is "Lower level [English language learners] need more direction—language knowledge." This guideline was supported by our resident experts (i.e., those of us who had degrees and taught in TESOL) as well as by our collective experiences. Using scholarly sources helped with understanding, and the guidelines helped with collective buy-in. These are approaches that I would not have taken to this extent with peer tutors, where my authority and greater experience alone, or that of one guidebook, may have been enough for them to accept my guidelines. However, I needed to respect and treat faculty tutors as my peers and take their previous experience into account.

Besides the value of using extant tutoring guides to examine tutoring-specific pedagogy, chapters and books on focused topics also prove useful for training faculty tutors. Although general tutoring guides, such as Ryan and Zimmerelli's, provide chapter-long overviews of the writing process and professionalism in the workplace, which apply more to peer tutors than to faculty, the chapters on specific tutoring situations and strategies can be equally relevant. In particular, experienced faculty and professional tutors often look for new strategies to meet the needs of individual students or who may be new to working one on one with English language learners and students with learning disabilities (Ryan and Zimmerelli 2016). For example, in one training, we discussed Nicole Kraemer Munday's (2005) "(Non)Meeting of the Minds" from *A Tutor's Guide: Helping Writers One to One* (Rafoth 2005). The situation described, in which a student does not understand where the tutor is coming from and does not feel she is being satisfactorily helped, is a common one for faculty as well as peer tutors. In fact, the situation can be exacerbated because more may be expected of a faculty member, and the stakes may even be higher, if a student decides to complain to the faculty member's department. Faculty tutors shared experiences and strategies with one another, and brought insight from classroom situations as well, to form strategies to deal with upset or stressed students. For example, faculty agreed on the importance of setting expectations in the beginning and also to take a limited amount of time (one to five minutes) to address the student's emotional concerns, whether that's the stress they're feeling about the paper or something else, and then refocus on the paper by explaining that's what we can help with right now.

This same situation is equally relevant in a peer tutor discussion, but peer tutors may not have the same depth of experience to address it themselves in the same way. Similarly, as part of our ongoing discussions on working with English language learners, we read and discussed Cynthia Linville's "Editing Line-by-Line" from Shanti Bruce and Ben Rafoth's specialized tutoring guide, *ESL Writers: A Guide for Writing Center Tutors* (Bruce and Rafoth 2009). The essay supported our consensus from a previous discussion that English language learners need more direct help than is advocated in traditional tutoring pedagogy, and we further explored how to best help these students. In addition to these, topics we have explored include tutoring students with disabilities, students with linguistic diversity, and students suffering from post-traumatic stress disorder (Babcock, Day, and Daniels 2017; de Kleine and Lawton 2015; Sinski 2012). Although peer tutors should and do engage in discussion of best practices, faculty tutors already bring a scaffold of knowledge of educational experience and pedagogy. Instead, it's up to the administrator to conduct higher level professional development, using scholarly evidence and, if relevant, bringing in their tutors' experiences to share for mutual enrichment.

MAKING TIME FOR FACULTY TUTOR TRAINING

Adjusting the timing and duration of training to faculty tutors' schedules is one of my most significant considerations in planning and scheduling training for faculty tutors. Faculty tutors have significant time constraints outside of the center that are often beyond those of peer, graduate, and professional tutors. In addition to teaching classes, faculty tutors meet with their own students, plan lessons, and participate in other activities and meetings on campus. Unlike students, faculty usually do not live on campus and often have family obligations that peer tutors may not. Even at community colleges, where students are more likely to have family obligations, they are also more likely than faculty to live in the community the college serves. Furthermore, adjunct faculty may be teaching at additional schools and therefore cannot be on campus on certain days. This is particularly acute at public two-year schools such as community colleges, which are more likely both to have more adjunct faculty and to have more, or only, faculty tutors (Gladstein and Fralix 2013; National Center for Education Statistics 2016).

All these factors coincide so that it may seem nearly impossible to gather all, or even a significant number of, tutors together at one time. This situation is opposed to typical ongoing training methods for peer tutors, which, if they do not involve a specific co- or prerequisite course, often involve in-person group meetings or discussions throughout the semester or year. Most tutoring guidebooks presume the existence of a tutor-training course or at least ongoing professional development. For example, the *Bedford Guide* suggests that the book may be adapted for large or small classes, while the *Oxford Guide* begins with a note directed to students, individual tutors, and instructors preparing to teach tutors; most guidebooks include exercises and discussion points at the end of each chapter, often explicitly intended for class use (Fitzgerald and Ianetta 2016; Ryan and Zimmerelli 2016). These circumstances are more realistic for undergraduate and graduate peer tutors rather than faculty tutors.

In order to adjust to faculty tutors' schedules, I placed training during our college's professional week or the week before classes start. Both full-time and adjunct faculty are usually on campus this week for departmental and other meetings, but they are not yet in the midst of teaching and grading. This is the ideal, if not only, time during the semester to meet. For the past two years when I have conducted these trainings, most tutors have been available. The professional week timing is also convenient because if the inevitable few tutors do need to miss it, it is easier to schedule any individual follow-up meetings during the first week of class, which is less busy for the center and often less busy for faculty. I also book toward the end of professional week, typically on Thursday, to avoid collegewide and relevant departmental meetings. I decided on a half-day length, which enables us to cover a lot of ground while considering faculty members' other personal and professional obligations.

I elected not to schedule any in-person follow-up meetings throughout or at the end of the semester, due largely to timing. The logistics of keeping the center open and navigating everyone's schedules make it difficult to meet during the semester, and once the semester is over, our largely adjunct population of faculty tutors is off campus. Instead, like Shiell at Walden University (chapter 3), the faculty tutors and I decided to use a tactic from peer tutor courses and create an online asynchronous discussion board for faculty tutors (Blazer 2015; Fitzgerald and Ianetta 2016). We used Blackboard to create a tutor community, but other learning management systems or online blogging platforms would also work. Although also useful for tutor training in general, similar to the once-per-semester training, the online discussions particularly address the desire to continue professional development while respecting the unique time constraints of faculty tutors.

FUNDING FACULTY TUTOR TRAINING

Funding faculty tutor training is a significant consideration for our center and others. At our school, as may be the case at other schools with only or primarily faculty tutors, funding is allocated specifically for tutoring and not for training. Unlike peer or graduate tutors—who pay to take a course, receive educational credit, or receive entry-level pay—faculty tutors must be paid commensurate with their experience, expertise, and degree level. Furthermore, since it may be assumed that faculty are not in need of training, training time may not be included in payment calculations. Finally, individual institutions may not be willing or able to allocate funds to any activities that do not involve direct interaction with students. As a result, at our school, as at many schools, it is not currently possible to pay faculty tutors to attend training. For example, gathering fifteen tutors for three hours would be equivalent to the funding for forty-five hours, or, at our center, almost four days' worth of tutoring, which is not a justifiable expense based on the amount of limited tutoring funding it would consume.

Instead, I provide breakfast both semesters and lunch once a year, as well as professional development credit. Fortunately, at some schools, including ours, professional development credit allows adjunct faculty to attain pay raises and seniority when receiving classes. Since I do not pay tutors to attend trainings, trainings are not mandatory. However, I find that most tutors attend and are deeply appreciative of our efforts to create a valuable training for them. This would concur with Sanyal and Shea's findings in their survey of Seton Hall University's faculty tutors, discussed in chapter 6, in that all but three of the seventeen faculty tutors surveyed agreed that faculty tutors need training.

KEEPING TRAININGS RELEVANT FOR FACULTY TUTORS

My most important ongoing consideration is keeping training topics relevant for faculty tutors. In order to respond appropriately, I base our format and content changes in successive semesters on direct and indirect feedback from faculty and professional tutors. For example, when I surveyed tutors after our first training, I received feedback that they would appreciate more discussion during trainings. Therefore, I adjusted our next schedule to be primarily discussion.

I often base our discussions on a relevant reading from writing center guides or literature, although, in some cases, it is more relevant to learn from each other's experiences. To add to our knowledge on working with students with disabilities, I initially turned to readings on the topic from *Writing Centers and Disability* (Babcock, Day, and Daniels 2017). Serving students with disabilities is a growing area of need for training in higher education nationwide, but faculty tutors are more likely to have experience in this area than peer tutors (National Center for Learning Disabilities 2014). For instance, one of our faculty tutors enhanced our discussion, citing an experience working with a student during office hours, which also worked well for tutoring. In this instance, our experiences correlated well with studies in the field and enabled us to build on our expertise.

On the other hand, for our discussion on time limitations, I found that most current tutor guides and writing center literature accept time limits as a given, which was not necessarily obvious to faculty (Fitzgerald and Ianetta 2016; Geller et al. 2007; Gladstein and Fralix 2013). Faculty members are used to meeting with their own students as long as they deem necessary, so ending a session to adhere to a predetermined time limit may seem arbitrary. As one of our faculty tutors explained, it may be an obstacle to learning if sessions end when students have just reached an "aha" moment in their writing process. Therefore, time limitations may require a discussion with faculty when, with peer tutors, an ultimatum would suffice. When this was brought to my attention, and after repeatedly observing faculty tutors who ignored the stated time limitations, I realized we needed to spend time exploring the goals of tutoring versus teaching and the logistical realities of the center as opposed to office hours. I also shared with faculty tutors the statistics from the "National Census of Writing" on average length of writing center consultations offered: 30 minutes for 49 percent of 143 two-year institutions and 5 percent with no limit; 30 minutes for 39 percent and 2 percent with no limit for 574 four-year institutions (Gladstein and Fralix 2013). However, I also took time to listen to faculty concerns. After the discussion, faculty tutors created their own guidelines for the time limits instead of having it handed down by me. In our case, tutors asked for five-minute time limit warnings from staff in order to assist them with keeping to the time. The training session led to a joint sense of purpose and joint solution in response to the concern.

Relevant expert speakers can also be particularly useful for faculty tutor trainings. Inviting internal college speakers is valuable for faculty since, unlike peer tutors, faculty tutors are professionally invested in the college's long-term goals and may, therefore, be more interested in hearing about the inner workings of new programs at the institution. Over past semesters, I have invited deans, department chairs, course coordinators, and college counselors to our trainings. For adjunct faculty members, especially, this may be a rare chance to hear directly from administrators. Furthermore, faculty tutors may themselves be involved in new programs. For example, at our last training, the course coordinator who spoke about the newly reorganized developmental English courses was also one of our faculty tutors. Last, but not least, expert speakers can address faculty at a level that respects their institutional knowledge and experience while enhancing their knowledge of program updates, which can improve their ability to perform their educational duties in addition to tutoring. Faculty tutors realize the value of this content, and I have consistently received posttraining feedback that they appreciated hearing from college stakeholders.

SAMPLE FACULTY TUTOR-TRAINING SCHEDULES

The schedule format in tables 1.1–1.3 is what I came up with for our faculty tutor trainings, based on time considerations, and adjusted each

Table 1.1. Faculty tutor training fall 2016 schedule

8:00–9:00 AM	Coffee, Tea, and Doughnuts
9:00–9:30 AM	Opening Remarks by Dean WRL Center Policies New Tutor Leave and Absence Policy
9:35–10:10 AM	Tutoring Appointments (New, Up to 45-Minute Appointments) WCOnline Client Report Forms Hillman Mentoring Program Tutor Resource Library/Website Science Writing
10:10–10:40 AM	AELP Exercise Packets Question Session with AELP Department Chair
10:45–11:15 AM	Article Discussions: Direct/Indirect Tutoring and Print/Screen Reading
11:20–11:40 AM	Share Insights/Form Guidelines on Direct/Indirect Tutoring and Print/Screen Reading
11:45 AM–12:30 PM	Mental Health on Campus for Tutors at Montgomery College Mental Health Services Coordinator
12:30–1:30 PM	Lunch
1:00–2:00 PM	WCOnline Open Lab (Optional for Spring 2016 Tutors)

Source: I relied on our own experiences for discussions on Appointment Time Limits and Print/Screen Reading. Discussions on tutoring students who use Disability Support Services (DSS) used information from internal presentations on students on the Autism Spectrum and drew on *Writing Centers and Disability* (Babcock., Day, and Daniels 2017).

NOTES
As mentioned, our first training was heavier on lecture.
AELP stands for American English Language Program (later changed to ELAP, English Language for Academic Purposes).
I used Steven J. Corbett's "Tutoring Style, Tutoring Ethics" and M. Julee Tanner's "Reading vs. Print," respectively, to jumpstart discussions (Corbett 2008; Tanner 2014).

semester based on time and content feedback. I recommend coordinating with relevant departments to assure the timing does not conflict with other meetings that faculty may have to attend. Once I had the basic format, I found it easier to adjust for each training as necessary. I hope that these examples below, including notes of how I have adjusted the needs of each training, will be useful to other centers planning faculty tutor trainings.

BUILDING A PROFESSIONAL LEARNING COMMUNITY

Building a professional learning community was a result of more than a goal; however, it has been the most valuable outcome of our trainings. My original goal was to familiarize or update faculty tutors about writing

Table 1.2. Faculty tutor discussions spring 2017 schedule

9:00–9:15 AM	Coffee and Snacks
9:15–9:30 AM	FA16 Center Statistics Presentation WRL Center Policy Updates– New AELP and Group Appointments Tutor "Choose Your Own Adventure" Training/Research Project
9:35–9:50 AM	Discussion: Tutoring for Speeches Share Insights/Form Guidelines
9:50–10:05 AM	Snacks/Break
10:05–10:40 AM	Discussion A: Strategies for Working with ELLs (Main Center area) Share Insights/Form Guidelines Discussion B: Strategies for Working with "Difficult" Students (Computer Lab) Share Insights/Form Guidelines
10:45–11:00 AM	Wrap Up/Establish Guidelines

NOTES

The SP17 schedule responded to feedback to add more discussion, as well as time constraints. All attendees were returning tutors.

I used "Editing Line by Line" by Cynthia Linville and "(Non)Meeting of the Minds" by Nicole Kraemer Munday, respectively, to jumpstart discussions (Linville 2009; Munday 2005).

center literature. However, I also wanted to hear from our knowledgeable faculty and incorporate their knowledge from the classroom and, in some cases, from years of tutoring, into our training and practices. Therefore, I brought our questions about policies I wanted to develop in the center to the tutors. This strategy could be, and has been, implemented with peer tutors; however, faculty tutors bring an even greater breadth and depth of knowledge of the institution and of teaching, which was useful in solidifying our decisions. For example, one of our first training discussions centered on whether students could bring drafts to the center on their laptops. Although I had done research and brought articles on the topic to discuss with faculty, I based our final decision on the discussion I had with faculty tutors and followed guidelines that we created as a professional community (Tanner 2014). Our approach to including faculty tutors in establishing guidelines and best practices demonstrates respect and takes advantage of their knowledge and expertise.

Using trainings as a time to establish guidelines and best practices for the center creates faculty buy-in and gives faculty tutors a stake in the writing center community. Furthermore, having tangible results in the form of guidelines makes the training a productive use of everybody's time. In addition, when faculty tutors are fully aware of what our policies are as well as how and why they were created, they are equipped to be

Table 1.3. Tutor training fall 2018 schedule

8:00–9:00 AM	Coffee, Tea, and Doughnuts
9:00–9:30 AM	Opening Remarks by Dean of ELAP Hello from ENGL Dept. Chair WRL Center Updates and Announcements Discussion Post Signup
9:30–9:50 AM	IERW Program Updates and Tutoring for IERW Students with IERW Coordinator
10:00–10:45 AM	Discussion A: Appointment Time Limits/Time Management Discussion B: Print/Screen Reading in the WRL Revisited Share Insights/Form Guidelines
10:45–11:00 AM	Establish Guidelines
11:00–11:15 AM	Hello and Tutoring for DSS Students with DSS Counselor
11:15–11:45 AM	Discussion A and B: Tutoring for DSS Students Share Insights/Form Guidelines
11:45–12:00 PM	Establish Guidelines/Wrap Up
12:00–1:00 PM	Pizza and Salad Lunch

NOTES

Our most recent schedule as of this writing includes a balance of speakers and discussion, in response to feedback. Time has been adjusted as well.

ELAP stands for English Language for Academic Purposes, for English language learners.

IERW stands for Integrated Reading and Writing, developmental English for native speakers. One of our tutors is also the course coordinator.

I relied on our own experiences for discussions on Appointment Time Limits and Print/Screen Reading. Discussions on tutoring students who use Disability Support Services (DSS) used information from internal presentations on students on the Autism Spectrum and drew on Writing Centers and Disability (Babcock, Day, and Daniels 2017).

incredible ambassadors to their departments and fellow faculty for and about the writing center.

To connect tutors with each other, and specifically with writing center literature, I decided to draw on a model sometimes used for peer tutor classes—online discussion posts (Blazer 2015; Fitzgerald and Ianetta 2016). We asked different tutors to ask a question of their choice each week on a topic of tutoring interest. Besides the time consideration, this method works well because faculty tutors are already versed in scholarly debate and speaking from positions of professional experience. Topics have included working with students on the autistic spectrum, using appropriate pronouns for students in writing client report forms, and emotional labor in the writing center. Since there is no lead poster, the discussion board acts more as an ongoing professional development learning community than a class.

The discussion from the trainings and the board has resulted in both spontaneous and deliberate "unending conversations" in our center throughout the semester. The in-person conversations typically occur spontaneously between overlapping tutors in the center. For example, I've overheard (and instigated) lively and respectful debates over the Oxford comma or the use of the singular "they." However, the online conversations stemmed from a deliberate effort to continue professional development while still meeting our time and funding needs.

Our professional learning community or "unending conversation" both online and in-person is an ongoing development and I have no doubt will continue to develop over time. Building such a community with faculty tutors can be particularly rewarding, as, unlike most peer tutors, faculty tutors often remain at the institution and continue to build on their professional development and contribute to improved training and learning for all tutors and writing center staff. Establishing sustainable ongoing professional development training for faculty tutors has been worth the time, effort, and funding possible to invest in the future of our center, and I encourage other centers with faculty tutors to do so as well.

Drawing on my experiences and those of the faculty tutors, there are a few key takeaways for administrators in a writing center staffed by faculty tutors or for faculty tutors themselves:

- Use scholarly sources in writing center or related fields, as well as tutoring guides, to start discussions, but also use the expertise of the faculty tutors at the table.
- Use articles and chapters on specific tutoring situations, such as working with English language learners or students with disabilities, as they tend to be of the most interest and relevance.
- Bring speakers from around and outside the college to speak on topics of internal college interests, such as a new English language program, or more general interests, such as helping students write a resume.
- Use faculty tutors as expert speakers as well, if they belong to a particular group or department or have some special expertise, such as technical writing.
- Use discussions to create guidelines on topics for your center, which you can incorporate into your tutor handbook and add to over time.
- Create an online discussion board, in order to encourage an ongoing conversation over time and between tutors who may never work the same shift.
- Have tutors volunteer to lead online discussions, so everyone's interests and concerns are addressed.

- Regularly continue these discussions with tutors when you see them, point out new articles ("Look! The IWCA agrees with me about 'they' as a singular pronoun . . .") and continue to learn.

REFERENCES

Babcock, Rebecca Day, and Sharifa Daniels, ed. 2017. *Writing Centers and Disability*. Fountainhead Press X Series for Professional Development. Edited by Allison D. Smith and Trixie G. Smith. Southlake, TX: Fountainhead Press.

Blazer, Sarah. 2015. "Twenty First Century Writing Center Staff Education: Teaching and Learning towards Inclusive and Productive Everyday Practice." *Writing Center Journal* 35 (1): 17–55.

Bruce, Shanti, and Ben Rafoth, ed. 2009. *ESL Writers: A Guide for Writing Center Tutors*. 2nd ed. Portsmouth, NH: Boynton/Cook Publishers.

Burke, Kenneth. 1973. *The Philosophy of Literary Form: Studies in Symbolic Action*. 3rd ed. Berkeley: University of California Press.

Corbett, Steven J. 2008. "Tutoring Style, Tutoring Ethics: The Continuing Relevance of the Directive/Nondirective Instructional Debate." *Praxis: A Writing Center Journal* 5 (2): 27–42.

de Kleine, Christa, and Rachele Lawton. 2015. "Meeting the Needs of Linguistically Diverse Students at the College Level." White paper (commissioned) for the College Reading and Language Association (CRLA). https://www.crla.net/images/whitepaper/Meeting_Needs_of_Diverse_Students.pdf.

Fitzgerald, Lauren, and Melissa Ianetta. 2016. *The Oxford Guide for Writing Tutors: Practice and Research*. New York: Oxford University Press.

Geller, Anne Ellen, Michele Eodice, Frankie Condon, Meg Carroll, and Elizabeth H. Boquet. 2007. *The Everyday Writing Center: A Community of Practice*. Logan: Utah State University Press.

Gladstein, Jill, and Brandon Fralix. 2013. "National Census of Writing 2013." http://writingcensus.swarthmore.edu/survey/2.

Harris, Muriel. 1995. "Talking in the Middle: Why Writers Need Writing Tutors." *College English* 57 (1): 27–42.

Jewell, Megan Swihart, and Joseph, Cheatle. 2016. "Toward a Professional Consultant's Handbook: Researching Support and Training Methods." *WLN: A Journal of Writing Center Scholarship* 41 (3–4): 10–17.

Linville, Cynthia. 2009. "Editing Line by Line." In *ESL Writers: A Guide for Writing Center Tutors*, edited by Shanti Bruce and Ben Rafoth. 2nd ed., 116–31. Portsmouth, NH: Boynton/Cook Publishers.

McKinney, Jackie Grutsch. 2013. *Peripheral Visions for Writing Centers*. Boulder, CO: Utah State University Press.

Moneyhun, Clyde, and Patti Hanlon-Baker. 2012. "Tutoring Teachers." *Writing Lab Newsletter* 36 (9–10): 1–5.

Munday, Nicole Kraemer. 2005. "(Non)Meeting of the Minds." In *A Tutor's Guide: Helping Writers One to One*, 2nd ed., edited by Ben Rafoth, 17–22. Portsmouth, NH: Heinemann.

National Center for Education Statistics. 2016. "Chapter 3: Postsecondary Education." *Digest of Education Statistics, 2016*. https://nces.ed.gov/programs/digest/d16/ch_3.asp.

National Center for Learning Disabilities. 2014. "The State of Learning Disabilities." 3rd ed. https://www.ncld.org/wp-content/uploads/2014/11/2014-State-of-LD.pdf.

North, Stephen M. 1984. "The Idea of a Writing Center." *College English* 46 (5) (September): 443–46.

Rafoth, Ben, ed. 2005. *A Tutor's Guide: Helping Writers One to One*. 2nd ed. Portsmouth, NH: Heinemann.

Ryan, Leigh, and Lisa Zimmerelli. 2016. *The Bedford Guide for Writing Tutors*. 6th ed. Boston: Bedford / St. Martin's.

Sinski, Jennifer Blevins. 2012. "Classroom Strategies for Teaching Veterans with Post-Traumatic Stress Disorder and Traumatic Brain Injury." *Journal of Postsecondary Education and Disability* 25 (1): 87–95.

Strang, Steven. 2006. "Staffing a Writing Center with Professional Tutors." *The Writing Center Director's Resource Book*, edited by Christina Murphy and Byron L. Stay, 291–300. New York: Routledge.

Tanner, M. Julee. 2014. "Digital Vs. Print: Reading Comprehension and the Future of the Book." *SJSU School of Information: Student Research Journal* 4 (2): 1–12.

2
MODULAR TRAINING FOR PROFESSIONAL WRITING CENTER CONSULTANTS

Fallon N. Allison

INSTITUTIONAL CHANGES

The late twentieth-century burgeoning of writing centers in the United States is described in Kenneth Bruffee's (1984a) familiar and much-quoted "Collaborative Learning and the 'Conversation of Mankind'" as a response to institutional pressures: "The roots of collaborative learning lie neither in radical politics nor in research. They lie in the nearly desperate response of harried colleges during the early 1970s to a pressing educational need" (637). As new institutional pressures arise, writing centers continue to respond (whether calmly or desperately) to them. As the coordinator of the Studio, the writing center for Illinois Central College (a large community college), I was recently tasked with creating a method of training professional consultants. Previously, my staff was composed of peer writing consultants and a handful of full-time faculty, but institutional pressures (cost effectiveness and centralization of academic support) created a new category of writing consultant: the professional consultant. While professional writing consultants may be common at other institutions (and scholarship suggests they are particularly common at two-year colleges), they were new to the Studio.

The training I designed for professional consultants is a series of online modules. It provides a comprehensive, trackable training course that is flexible enough to accommodate the complicated schedules of contingent, part-time employees. In addition to being flexible, online modular training is "low touch." Low touch methods are automated and require minimal direct interaction with the coordinator, as opposed to "high touch" methods, which use one-on-one guidance from, and frequent contact with, the coordinator. Any writing center that finds itself with an expanding staff, a new corps of professional consultants, or expansion of the coordinator's duties, may consider online modular training.

DOI: 10.7330/9781646420858.c002

WHO ARE PROFESSIONAL CONSULTANTS?

In the Studio, professional consultants work alongside peer consultants (peer consultants are paid minimum wage, and professional consultants are paid according to their level of education and experience). The professional consultants at ICC are recent graduates from the college, undergraduates from nearby four-year institutions, adjunct instructors of English, professionals "moonlighting" from other occupations (we currently have two social workers as part-time writing consultants), and, possibly, professional tutors from other disciplines. The term "professional" might mask the need for training; some of the professional consultants, such as adjunct instructors and those working for us while furthering their education at other institutions, are new to writing centers. Professional writing consultants need specialized training, regardless of their academic degrees, experience with teaching composition, or experience writing professionally. In "Professional Tutors, Shifting Identifies: Narratives from the Center" (chapter 5), Kimberly Fahle Peck et al. advise writing center administrators to be mindful that their professional consultants wear many hats and to "support them as they navigate the challenges of a work life built on patchwork employment and simultaneously held professional identities." Flexibility in training is particularly important for professional consultants, who may have competing demands on their time.

SPECIAL CHALLENGES FACED BY PROFESSIONAL CONSULTANTS

Training time is the first challenge faced by professional consultants. Peer consultants participate in twenty hours of paid onboarding and training prior to the semester in which they begin work. During that semester, they take ENGL 140: Introduction to Writing Center Theory and Practice, a three-credit course. This training course allows for tracking of progress, reiteration of values, and a steady accretion of writing center knowledge. Professional writing consultants at the Studio do not have the luxury of the semester-long training course that prepares peer consultants. They are unlikely to have even the small luxury of the twenty hours of presemester training that peer consultants receive, since it is costlier to train professional consultants. Miriam E. Laufer (in chapter 1, "Redefining Training for Faculty Tutors") notes that many institutions are not willing to pay professional tutors to attend presemester training. Because my institution uses professional consultants to staff times of day that are difficult to cover and to staff the smaller writing center outpost on a satellite campus, they need to be onboarded faster. Their training must take place on the job and must take less time than the training peer consultants receive. Although training for professionals is abbreviated, it must prepare them to maintain the standard of competency expected of peer consultants. The issue of competency is critical. It would be dangerous to assume that professional consultants are, by nature of having a college degree, more prepared for writing center work than their peer consultant colleagues.

Peer consultants bring some unique advantages to writing center work. As Jill Reglin (2017) notes in "Creative Staffing for the Community College Writing Center in an Era of Outsourced Education," peer tutors are "qualified in ways others are not because they share a social status or space with other students—regardless of level of study or age difference. The power of equal footing cannot be mimicked or taken for granted" (16). Peer consultants have an easier time creating a collaborative atmosphere (as opposed to a teacher-student hierarchy) by dint of the fact that they too are students. They also share a discourse community with their peers (Harris 1995). The advantage peer consultants bring to the writing center extends beyond sharing a community; they are familiar with the "contexts of assigned readings and class discussions in which the various writing assignments are supposed to be prepared," as Louise Smith puts it (1986, 4), and moreover, they are immersed in writing across the disciplines as part of their educational experience. They are continually negotiating audience, style, and format as they tackle writing assignments designed by instructors across varied disciplines, so they are limber and prepared to renegotiate their expectations of writing projects. Professional consultants might not have the same ease switching among genres and disciplines of writing if they have not been actively engaged in writing across the curriculum. In short, they may struggle with writing that is outside of their wheelhouse.

Professional consultants bring knowledge of the writing process and a strong understanding of grammar and mechanics to their work in the Studio. This contribution can itself be a blind spot that training must address. Professional consultants must set aside their talent as copyeditors in order to adopt a facilitative approach focused on holistic writing improvement rather than a prescriptive approach focused on correcting surface errors. As Alison Bright (2017) cautions in "Cultivating Professional Writing Tutor Identities at a Two-Year College," "varied backgrounds and experiences [of the mix of professional, faculty, and peer tutors at two-year colleges] can potentially enrich the tutorials of student writers at two-year colleges, they can also potentially result in a disconnect between the writing tutors' expectations for the tutorial and the best practices in the field" (12). Professional consultants might be unaware of best practices in writing centers and may also struggle to adapt to new ways of approaching writing. Adjunct instructors who also work as professional consultants may find this a particular stumbling block, as Laufer (in chapter 1) notes, faculty members are accustomed to being experts in, and teaching within, their own subject areas and therefore may have to adjust to acting as non-expert readers. The institutional administration's view of professional consultants is that they should need very little training, but early discussions with my professional consultants and observations of their work indicated that they struggled with four particular problems: (1) the desire to proofread, (2) a tendency toward overzealousness (i.e., feeding ideas to students, as Elizabeth Boquet [1999] describes in "Our Little Secret"), (3) lack of familiarity with the wide variety of genres being deployed in college writing, and (4) lack of community with other writing center consultants. Drawing on my experiences and those of the professional consultants, I designed training modules with these four problems in mind.

WHY MODULAR TRAINING?

Modular training meets four goals: it is an efficient and comprehensive alternative to the semester-long training course that develops our peer consultants; it is flexible to accommodate adjunct faculty teaching schedules and the work schedules of other part-time, contingent professionals; it is relatively low touch; and it helps build a sense of community for professional consultants.

I toyed with a number of potential training solutions for professionals before identifying modular training as the best option. Modular training allows me to keep some aspects of high-touch training while substituting many parts of the peer consultant training course with low-touch alternatives. Our training class for peer consultants includes weekly class meetings along with homework readings, exercises, research essays, and multimedia projects. This classwork reflects upon and is extended into practical applications during consultations. In *Key Concepts in Adult Education and Training*, Malcolm Tight's (1996) distinction between education and training may be useful in distinguishing the inherent difference between the training class taken by peer consultants and the modular training of professional consultants: "Education is not a speedy process, but takes a lengthy, though perhaps not continuous, period of time. Learning, by contrast, could be seen as not necessarily involving instruction, and as often occurring over a shorter timeframe and in smaller chunks" (17). The peer consultant course has education as its goal: it builds knowledge of the missions and methodologies of writing center work and deepens the student's understanding of how to execute those methodologies. Modular training for professionals is "more likely to be involved with the development of specific identified skills" (19). The modular training uses some of the readings required in the peer course, but it does so with guides for on-the-job application, and it requires written reflections that are visible to all members of the staff. Because the work in the module is codified and visible, it engenders regular discussions in both the Studio and at staff meetings. These meetings allow me to "close the loop" by connecting the work new professional consultants are completing with larger community discussions. Further, the codification of the work is an indication that learning to be a good writing consultant is a process, and the work of our writing center is based on methodology, not just content expertise.

Modular training can help create scaffolding in the training process, for various knowledge and skills I want different groups of consultants to acquire. Modules can be easily manipulated to add and remove information and entire topics. The order in which the modules are deployed can be changed to suit a particular cohort of professional consultants or to respond to issues facing our, or any, writing center at a particular moment. I chose to house the modules online within the Blackboard learning management system. I tested the modules using other platforms—such as Canvas, Sakai, and Microsoft Teams—and have found that they are easily transportable to other systems.

Finally, I created the modules not to replace in-person training but to help facilitate professional consultants' abilities to join in the conversation. Bright emphasizes the importance of training programs that engage consultants in writing center discourse (Bright 2017). In-person training has been, and always will be, an extremely important hallmark for writing centers. Splitting professional training between online modules and in-person tutorials allows professionals to acquire important information in a structured way that they can then apply practically to their work in the writing center. Further, a distinct professional writing consultant training program "[gives] new tutors the opportunity to create a tutor identity that [is] distinct from their other professional or academic identities" (Bright 2017, 12). The modules also allow consultants to do what Bright calls for: immerse themselves in the discourse community.

The structure of the modules follows the "online collaborative learning theory" (OCL), of Linda Harasim, a pioneer of online education, by requiring participants to generate ideas, confront new ideas and organize them, and, finally, through online discussion, construct knowledge. Harasim (2017) describes the three phases of successful online collaboration:

Idea Generating. The first phase, "Idea Generating," refers to divergent thinking within a group: brainstorming, verbalization, generating information, and thus sharing of ideas and positions on a particular topic or problem. Many perspectives emerge. The role of the instructor is to facilitate idea generation and encourage active participation by all members of the group.

Idea Organizing. Phase 2, "Idea Organizing," is the beginning of conceptual change. As participants confront the new or different ideas that had been generated by their peers or encountered in the course readings, they begin to discuss in a more focused way to clarify and cluster these many ideas according to their relationship and similarities to one another. Idea organizing behavior demonstrates intellectual progress and the beginning of convergence as students discuss and/or debate to select the strongest positions and weed out weaker positions (using such processes as referencing, agreement, disagreement, or questioning).

Intellectual Convergence. The third phase, "Intellectual Convergence," is typically reflected in shared understanding, a shared position (including agreeing to disagree), or a mutual contribution to and construction of shared knowledge (Harasim 2017, 122).

Each module asks professional consultants to bring their assumptions, ideas, and questions through set induction exercises. Curated readings followed by application of the ideas in the readings ask consultants to combine their knowledge of the writing process with new ideas about writing center work. Finally, several types of discussion encourage consultants to transform their new knowledge into practice. Static online training modules that did not require input from a coordinator and did not require discussion and collaboration among consultants would not create a community and would not challenge professional consultants to create shared knowledge.

CURRENT SET OF MODULES, IN DEPLOYMENT ORDER

I currently use ten modules to train professional consultants: The History and Mission of Writing Centers, Higher Order Concerns, the Non-Directive Method, Diverse Learner Populations, Writing Across the Curriculum, Modeling Resources, Synchronous Online Consultations, the Writing Center Gets Political, Learning Theories, and Empowering Students/Cognitive and Motivational Scaffolding.

Not all training has a module, of course, because some topics I like to handle in wholly discussion-based training sessions, even with the synchronous and asynchronous staff discussion that I attach to most modules. For instance, dealing with interpersonal challenges is a topic that should be handled in person. Another significant training topic that does not have a module is special strategies for working with strong writers, again because I have found that larger group discussion is most productive with this topic. And not all of the scholarly reading and engagement with the writing center community are linked to modules. I distribute optional articles from *WLN*, *The Writing Center Journal*, and *Praxis* on a regular basis and encourage the staff to have informal chats about them during downtime.

THE STRUCTURE OF THE MODULES

The training modules combine asynchronous online work, discussion, and assessment with on-site training and in-person discussion and mentoring, so they are nigh impossible to transcribe simply in writing (the irony!). They follow a consistent format that aligns with Harasim's guidelines for OCL, comprising asynchronous online and in-person work:

I. Set induction question(s)—completed in the test canvas on Blackboard

II. Theoretical reading—posted on Blackboard

III. Application of the theory—work completed on Blackboard or in person

IV. Reflection/Bridge to other modules—completed on Blackboard Discussion Board, requiring interaction with fellow consultants

V. Closing the loop—assessment and feedback handled by the coordinator

THE HISTORY AND MISSION OF WRITING CENTERS

The goal of this module is to introduce consultants to the history of writing centers, the terminology they will encounter in the writing center discourse community, and the history and mission of our particular writing center. The module challenges preconceived notions new consultants might have about the writing center and the work of writing consultants. For peer consultants, introduction to the history and mission of writing centers occurs during presemester training sessions. Professional consultants might participate in this training, depending on the timing of hiring and whether or not the institution will fund presemester training for professionals. This module aids with midsemester onboarding and acts as a safety net for maintaining quality despite uncertain budgets. The format, with accompanying questions, follows:

I. Set induction:

Why do you think writing centers were created?
When do you think writing centers became part of education in the United States?
Do you think education systems in other countries use writing centers?
Which students is the Studio designed to serve?

II. Reading:

Carino, Peter. 1995. "Early Writing Centers: Toward a History." *The Writing Center Journal* 15 (2): 103–15.
North, Stephen M. 1984. "The Idea of a Writing Center." *College English* 46 (5): 433–46.

III. Application:

Group discussion of the readings, among all new members of the staff, scheduled with the coordinator. This discussion covers foundational documents for the Studio as well.

IV. Reflection/Bridge:

How do we improve the writer?
As you formulate your answer, think about what has helped you improve as a writer—a concept you read and learned, the work you did for a particular assignment, and so forth.
Please also respond to at least one post from a fellow consultant.

V. Closing the Loop:

Each Discussion Board thread receives a reply from the writing center coordinator.

HIGHER ORDER CONCERNS

The goal of this module is to direct attention to higher order concerns in writing (which will help new professionals resist the urge to merely proofread and faculty consultants resist using the red pen). Many strong writers don't need to consciously reflect on higher order concerns when writing; this module will help them to see the concerns to which they naturally pay attention during their writing processes, concerns of which less adept writers may need to be made explicitly aware. The work of this module helps consultants craft their approaches so that they truly engage the writer in a productive discussion about the writing process.

I. Set induction:

Part 1: Please take a few minutes to list the elements of strong writing.
Part 2: In the Studio, you will often hear discussion of higher order concerns in writing. Put the following list of writing concerns in order, with #1 as the highest order concern:

Sentence Variety; Spelling; Development/Specificity of Ideas; Word Choice; Tone; Punctuation; Citation; Sentence Structure; Grammar; Transitions between Paragraphs; Paragraph Unity; Thesis/Focus; Clarity of Ideas; Organization.

II. Reading:

Allison, Fallon N. (2016). "Errors and Mistakes." Illinois Central College, April 20.

III. Application:

Read the sample paragraph, a real piece of student writing from our institution, posted on Blackboard. This paragraph has multiple problems. Pick one or two higher order concerns that you would address if you were able to talk to the writer of this paragraph. Name the concern(s) you picked, and briefly justify your choice.

IV. Reflection/Bridge:

Choose one item—any item—from the Higher Order Concerns list that you prioritized earlier. Reflect on how you would help a writer improve his or her understanding of that concept.

V. Closing the Loop:

Full staff meeting in which we examine the various orders we created for the higher order concerns lists from the set induction activity. Discussion of the differences among our lists, particularly with an eye for how different genres of writing might require a consultant to adjust the order of his or her list.

THE NON-DIRECTIVE METHOD

The goal of this module is to help new consultants develop strategies for engaging students in improving their writing and strengthening their understanding of their writing process. I believe this module is key for helping faculty, graduate students, and other categories of professional consultant wear a different hat when working as a writing consultant. This is our lengthiest and most comprehensive module, and consultants must complete this module in order to move from observations and team consultations to solo work. Veteran consultants are a crucial ingredient, as the module is interactive and requires veterans to bring their knowledge and creativity to work in role-playing exercises. The "closing the loop" component has a greater scope as well. I hope to eventually develop video examples of productive use of the non-directive method.

I. Set induction:

> Read Jeff Brooks's (1991) "Minimalist Tutoring: Making the Student Do All of the Work," *Writing Lab Newsletter* 15 (6): 1–4.
> List two improvements you might hope to see in a student's piece of writing.
> For each hypothetical improvement, write at least one question that you could ask to lead the student writer to address that area of concern.

II. Reading:

> Boquet, Elizabeth H. 1999. "Our Little Secret: A History of Writing Centers, Pre- to Post-Open Admissions." *College Composition and Communication* 50 (3): 463–82.
> Bruffee, Kenneth. 1984b. "Peer Tutoring and the 'Conversation of Mankind.'" *Writing Centers: Theory and Administration*, edited by Gary A. Olson, 87–98. Champaign, IL: National Council of Teachers of English.
> Newkirk, Thomas. 2007. "The First Five Minutes: Setting the Agenda in a Writing Conference." *The Longman Guide to Writing Center Theory and Practice*, edited by Robert W. Barnett and Jacob S. Blumner, 302–15. London: Pearson.

III. Application:

> Part 1: Submit a brief summary of Boquet, Bruffee, and Newkirk on Blackboard. Comment on which article contributed the most to your new understanding of writing center work.
> Part 2: Watch the "Allowing Students Time to Think" video posted on Blackboard.
>
>> This video shows thirty seconds of a student thinking, in order to encourage patience. At the end of the video is a quote from Mina Shaughnessy: "To do things for the student[s] that [they] can do for [themselves] is not generosity but impatience."
>
> Part 3: The consultant who worked with Judy in Boquet's "Our Little Secret" did not practice the non-directive method. This short-changed Judy, who could have grown from being challenged to conceive of her own topic and from being asked to explore the process of shaping an essay topic. Without the experience of challenge-growth, the writer's recourse is to return to the writing center the next time she needs a topic. Let's practice challenging writers to help them grow:
>   - Read the writing sample (titled *Non-Directive Sample*) posted on Blackboard.
>   - Create an agenda of the concerns you would like to address with the writer of this sample.

- Draft three leading questions you would use to challenge the writer to improve.
- Check your work schedule. You will see that you have been assigned to pair with a veteran consultant for a role-playing exercise. Use your agenda and questions in this exercise.

IV. Reflection/Bridge:

Reflect on the success of the questions you used to engage the mock writer in collaborative work. Were they too broad? Too narrow? Were there any surprises?

V. Closing the Loop:

The coordinator reads the summaries of Boquet, Bruffee, and Newkirk, and responds to each consultant with a written comment. Once all new consultants have completed this module, the coordinator schedules a staff meeting.

THE IMPETUS FOR CREATING THE MODULES

I must admit that I dreamt up a modular training system as a defensive move: the relocation and reorganization of our writing center threatened the Studio's well-established, theoretically grounded practices. Many writing centers are currently in the midst of the trend of co-location with other types of academic support, housed in the one-stop-shop of a library or information commons. When the Studio moved out of an academic department and into the library, there was an immediate pressure to anoint professional tutors from other disciplines as writing consultants, with only a few hours' "crash course" training. The administration's argument is that if our peer consultants from various majors can do the work (and, as Clint Gardner notes, "Our Students Can Do That"), anyone with a degree, no matter the discipline, must also be qualified to be a writing center consultant. The modules provide administrators and would-be untrained professional consultants with a clear picture of the dimensions of the work. Those less fit for the work have self-eliminated once it has become apparent that writing center work requires more than merely "putting a comma in wherever you pause." Creating modular training for professional consultants has helped me continue to hold our thin red line and maintain theoretically sound writing center practices. I hope that the modules align with Bruffee's description of early collaborative learning that "did not seem to change what people learned . . . so much as it changed the social context in which they learned it" (1984a, 638).

APPLICABILITY IN THE WIDER WRITING CENTER COMMUNITY

The modules were created to adapt to the Studio's changing environment, but they were not created to replace in-person training for consultants. Instead, the modular program instills a sense of community in new professional consultants by requiring them to actively engage with their fellow professional and peer consultants in new, structured ways. I believe that by making the foundations of our work clear—the coalescence of reading, reflection, rhetorical knowledge, and interpersonal interactions—the modules help new professional consultants join the reflective conversations that I consider to be the hallmark of the Studio at Illinois Central College. As other institutions face changes similar to those at Illinois Central College—reorganization and new reporting lines in academic support—I hope the design of the modules and the templates I have provided here will be useful.

For a coordinator, one particularly useful and interesting aspect of the modules is that they capture the ways in which new consultants might misunderstand, reject, or repurpose the readings and applications. They not only make necessary knowledge and skills visible to the consultants; they also make my assumptions and the varied perspectives of my staff visible to me. The programmatic nature of the modules does not mean the work or the community of the writing center is programmatic—quite the contrary, as the "conversation of mankind" continues in new forms and contexts.

ACKNOWLEDGMENTS

I'd like to thank Alexandra Hoover for her contributions to an earlier draft of this chapter.

REFERENCES

Allison, Fallon N. 2016. "Errors and Mistakes." Unpublished training document. Illinois Central College, East Peoria, IL.

Boquet, Elizabeth H. 1999. "Our Little Secret: A History of Writing Centers, Pre- to Post-Open Admissions." *College Composition and Communication* 50 (3): 463–82.

Bright, Alison. 2017. "Cultivating Professional Writing Tutor Identities at a Two-Year College." *Praxis: A Writing Center Journal* 15 (1): 12–14. http://www.praxisuwc.com/151-final.

Brooks, Jeff. 1991. "Minimalist Tutoring: Making the Student Do All of the Work." *Writing Lab Newsletter* 15 (6): 1–4.

Bruffee, Kenneth. 1984a. "Collaborative Learning and the 'Conversation of Mankind.'" *College English* 46 (7): 635–52. National Council of Teachers of English.

Bruffee, Kenneth. 1984b. "Peer Tutoring and the 'Conversation of Mankind.'" *Writing Centers: Theory and Administration*, edited by Gary A. Olson, 87–98. Champaign, IL: National Council of Teachers of English.

Carino, Peter. 1995. "Early Writing Centers: Toward a History." *Writing Center Journal* 15 (2): 103–15.

Gardner, Clint. 2017. "Our Students Can Do That: Peer Writing Tutors at the Two Year College." *Praxis: A Writing Center Journal* 15 (1): 47–54.

Harasim, Linda. 2017. *Learning Theory and Online Technologies.* New York: Routledge.

Harris, Muriel. 1995. "Talking in the Middle: Why Writers Need Writing Tutors." *College English* 57 (1): 27–42.

Newkirk, Thomas. 2007. "The First Five Minutes: Setting the Agenda in a Writing Conference." *The Longman Guide to Writing Center Theory and Practice*, edited by Robert W. Barnett and Jacob S. Blumner, 302–15. London: Pearson.

North, Stephen M. 1984. "The Idea of a Writing Center." *College English* 46 (5): 433–46.

Reglin, Jill. 2017. "Creative Staffing at the Community College Writing Center in an Era of Outsourced Education." *Praxis: A Writing Center Journal* 15 (1): 15–18.

Smith, Louise Z. 1986. "Independence and Collaboration: Why We Should Decentralize Writing Centers." *Writing Center Journal* 7 (1): 3–10.

Tight, Malcolm. 1996. *Key Concepts in Adult Education.* New York: Routledge.

3
EXAMINING ASSUMPTIONS ABOUT TRAINING AND DEVELOPMENT FOR WRITING CENTER PROFESSIONAL CONSULTANTS

Anne Shiell

Tutor training is a recurrent topic in the writing center field, appearing frequently in the scholarly literature, conference presentations, and WCENTER listserv inquiries. However, explorations of professional consultants (PCs)—not faculty, but part- or full-time staff members with professional degrees—have been sparse. Most of the conversation, examples, and research on writing center tutor training are aimed at administrators training student consultants. Similarly, widely used tutor-training manuals are primarily meant for use with undergraduate peer tutors (Jewell and Cheatle 2016). The training and development of PCs have largely gone unexamined or, at least, unpublished.

That tutor training and development discussions focus on student consultants is unsurprising. Writing centers began staffing peer tutors in the latter half of the twentieth century (Boquet 1999), around the same time professional writing center organizations and publications began forming and disseminating scholarship. The first issue of the *Writing Lab Newsletter* ran in 1977, the *Writing Center Journal* launched in 1980, and the International Writing Centers Association was founded in 1983. Currently, peer tutors make up the most common staff model for writing centers (the Writing Lab and the OWL at Purdue and Purdue University 2019). However, the limited discussion around PCs is surprising given that the consulting staff in many centers also partially or fully comprises professionals. Nearly a quarter (24%) of four-year institutions and more than half (55%) of two-year institutions surveyed in the "National Census of Writing" employed professional tutors as of 2013 (Gladstein and Fralix 2013). In more recent data from the Writing Centers Research Project Survey 2016–17, 29 percent of all institution

DOI: 10.7330/9781646420858.c003

types surveyed have professional staff (the Writing Lab and the OWL at Purdue and Purdue University, 2019).

Some administrators train PCs through courses, meetings, or pre-semester workshops and provide development opportunities such as meeting with the director, reading professional journals, and participating in conferences, but not all center administrators provide such opportunities for their PCs (Gladstein and Fralix 2013). Around a fifth of center administrators (20% at two-year institutions and 22% at four-year institutions) responding to the "National Census of Writing" survey reported that they did not require any training for their PCs, and roughly 10 percent of respondents (12% at two-year institutions and 8% at four-year institutions) reported having no development opportunities available for PCs (Gladstein and Fralix 2013). The lack of conversation about training and developing PCs does not seem to stem from a lack of PCs themselves.

Some writing center administrators assume PCs do not need training or development because they are professionals, while others believe in the value of these offerings but question how to provide them given time and budget challenges. In this chapter, I use a narrative format to explore some of these assumptions and challenges that I have heard and experienced as a manager of PCs. While my story does not heed the call for replicable, aggregable, and data-supported (RAD) research in the field, there is still value in lore, which "acknowledges the wisdom, tradition, and experience that writing center folks bring to their work" (Kinkead 2017, 10). By sharing my experiences, I hope to encourage conversations about this relatively unexplored group of writing center staff.

Presenting training and development content ideas is not my primary purpose, as the content of training and professional development for any writing center staff member should be "based on what writers *in your context* need and how your writing center can support them" (Jackie Grutsch-McKinney, as cited in Bleakney 2018; emphasis added). Writing center contexts vary widely between student demographics, student needs and challenges, mode of education (brick and mortar, distance, hybrid), and relationship to the institution or community. Consultants in Walden University's Writing Center (WUWC)—full-time, remote, professional staff at a large, for-profit, online university whose student body primarily comprises working adults around the world—should receive different training and development than consultants who, for example, tutor undergraduate students face-to-face at a small liberal arts college. Context informs training and development logistics and technologies as well as content, so I aim to address assumptions about PCs and discuss considerations for training and development that will be useful to administrators of centers with contexts differing vastly from my own.

My own context is as a former PC now managing a PC team at the WUWC, a large center that transformed dramatically in the past three years in size, culture, and professionalization (see Sharkey-Smith, chapter 7). To revise the training and development offerings to better suit this new team of twenty-two professional educators, center administrators turned to existing writing center literature. We sought to discover several things: What training and professional development best practices for PCs exist? How much and what kind of training and development should be offered for consultants with writing center work histories, teaching backgrounds, and tutoring experience? Should it be required? How can administrators balance the training and development needs of staff and the needs of students? We found a plethora of articles, handbooks, course syllabi, and other resources for training student peer tutors but few recommendations or considerations for PCs. So we adopted and adapted peer tutor-training methods, reflected on our previous practices, and revised them through focus groups, pre- and post-training and development surveys, and lots of experimentation.

As we learned more about training and developing PCs, we continued to make and hear need, time, and funding assumptions worth questioning. These assumptions may cause centers with professional staff to miss opportunities that would benefit the PCs and the students they serve. The assumptions may also prevent center administrators without PCs from considering this demographic as part of their staffing model, a model that has proven successful for students and expands career options in the writing center field. This chapter addresses these assumptions and our learnings to reexamine barriers for centers with, or with the potential for, PC staff.

ASSUMPTIONS ABOUT THE NEED FOR TRAINING

Professional Consultants Do Not Need or Want Training

One of the most common assumptions we have heard is that PCs do not need or want training or development because they are adults with graduate degrees and work experience. As one "Writing Centers Research Project Survey" respondent noted, tutors conducting online consultations need "very little [training] because they are professional tutors" (the Writing Lab and the OWL at Purdue and Purdue University 2018). Unlike student consultants who are new to writing center work or may have tutored for a few years, PCs hold degrees and have experience, sometimes extensive, in writing centers, one-to-one tutoring, and/ or classroom teaching. The "instructional authority" that comes with this prior experience "seems to imply they [nonpeer consultants] do not need training" (Jewell and Cheatle 2016, 11). As Fallon N. Allison (chapter 2) notes, however, a PC who holds a college degree is not necessarily better prepared than a peer consultant for writing center work. Administrators should not assume that because of PCs' qualifications, they do not need training or want development opportunities.

We have found that PCs want and benefit from both and that the topics and content should be tailored to their experience and interests. Using common training guides, such as *The Bedford Guide for Writing Tutors*, can be useful—to an extent—with PCs, but some of the topics are more appropriate and relevant for student employees with limited work experience. As Steven Strang (2006, 293) noted, "professional tutors bring to the center a plethora of teaching styles that have grown out of their own theories and experiences of teaching"; PCs may even have been hired as specialists (Strang 2006), such as in working with multilingual students. Instead of discussing appropriate conduct and dress in the workplace, we discuss topics such as emotional intelligence and conflict resolution strategies. Rather than learning the stages of the writing process, we share ideas on effective feedback and encouragement for adult students with little time for revision. While student tutors might watch *Writing across Borders*, a documentary on international students and academic writing expectations at American colleges and universities, we read Bobbi Olson's (2013) "Rethinking Our Work with Multilingual Writers: The Ethics and Responsibility of Language Teaching in the Writing Center" and grapple with our role in upholding or questioning those expectations and the language of the academy. When shared and examined through training and development, consultants' prior experience and expertise allow for a richness of conversation and inquiry that benefits their tutoring practices and their job satisfaction, ensuring they are prepared to help students in their institutional context and preventing stagnation in effective tutoring practices.

Classroom Teachers Do Not Need Tutor Training
On the other hand, we have also found that teaching expertise does not always translate to effective tutoring; we shouldn't assume that PCs with classroom teaching experience do not need training in tutoring. Even experience working one to one with students in a faculty role does not always equate to strong tutoring (Moneyhun and Hanlon-Baker

2012; Jewell and Cheatle 2016; and Miriam E. Laufer, chapter 1); as Laufer identifies, teaching pedagogies and tutoring pedagogies have distinct goals and outcomes, and faculty members may not be familiar with or up to date on writing center practices. Traditionally, writing center pedagogies champion a collaborative, nonhierarchical approach in tutoring sessions; different authority and power dynamics are at play in a teacher-student relationship versus a tutor-tutee relationship. This relationship becomes further complicated if the PCs are working with adult students (see Sharkey-Smith, chapter 7). Falling into an authoritative role or being viewed in that light, particularly by younger students, is one of the biggest tutoring challenges for PCs (Strang 2006). We have found that consultants with teaching experience, but without a writing center work history, are more inclined to tutor with an overly directive or even editorial approach. We have also found that these consultants can become excellent tutors and that they benefit from a study of foundational writing center literature and selections from canonical peer–tutor training guides, as well as mentoring and coaching from peers or administrators. These activities can help the consultants hone their tutoring practice and draw from a broader range of pedagogical choices. In addition, learning the history, theories, common language, and concerns of writing center work can help them become more comfortable with and active in the center's discourse community.

Human Resources Onboarding Provides Enough Training

We encountered a third assumption—this one, our own—that new PCs will learn what they need to know about the institution from human resources onboarding, a formal process that introduces new employees to the university. Students and faculty consultants may go through human resources onboarding as well, but they have the advantage of already being a part of the institutional community when they are hired. Or, if they are new to the institution and starting both their work at the writing center and their role as a student or faculty member, they are simultaneously entrenched in the institution's culture through taking or teaching classes. This affiliation beyond the writing center allows them to bring experiential understanding of the institution, its student body, the faculty structure and dynamics, and campus perception of the center to their consulting role. Unless they are already familiar with the institution, a newly hired PC will not have these same insights and will need to learn them another way.

New PCs will typically go through an onboarding process with the human resources department to learn about various aspects of their new employer and job. When we doubled our consulting staff in 2015, we incorrectly assumed that they would learn all the institutional knowledge they needed to know through this university orientation, our center's own onboarding program, and on-the-job learning. We also shifted their nontutoring responsibilities from answering student emails to focusing on the center's services, such as webinars, that we thought required greater expertise appropriate to their level of education and experience. What we didn't realize until later in the year was the degree to which consultants had learned institutional knowledge through staffing the email service. Answering student emails helps consultants learn the names and nuances of different departments and their services, where to direct students with noncenter questions, what challenges students face when making tutoring appointments, and other valuable information more quickly and thoroughly than through solely tutoring. New consultants now answer student emails as a regular responsibility, and they appreciate the way this work has immersed them in the university. For centers that do not offer email support, consultants could feasibly gain a similar learning experience through answering student phone calls, staffing a chat service, or working at a center's front desk.

Consultants Only Need Training When They Are New

While center administrators often organize ongoing training for peer staff, some feel that PCs—being professionals with more experience and education—don't need training beyond their initial new-hire onboarding. At our center, training doesn't stop once PCs have become comfortable and competent in their positions. Ongoing training can still be useful to help consultants pursue a goal and feel connected to the center, fulfill a request for specific learning, and/or address a need, as illustrated in the following three examples.

Goal-Based Training

Training can help consultants work toward, and understand their contribution to, center goals, such as the WUWC's 2016 goal of working to better support multilingual writers. That year, our PCs attended an internally created, six-session Multilingual Student Writing Support Series training series on topics including language interference and culturally diverse educational experiences. The training continued the following year with less formal, optional drop-in meetings to discuss questions, concerns, successes, challenges, and tips for supporting multilingual writers. Training based on a center goal not only helps consultants accomplish the goal itself (in this case, better supporting multilingual students), but also helps consultants feel involved in collectively working toward a goal as a team or center, which makes the goal more meaningful and serves as a "philosophical inducement" (Devet 2006, 19) for retention.

Requested Training

PCs may have professional development goals unrelated to centerwide goals, and asking for staff input is another way to develop training topics. Providing effective feedback for students with disabilities is an example of a training series that our consultants requested. The training aimed to help consultants better understand writing challenges that students with disabilities face, teach methods for effective feedback, and raise consultants' confidence in working with this population. Even though some PCs came to their positions with expertise in this area, the training allowed them to learn from each other and develop further, ultimately benefiting both staff and students.

Need-Based Training

Training can also be organized to strengthen skill gaps. For example, in 2018, manager evaluations, peer observations, and self-reflections illustrated that the WUWC PC team needed additional training in APA style. We developed an "APA at Walden" training series that included a panel discussion with center staff who had expertise in answering nuanced APA questions from students and faculty and were familiar with university expectations. The series also included an activity in which consultants collectively reviewed a paper for APA style and an "APA Refresher" activity in which consultants rotated each week in summarizing an APA rule for the team's bulletin communication. Through a pretraining survey and posttraining survey, we found that the training increased consultants' knowledge of APA style and comfort level with teaching it to students.

ASSUMPTIONS ABOUT TIME

Even if we acknowledge that PCs do need and want training and development, administrators must be able to find and justify the time involved for themselves, the consultants, and students.

Part-Time and Staggered Schedules Make Training Impossible
A challenge of training PCs is having enough individual or common time. Not all centers with PCs are able to offer full-time positions, and part-time consultants' working hours are often staggered to help ensure appointment availability throughout the week. As Laufer (chapter 1) says of faculty tutors, who face some of the same time issues as PCs (such as living off campus, having family responsibilities, and holding other positions), finding common time can feel near impossible. However, it is prudent to consider Strang's (2006) claim that the quality in tutoring work that results from training professional staff is worth the scheduling challenges, and new technologies can make scheduling easier. If consultants aren't able to meet on campus but do have common time available, synchronous online training can be an option. For example, "shadow reviews" are our online version of appointment observations, a common training practice in writing centers. Because our staff is entirely remote, we conduct these sessions using online meeting software with screen-sharing functionality (currently, Skype for Business), so that participants can view the presenter's computer screen. During a shadow review, an experienced consultant screen-shares and talks through a review, either in real time or in reflection. The consultant also answers questions and facilitates discussion. We typically hold shadow reviews as part of training on a new skill or process, such as when we focused on accessibility in asynchronous feedback, or to highlight a consultant's specific practice or strategy.

Part-time schedules can still make synchronous training or development sessions difficult, but asynchronous online communities—through which teachers can post questions and ideas, reflect on and discuss practices, and share resources—make participation more possible. Our consultants regularly use Yammer, an enterprise social network, for asynchronous conversations about tutoring practices and extended discussions originating in synchronous professional development sessions. Other platforms used for peer or faculty tutor professional development, such as blogs (Blazer 2015; Hall 2017), Facebook (Naydan 2013), internal listservs (Davis, Mooney, and Sargent 2016), or virtual discussion boards (as Laufer, chapter 1, suggests) could be adopted for PCs.

Training and Development Takes Too Much Time for Administrators
Providing training and development opportunities does take a lot of time for administrators, and it's important to acknowledge the truth of this challenge. However, it is also worth weighing the time investment in ongoing training and development in comparison to the time—and

cost—should a consultant feel stagnant in his or her career and leave the center. Lack of growth and development is a common reason for employee turnover (Sears 2017). While researchers disagree on the monetary cost of turnover, there is consensus that turnover costs are significant, both in terms of direct costs and "indirect costs" such as loss of institutional knowledge and the time needed to hire and onboard a replacement (9). Some research even suggests that the time involved in interview processes is increasing (Chamberlain 2015). Therefore, administrators might think of training and development as a challenging but positive long-term investment in the consultant and in the center. Because of the time required to organize, conduct, evaluate, and revise training and development programs or sessions, writing center administrators with PCs can help each other by sharing experiences, resources, and ideas.

Training and Development Take Time away from Students

Consultants' time spent on training and development does take time away from students, an assumption that is also true though less straightforward than it might seem. In our case, each hour that a consultant spends on training and development is one fewer tutoring appointment with a student. However, consultants have reported, and we have consistently observed, that training and development help consultants feel engaged, reflect on their tutoring approaches and choices, flex their intellectual muscles, and explore new strategies for working with students. In short, it improves their work, which benefits students, and their job satisfaction.

Job satisfaction contributes to employee retention, which also benefits students. Centers with student consultants expect regular staff turnover as those consultants graduate, yet still find value in offering training and development. Professional consultants have even more of an opportunity than do peer consultants to use training and development to benefit students. When consultants stay in their positions, the center builds a "strong continuing core of tutors from one academic year to the next, a stable and continuing workforce whose skills and knowledge of the center's clients becomes more and more sophisticated" (Strang 2006, 293). Their training experiences and continued growth can also help inform future training (Laufer, chapter 1). While training and development opportunities for staff do mean fewer direct interactions with students, there are valuable trade-offs with PCs' growth and retention. To minimize the time taken away from tutoring and other center services, administrators can use breaks in the academic calendar and center traffic trends to schedule training and development during historically slow times.

ASSUMPTIONS ABOUT COSTS

Admittedly, and thankfully, the WUWC's full-time, salaried PC positions mean that training and development is in our control; we have not needed to justify the importance of these activities to university administration, nor do we face the obstacle of an institution only funding time spent directly working with students. Laufer (chapter 1) presents some incentive suggestions for when centers can't pay tutors for their training time. For centers that can offer compensated training and development, different cost assumptions and considerations come into play.

Professional Development Is Expensive

Conference participation is one of the more common forms of professional development for PCs (Gladstein and Fralix 2013). We encourage our PCs to attend and present at the International Writing Centers Association's annual conference and other national and regional conferences, but we have also identified opportunities that have low or no budget requirements outside of staff time. The following collaborative opportunities do not require additional funding and could be offered in a face-to-face setting or online using meeting software with screen-sharing and video-conferencing capabilities, such as Zoom. We use the following professional development activities to create space for inquiry, learning, and reflection.

Think-Pair-Share

Think-Pair-Share discussions involve small groups of PCs that individually review the same student paper and then meet online for an hour to discuss their approach, questions, and challenges. Each meeting focuses on a theme, topic, or tutoring strategy, such as considerations for reviewing papers of a particular genre (e.g., a doctoral student's dissertation prospectus). Participants takes turns sharing their screen to visually walk through their review, explaining their pedagogical choices and inviting discussion. Think-Pair-Share meetings often lead to consultants trying new and different approaches in their reviews; we have seen direct impacts on consultants' practices and on students' satisfaction. Even if consultants do not change their practices, they find that the collegial sharing provides a valued space for reflection and reinforces our philosophy that there is no single "right" way to tutor.

Journal Club

Journal Club meets monthly to discuss an article related to writing center work or higher education. The meetings create an avenue for consultants to read, grapple with, and discuss literature in the field and reflect on how their own practices and our center's approach to paper reviews is affirmed, challenged, or informed by this scholarship. For our Journal Club, senior writing consultants, with input from managers and colleagues, select readings to inform the center's yearly goals, extend organic discussions among consultants, or address a training need. Consultants might choose recent articles to stay abreast of current literature, or they might propose articles based on areas of personal interest. Many institutional libraries offer access to journals such as the *Writing Center Journal* and *WLN: A Journal of Writing Center Scholarship*, while other publications, such as *Praxis: A Writing Center Journal*, are freely available online. Whether held virtually or face to face, Journal Clubs can help consultants engage in reflection, learn from colleagues, and feel more connected to the field.

Spotlight Sessions

Administrators originally organized "spotlight sessions," led by the new consultants who joined our center in 2015, for the current team to get to know new colleagues and recognize the experiences they brought to the position. Each new consultant chose a topic of interest for presenting to and/or discussing with the team, based on their past work, research, or professional interests. Example topics included andragogy theory, code meshing, publishing with academic journals, and tutor/teacher identities. After the first year, the spotlight sessions continued due to consultants' requests. Consultants have reported appreciating the spotlight sessions as a learning opportunity and a chance to practice presentation skills, but also as a form of community building.

Invited Speakers

When we have had funding available for professional development but not enough for each consultant, we have invited other professionals in the field to speak with our team. Inviting a guest speaker for a fee is likely to cost far less than funding multiple, or sometimes even one, PC for attendance at a conference. Costs may be reduced further if a speaker is willing to engage with consultants online through an online meeting platform such as Google Hangouts or Zoom. In the spirit of collegiality, a speaker may even be willing to visit (physically or virtually) pro bono or in return for a speaker swap. Guests might talk about their career path, a published article or book, an area of pedagogical expertise, or advice, such as on writing for publication or conducting writing center research. With such a large, active, collaborative field of writing center scholars and professionals, there is ample opportunity for tapping into expertise and growing professional networks.

Another cost-effective option is to host a speaker from within the institution. Laufer (chapter 1) describes the benefits, such as opportunities to gain institutional knowledge and interact with administrators, of inviting deans, department chairs, and other guests to speak with tutors. Large centers such as the WUWC can even look within for speakers and topics. Our monthly PC team meeting regularly includes visits from center leaders, who share insights into their role and updates on university initiatives.

FURTHER CONSIDERATIONS

Training and Development as Strategies for Staff Engagement and Retention

When weighing the time and monetary costs of training and development, it's important to consider the potential positive impact training and development can have on retaining trained consultants, which is "a goal, a desire, an ideal" for center directors (Devet 2016, 24). Staff turnover, sometimes as often as each semester, is an expected, unavoidable reality of writing centers with student consultants. Volunteer faculty consultants' time at the center may dwindle as they become tenured or take on other responsibilities, such as committee and service work. Centers with PCs, however, have the opportunity and the challenge of retaining those consultants. Engagement is crucial to employee retention, and thoughtful, strategic training and professional development can help consultants stay engaged in their work, particularly because they are educators who highly value continued learning. We strive to offer opportunities that take an "inquiry stance" by encouraging active participation and reflection through "relentless questioning, asking why, wondering, researching, generating alternatives, testing, reviewing, and revising options" (Hall 2013, 2). We have found it important for consultants to feel that they are the makers, not simply the receivers, of knowledge.

Another factor in employee retention that is particularly challenging for writing centers is the lack of organic opportunities for employees to grow professionally. Writing centers typically do not have many opportunities for advancement, which is not problematic for student and faculty consultants who likely expect limited, if any, promotions. Expectations or desires for advancement may be greater, however, for PCs who consider their writing center work as a step—perhaps even the final one—on their career path. While development opportunities are not akin to a promotion, they allow employees to continue to learn and grow in their professional skills and knowledge.

It's important to acknowledge that training and development for PCs present a catch-22; as we work to retain consultants by providing opportunities for them to grow professionally, we are, in a sense, preparing them for roles that may not be available within our centers. We have faced this challenge, as consultants have outgrown their roles and left for promotions and greater responsibilities within other academic centers at the university, or who have moved on to administrative positions at other writing centers. While we are saddened to lose these team members, we are proud that they were able to build the skills needed in their consultant positions to take on more leadership within the university and/or writing center field.

REFERENCES

Blazer, Sarah. 2015. "Twenty-First Century Writing Center Staff Education: Teaching and Learning Towards Inclusive and Productive Everyday Practice." *Writing Center Journal* 35 (Fall/Winter): 17–55.

Bleakney, Julia. 2018. "Tutor Education." Presentation, the International Writing Centers Association Summer Institute, Indianapolis, July 17.

Boquet, Elizabeth H. 1999. "'Our Little Secret': A History of Writing Centers, Pre- to Post-Open Admissions.'" *College Composition and Communication* 50 (3): 463–82. https://doi.org/10.2307/358861.

Davis, Jeffry C., Shannon Mooney, and Emma Sargent. 2016. "Building an E-community of Consulting Problem Solvers: Utilizing Online Conversation in the Writing Center." *Synergy* 9 (June 1). https://www.myatp.org/synergy.

Devet, Bonnie. 2016. "Retaining Writing Center Consultants: A Taxonomy of Approaches." *WLN: A Journal of Writing Center Scholarship* 41, nos. 3–4 (November/December): 18–25.

Chamberlain, Andrew. 2015. *Why Is Hiring Taking Longer? New Insights from Glassdoor Data*. Glassdoor. Accessed September 27, 2018. https://www.glassdoor.com/research/app/uploads/sites/2/2015/06/GD_Report_3.pdf.

Hall, R. Mark. 2013. "Problems of Practice: An Inquiry Stance toward Writing Center Work." *Writing Lab Newsletter* 37 (January/February): 5–6. https://wlnjournal.org/archives.

Hall, R. Mark. 2017. "Blogging as a Tool for Dialogic Reflection." In *Around the Texts of Writing Center Work: An Inquiry-Based Approach to Tutor Education.* 105–24. https://doi.org/10.7330/9781607325826.c005.

Gladstein, Jill M., and Brandon Fralix. 2013. "The National Census of Writing." Accessed September 26, 2018. http://writingcensus.swarthmore.edu.

Jewell, Megan S., and Joseph Cheatle. 2016. "Toward a Professional Consultant's Handbook: Researching Support and Training Methods." *WLN: A Journal of Writing Center Scholarship* 41 (3–4) (November/December): 10–17. https://wlnjournal.org/archives/v41/41.3-4.pdf.

Kinkead, Joyce. 2017. "The Writing Center Director as Archivist: The Documentation Imperative." *WLN: A Journal of Writing Center Scholarship* 41 (9–10) (May/June): 10–17. https://wlnjournal.org/archives/v41/41.9-10.pdf.

Moneyhun, Clyde F., and Patti Hanlon-Baker. 2012. "Tutoring Teachers." *Writing Lab Newsletter* 36 (9–10) (May/June): 1–5. https://wlnjournal.org/archives/v36/36.9-10.pdf.

Naydan, Liliana M. 2013. "Just Writing Center Work in the Digital Age: De Facto Multiliteracy Centers in Dialogue with Questions of Social Justice." *Praxis: A Writing Center Journal* 11 (1). http://www.praxisuwc.com./naydan-111.

Olson, Bobbi. 2013. "Rethinking Our Work with Multilingual Writers: The Ethics and Responsibility of Language Teaching in the Writing Center." *Praxis: A Writing Center Journal* 10 (2). http://www.praxisuwc.com/olson-102.

Sears, Lindsay. 2017. *2017 Retention Report.* Work Institute. Accessed September 27, 2018. https://cdn2.hubspot.net/hubfs/478187/2017%20Retention%20Report%20Campaign/Work%20Institute%202017%20-Retention%20Report.pdf.

Strang, Steven. 2006. "Staffing A Writing Center with Professional Tutors." In *The Writing Center Director's Resource Book,* edited by Christina Murphy and Byron Stay, 291–99. New York: Routledge.

The Writing Lab and the OWL at Purdue and Purdue University. 2018. "WCRP Survey 2014–15." *Writing Centers Research Project Survey.* https://owl.purdue.edu/research/writing_centers_research_project_survey.html.

The Writing Lab and the OWL at Purdue and Purdue University. 2019. "WCRP Survey 2016–17." *Writing Centers Research Project Survey.* Accessed March 5. https://owl.purdue.edu/research/writing_centers_research_project_survey.html.

4

READING BETWEEN THE LINES
Professional Tutor Training with the Stanislavski System for Actors

Irina Ruppo

INTRODUCTION

This chapter presents exercises developed in an Irish university writing center for postgraduate, or what I term "professional," writing center tutors. Drawn from the work of Constantin Stanislavski, these exercises have been created to help tutors to engage with the student's text at a deep level without judging or criticizing the text and thus compromising the writing center's identity as a nonjudgmental and supportive space. In designing these exercises, I drew on my experience as a manager of the Academic Writing Centre (AWC), a busy writing center catering to the entire student population of the National University of Ireland Galway (NUIG). While the structure of the AWC, which I describe in more detail in the next section, might differ from its counterparts elsewhere, I believe the lessons learned here are applicable to writing centers worldwide. The main challenge currently faced by the AWC in relation to tutor training has to do with the insufficient time available for training; the exercises were developed in order to address this problem, but they can also be used in less time-poor environments as part of a longer tutor-training course in meaningful textual analysis.

The work of the seminal theater practitioner Constantin Stanislavski might strike one as an unusual source of inspiration for writing center work. The use of acting methods for teacher training is a long-standing, though relatively poorly explored, field (Özmen 2011, 36), and the connections between acting and writing have not yet been fully explored (Henney 2012). Moreover, Stanislavski is often associated with Method Acting, which was a methodology developed in the United States and influenced by his teachings, and its use of emotion for character embodiment. This chapter, however, discusses a different aspect of Stanislavski's work, namely, the centrality of textual analysis for his work with actors.

DOI: 10.7330/9781646420858.c004

The analysis of a student paper constitutes a major part of a tutorial session; it would be impossible for the tutor to conduct an effective session without understanding the student's text and the clues it provides as to the student's needs. Yet most of the conversation on tutoring techniques avoids the subject of textual analysis. It is presumed that tutors' advanced writing and reading comprehension skills would enable them to engage with the text successfully; the challenges explored in most manuals have to do with interpersonal relations and teaching techniques. However, if no guidance on textual analysis is offered, the tutors are likely to fall back on their earlier experiences as students or, in some cases, editors or proofreaders. The problem is that editing, proofreading, or marking are all processes lacking an empathetic engagement with the text; the objective is to find flaws. By contrast, Stanislavski's approach to textual analysis is not evaluative; the actors do not seek to correct the text but to understand and transform the emotions and ideas hidden between the lines.

The exercises examined here were designed to meet the needs of the AWC tutors but can be used with other postgraduate tutors or professional consultants rather than undergraduate peer-tutors. In other words, they are more likely to be of benefit to tutors who, like the AWC tutors, possess excellent writing skills and an interest or experience in teaching. Postgraduates or professional tutors have unique needs. As Matthew Sharkey-Smith explains (in chapter 7) near-professional or professional tutors occupy a liminal "role between that of peer and faculty," so their ability to provide peer support is tempered by their greater sphere of experience and their authorial role, yet they do not have access to such pedagogical tools as grades and regular sessions. Another challenge has to do with the need to tutor outside the sphere of one's expertise, a challenge outlined in chapter 8, by Catherine Siemann. Finally, professional or postgraduate tutors may be allocated less time for training than their undergraduate counterparts. This shortage of time may, in turn, affect the tutors' ability to integrate writing center pedagogy and, as we shall see, impact their ability to negotiate between directive or non-directive approaches to tutoring, something that happens because the choice to hire postgraduate or professional tutors may be motivated by the shortage of time and resources available for training. This predicament is indeed the case of the AWC, whose structure is outlined below.

BACKGROUND

The AWC was founded as a pilot project in 2009. In 2011, it relocated to the university library. Depending on budget allocation, the AWC opens for twelve to eighteen hours a week, offering a combination of morning, midday, and evening hours. During opening hours, two tutors are responsible for working with students who arrive for drop-in appointments. On occasion, we have used scheduled appointments, but our preferred method is to work with drop-ins on the first-come-first-served basis. Tutors are hired at the start of the academic year. They are recruited from various year-long taught master's programs such as the MA in English, LLM in human rights, and MSc in science. Between seven and nine tutors are recruited every year for the duration of six months. One of the tutors is hired to provide the service through the medium of the Irish language (Gaeilge). Tutors' employment commences on October 1, which is when the AWC opens its doors, and ceases on the last day of teaching, which is also when the AWC closes for the summer. It should also be noted that the teaching terms at NUIG are only twelve weeks, with the AWC usually being open for only ten weeks in each term.

The demand to attend AWC is quite high. During busy times, the two tutors on duty are sometimes compelled to see as many as eight students during the four-hour slot. In spite of these challenges, the anonymous feedback remains positive, with students reporting high levels of satisfaction and a desire to come to the AWC again. The AWC has one manager (the author of this chapter), who works eighteen hours a week from September to May. Usually, the manager provides one 2-hour training session before the start of the first term, followed by monthly 90-minute training sessions throughout both terms.

This is not the place to discuss the reasons for the NUIG adopting this particular model, which is, moreover, likely to change and evolve in the future. Rather, I would like to present the particular challenges faced by the AWC as extreme versions of the problems facing writing centers elsewhere. The NUIG's response to these challenges, especially in the field of tutor training, should be of use to managers of other writing centers, even if they operate within less time-poor frameworks.

The main challenge is shortage of time. All of the tutors are hired in September. With only one part-time manager completely responsible for the selection process, there is little to no time or budget allocated for training. However, the standards of the AWC are high. Students are assured that their difficulties with writing will be addressed in a safe and judgment-free place; that the tutors will work with them on their strengths as well as areas of improvement; that they will be warmly welcomed; and that they will get useful advice specially tailored to their needs, whatever these might be. Advanced writers are told that they are as likely to benefit from a tutorial at the writing center as novice writers because the AWC caters to all levels of experience and all disciplines. How can the AWC provide this level of service if there is so little time to train new tutors? The answer is that we hire postgraduates who may be described as near professionals. They have primary degrees, excellent writing skills, and either a talent for teaching or some teaching or tutoring experience. The selection process is rigorous, with prospective writing tutors required to submit academic writing samples as part of their application and having to do a mock tutorial at the interview.

While some centers hire predominantly peer tutors and other centers rely on professional (nonstudent) tutors, the NUIG approach occupies the middle ground between these two. Our tutors are students, but they are not true peer tutors, as, unlike undergraduates, they already have degrees. Our tutors often have some teaching experience, but this does not quite put them in the same category as people with several years of teaching practice. They are, in fact, near professionals. Their training needs are close to those of professional tutors; they are rightly proud of their existing writing skills and pedagogical experience. Training such people using a program designed for undergraduate tutors might be demotivating. Instead, a method is required—as explained by Anne Shiell in chapter 3—that allows them to examine their prior experience and expertise and create "a richness of conversation and inquiry that benefits their tutoring practices and their job satisfaction."

Moreover, the tutors' limited knowledge and experience of writing center pedagogy means that they find it difficult to put their writing and editing skills to full use without sounding judgmental and adopting the role of a teacher or a critic. As postgraduate tutors, they may indeed appear to undergraduates as figures of authority. They may intimidate or overwhelm their students to a greater degree than peer tutors. Yet should they adopt a completely passive role or limit their utterances to expressions of sympathy or icebreakers, they are likely to make students feel that their writing needs have not been addressed. It is not easy to strike the right balance.

This is not a new problem. Non-directive approaches, such as the one advocated by John Trimbur (1987) and Jeff Brooks (1991), have been the mainstay of tutoring pedagogy since the early days of the writing centers. However, non-directive approaches came under a great deal of criticism for being unrealistic and unconnected to the mainstream pedagogical traditions (Shamoon and Burns 1995), for being a falsehood perpetuated by writing centers out of political reasons (Clark and Healy 1996), and for preventing nontraditional students from accessing "insider knowledge" about writing conventions (Grimm 1999). More recently, Peter Carino (2003) has suggested that tutors need to be taught to switch between directive and non-directive approaches depending on the student's ability. John Nordlof (2014), in trying to steer the conversation away from the debate about a directive-versus-non-directive approach, proposed "scaffolding" as the most practical approach to tutoring. Both of these approaches are promising; they preserve the nonjudgmental and egalitarian aspects of the traditional non-directive methods while giving tutors flexible pedagogical tools. However, training new tutors in one of those approaches might require more time than is currently at our disposal at the AWC.

Carino's formula goes as follows: "More student knowledge, less tutor knowledge = more non-directive methods. Less student knowledge, more tutor knowledge = more directive methods" (2003, 110). However, if inexperienced tutors are given Carino's advice, they might start to differentiate students on the arbitrary principles of knowledge and ability. The unfortunate result might be that higher-achieving and cognitively more advanced students would experience the AWC as a nonjudgmental safe space, while novice writers and students with particularly pronounced writing or reading comprehension problems would feel judged and disempowered. Besides, given the diverse population of students at NUIG, I am wary of suggesting that tutors adjust their treatment of students based on their belonging to a particular group. In a long-term training course, which would allow tutors sufficient opportunity to workshop and discuss the potential pitfalls of various pedagogical strategies, Carino's advice would be helpful. Outside the supportive context such a course would provide, this advice carries too much risk.

According to Nordlof's method of "scaffolding," which builds on the psychologist Lev Vygotsky's "zone of proximal development," the tutor should identify the "skills the student is in the process of developing" and decide on the "proper scaffolds to help the student work on those skills" (Nordlof 2014, 59). Having examined previous studies of tutor strategies, Nordlof explains that successful tutors use both "cognitive scaffolding," which is the practice of simplifying problems and using prompts and questions to help the student get to a higher level of proficiency, and "motivational scaffolding," which refers to using empathetic and positive language as well as praise to "build a supportive learning environment for the student" (Nordlof 2014, 57). Nordlof contends that these strategies should completely replace the need to prevaricate between a directive and non-directive approach. However, scaffolding precludes a true relationship between peers. The metaphor that is frequently used to explain the approach is that of a parent holding onto the saddle of a child's bicycle so that pedaling can be mastered before balancing (56); this metaphor makes the hierarchy and authority in a tutorial only too clear. Again, it allows or tacitly encourages tutors to look down on students, especially on those with less well-developed writing skills. The local problem with this approach at the AWC is that tutors are overwhelmed with the sheer number of students who arrive in October; high demand coupled with few available hours mean that students cannot be easily asked to come back for a follow-up session. In a time-poor and pressurized situation, "scaffolds" can easily morph into simple directive advice.

There is a further complication in working with professional and postgraduate tutors. Just like undergraduate students, they need praise and encouragement to flourish. In fact, this might be particularly the case with postgraduates who are at a difficult and vulnerable stage in their academic careers. Over-coaching them and ignoring their existing skills might demotivate them or make them mistrustful of the tutor's advice. The need to offer concrete and transformative advice that would accommodate a variety of personalities is one of the reasons to turn to Stanislavski. "Never lose yourself on the stage," Stanislavski writes; "Always act in your own person, as an artist" ([1936] 1980, 177). Respect for the actor's self is matched in Stanislavski's system by respect for the play-text. When applied to the writing center situation, this approach translates into knowledge of oneself as a tutor and writer and into profound curiosity about the text and respect for the student as a partner in bringing out its potential.

THE "SYSTEM" AND THE TUTORS

"Through conscious means," writes Stanislavski, "we reach the subconscious" (176). This principle applies equally to the preparatory work of the actors on themselves, which would include recovering relevant memories and putting them to work, and, more important for our purpose, to the work on the play-text. A significant part of the Stanislavski rehearsal process is a careful analysis of the text. Actors are asked to read the text without thinking about acting. It is of paramount importance that "the author's text must be respected, studied and served" (Benedetti 1998, 105). They need to pay attention to the minute hints contained in punctuation, pauses, and other textual clues in order to uncover the subtext (88–89). By studying the "given circumstances" of the play—its historical period, social situation, and reconstruction of the characters' background stories from textual clues—actors can gain invaluable insight into the characters' inner world. This exercise in imaginative criticism allows actors to say their lines with the depth of the undercurrent emotions that one finds in real life. The idea of the subtext is a powerful tool for tutors.

The subtext can be seen as the gamut of ideas relating both to the essay content and structure; some of these ideas make it to the essay, and some are not fully articulated by the student. They may be guessed at through such clues as unusual vocabulary or punctuation, clichés, generalizations, structural inconsistencies, and other writing features, which are regarded as flaws by teachers. For a tutor, however, these are not flaws but aids in designing the right questions that would allow the student to bring the subtext to the surface. This way of seeing student writing differs from the well-known advice to see any student's paper, regardless of the stage of completion, as a "rough draft" in order to "discuss aspects of the paper in terms of what might be *more effective* instead of *inadequate* or *wrong*" (Ryan and Zimmerelli 2010, 53). "Effective" is a glib word. To the student, it suggests the need to impress an audience, while the tutor sees "more effective" as a polite euphemism. By contrast, the belief in the existence of the subtext allows the students to feel that they are understood in spite of all the shortcomings in communication; and the tutors, instead of being annoyed by errors (and possibly transferring this sense of annoyance to the students) now see them as moments of opportunity and discovery.

Consider this extract from a third-year undergraduate essay on Vladimir Nabokov's short story "Cloud, Castle, Lake": "It emerges that the macabre carnival of 'Cloud, Castle, Lake' is not, as in *Crime and Punishment*, a vision of the world, wherein immoral and sinful characters exist, but it is limited to the crowd. The individual sets himself apart from it, and the result is disastrous." The first sentence is difficult to understand; let us first look at the slightly easier second sentence and see if its syntax might be a clue to the subtext. The writer uses a compound sentence, where a complex sentence would seem more natural. The question is why she does not write: "When the individual sets himself apart from it, the result is disastrous." The answer might be: because it is not a matter of "when." The individual is apart from the crowd—this is what turns a person into an individual—some people cannot be absorbed by the crowd, and they are eliminated.

The discovery that the subtext is about crowds eliminating those it cannot absorb might help us tackle the first sentence. Here the word "it" in the final clause has an unclear reference; syntactically, it could refer to "the macabre carnival" or "a vision of the world"; semantically, it refers to the existence of "immoral and sinful characters." Of course, this is syntactically incorrect, but what is more important is why the student structures the sentence this way. The answer might be: because for her the two are one. She wants to speak of "the macabre carnival" as Nabokov's "vision of the world," and she also wants to contrast it with Dostoyevsky's vision of immorality and sinfulness. These two ideas—that the macabre carnival is the world and that this world is different from Dostoyevsky's vision—are intertwined in the sentence because they appeared almost simultaneously in the student's mind. She does not fully explain the reference to *Crime and Punishment* because for her it is already explained—it is opposite from the situation in "Cloud, Castle, Lake."

A careful tutor could help this student uncover the relationship between her ideas. A newer version of the text, closer to the subtext might read as follows:

> The macabre carnival of "Cloud, Castle, Lake" is Nabokov's vision of the world as a clash between crowds and individuals. Crowds embody immorality and sinfulness. They eliminate those they cannot absorb. This is different from the world of *Crime and Punishment,* where the seat of evil is the human soul and where sinfulness is linked to individualism. Unlike Dostoyevsky, Nabokov sees evil as the abandonment of individuality for the needs of the crowd.

Here, the comparison with *Crime and Punishment* is introduced only after the vision of the world in "Cloud, Castle, Lake" has been described. The point of comparison is made clearer through the repetition of the word "evil."

It might not be possible for the student to rewrite her paragraph in the manner above because it might still lie outside her current abilities. Regardless, tutors should be able to glimpse this version (or an even better one) behind what the student has written. Tutors' writing and reading skills are working at full capacity as they try to uncover the subtext. Instead of just spotting errors, they are actively engaged in discovering the text's true potential, and the only person who can help them on their quest is the student. The student thus turns into a helpful partner.

Stanislavski's analysis of the play requires the use of imagination and attention to detail. Actors are meant to identify points in the play that beg the questions "why" and "where." For example, in the group analysis of *Othello*, described in *Creating a Role*, the director pauses at the following lines in Othello's speech before the senate: "Most potent, grave and reverend seigniors, / My very noble and approv'd good masters." The director asks the actors about the nature of the relationship between

Othello and these senators whom he calls his masters: "Is he . . . a kind of minister of war, and are they a council of ministers, or is he simply a mercenary soldier, and are they plenipotentiary governors who make all the binding decisions in the country?" (Stanislavski [1957] 1961, 158). He explains that this information is vital for appreciating the play's conflict of classes and different nationalities and is essential for the actor playing the role. Anchoring his study of the text in such minute details, Stanislavski relies equally on appraisal of facts and imagination. He urges the actors to look outside the bounds of the play's plot and imagine the characters' past and future: "Do not conceal from us the hints you yourselves get from beneath the words, between the lines, the things suggested by Shakespeare just as you yourselves see, hear, and sense the life of a human spirit in the play. Be creators, not mere narrators" (160).

Textual analysis fueled by imagination can be useful in tutor-training sessions. A careful reading of a student's essay reveals useful information about the student and about the subtext. In this scenario, tutors would be given a copy of an anonymous student's essay (with the student's prior consent). After reading a two-page essay, tutors are asked if they have comments and questions. After an initial volley of comments, it is helpful to ask them to focus their attention on a single paragraph:

> An interesting factor develops from Amelia's nursing of her younger brother as we see the opinion of the local doctor. Through all the turmoil in Amelia's life she triumphs as this strong hardworking young woman who begins to defy Traditional gender roles as she announces that she wishes to be a doctor when she grows up. Amelia's announcement initially does not sit well with Dr. Mitchell as traditionally a doctor's job was only to be held by a man.

At first, tutors are likely to comment on the supposed flaws: the unnecessary capitalization, the way ideas seem to be jumbled together, and the overuse of adjectives in the second sentence. Sometimes, especially if essays happen to have spelling errors, tutors might start to laugh. At this stage, it is useful to ask them to use textual clues to try and guess the student's state of mind and their wishes at the time of the writing. The following are possible answers:

- The student wants to imitate writers of an older generation (the use of the word nursing).
- The student wants to emphasize the importance of tradition in the novel (the unusual use of capitalization).
- The student is writing in a rush and might be stressed out (the absence of commas).

- The student wants to make a point about Amelia's personality (the colloquial use of "this" and the string of adjectives in the phrase "this strong hardworking young woman").
- The student is worried about including too much plot summary (the lack of clarity as to the events of the novel; the structure of the passage).

Now the tutors seem to be more empathetic to the student. They stop looking for flaws and begin to develop a curiosity about the text and its author. They realize that each of these observations can be turned easily into a question that would satisfy their curiosity about the subtext and help the student express their ideas with greater clarity.

Next, the tutors are asked about the phrase "an interesting factor" at the start of the passage. For Stanislavski, a great deal of information is contained within pauses (Stanislavski 1988, 141). In academic writing, of course, there are no actual pauses. Their equivalents are empty phrases, and these are just as revealing. Here "interesting factor" is a type of pause, an empty phrase that does not lead anywhere. The student has not explained what that factor is and why it is interesting. What are they trying to say? Possible answers include:

- Taking care of her brother is a key event in Amelia's life.
- Taking care of her brother helps Amelia discover her vocation and leads her to defy traditional gender roles.
- When she takes care of her brother, Amelia becomes inspired by Dr. Mitchell, who, however, is not supportive of her decision to become a doctor.

Why is the student reluctant to commit to any of these summaries of Amelia's situation? It is possible that they have not decided which aspect of the novel is important to their argument; it might be Amelia's vocation, it might be the reaction of Dr. Mitchell, and it might be the experience of "turmoil" caused by her brother's illness. Possibly there is a sentence that would relate all these aspects of the plot to each other and to the problem of gender roles. It is outside the student's reach, and, for the moment, it is not accessible to the tutors either. As the tutors look for the perfect way to relate these ideas, they have a sense of having glimpsed the subtext behind the empty phrase "interesting factor." The tutors' task becomes akin to that of Stanislavski's actors, who, having sensed the true emotion contained in a particular line, need to work on their own emotional memory to help them execute the words with a sense of truth.

The exercises above are not meant to replace such classic training methods as mock tutorials, role-playing games, or simple debriefing and airing of concerns. They are supplementary exercises meant to aid advanced writers in becoming engaged and efficient tutors. Throughout my work at the AWC, I have found that postgraduate tutors usually fall into one of two types: those who seem to be more interested in improving the text and those who seem to be more interested in reassuring the student. The former may at times lack empathy, can easily overwhelm the student, and can adopt an overly directive approach. The latter may be careless with time and give the student little practical advice or guidance on how to improve their written work. The Stanislavski-inspired exercises allow tutors to gain a new perspective on the text and its author and thus revise hard-set practices in working with students.

CONCLUSION

Many of the challenges faced by postgraduate tutors and professionals alike have to do with the search for balance: balance between authority and peer support, experience, and open-mindedness, and balance between the needs of students and their text. While the student may need reassurance, empathy, and support in developing as a writer, their text might need different things. The text (if I may be pardoned of anthropomorphizing the written word) may need editing for clarity and logic as well as attention to sentence structure. The text can also challenge the tutor, especially if its subject falls outside the tutor's discipline. Stanislavski-inspired exercises included here are meant to supplement the traditional training methods as an aid in finding the required balance between the conflicting demands of the tutorial situation.

In pointing out his negative comments on contemporary directors' management of their cast, Stanislavski might strike a note of recognition with some writing instructors. "In one way or another," Stanislavski writes, the director "has 'tipped off' actors about what he wishes them to do; somehow or other the actors succeeded in picking up a few crumbs of another man's spirit and will, having in the process successfully barred all the roads to their intuition and their creative work" (1988, 98). Stanislavski argues that this particular pitfall would be avoided through the use of his system, which relies, among other things, on a careful study of the play's text combined with exercises to enable the actors to find a way toward truly original and cliché-free acting true to the author's supposed intentions.

The use of clichés and the misunderstandings of one's source texts or ideas are indeed as problematic in academic writing as they are in acting. The danger of stifling a student's voice through overinstruction is as relevant to teaching writing and training tutors as it is to directing.

Stanislavski's insights into guiding actors, moreover, rest on the idea that I consider to be essential for a successful writing center session, namely, that the text and the actor, rather than any static vision of the director, are crucial sites of discovery. Like Stanislavski's director, who should carefully interpret the play text with the actors, a successful tutor should be able to read between the lines of the student's essay, seeing not only what is obviously stated but also the potential thoughts that might lie hidden therein and that can emerge through the effort of the student's imagination.

Yet, it has to be noted that Stanislavski is a difficult guide. His famous "system" is not a single and clear instruction manual; it resides within several sources, namely, a series of engaging, but somewhat truncated and often ambiguous books, told from the point of view of an imaginary student recalling the lessons of an imaginary director: *Actor Prepares* (1936), *Building a Character* (1948), *Creating a Role* (1957), and a similarly loosely structured book of stenographic notes posthumously translated and published in *Stanislavsky on the Art of the Stage* (1988). Stanislavski's main three books on acting are written from the perspective of a young actor studying in what the author imagined to be an ideally equipped and staffed theater school. Stanislavski's creative forays into the relationship between a small group of students and their teacher have a lot to offer a writing center director or tutor, not only by way of inspiration but also as cautionary tales. In his endeavor to school his students in his method, the director sometimes risks traumatizing students, as well as offending and stereotyping them.

For this reason, while I consider Stanislavski's books important to my development as a writing center manager, I rarely mention his name when using exercises inspired by his system. Besides, I use only some aspects of his system, so a study of his work would not necessarily be of help to the tutors. Stanislavski's early twentieth-century texts—with their politically incorrect terms used in relation to race and disability, and their sexism—are certainly not the best guides for twenty-first-century tutors.

However, Stanislavski in particular, and performance studies in general, might offer further insights for writing center directors and tutors. The tutorial session is at once a literary event, wherein a text is collaborated upon and transformed, and a performance. Approaching writing center, through the lens of performance studies can help us see how the student, the tutor, and the tutor's trainer participate in a complex performance where the roles of the audience, actor, and director are constantly changing.

REFERENCES

Benedetti, Jean. 1998. *Stanislavski and the Actor*. London: Methuen.
Clark, Irene Lurkis, and Dave Healy. 1996. "Are Writing Centers Ethical?" *Writing Program Administration* 20 (1/2): 32–48.
Brooks, Jeff. 1991. "Minimalist Tutoring: Making the Student Do All the Work." *Writing Lab Newsletter* 19 (2): 1–4.
Carino, Peter. 2003. "Power and Authority in Peer Tutoring." In *The Center Will Hold: Critical Perspectives on Writing Center Scholarship*, edited by Michael A. Pemberton and Joyce A. Kinkead, 96–113. Logan: Utah State University Press.
Grimm, Nancy Maloney. 1999. *Good Intentions: Writing Center Work for Postmodern Times*. Portsmouth, NH: Boynton/Cook Heinemann.
Henney, Pamela Ann. 2012. *Acting the Author: Using Acting Techniques in Teaching Academic Writing*. PhD diss., University of Akron, OH.
Nordlof, John. 2014. "Vygotsky, Scaffolding, and the Role of Theory in Writing Center Work." *Writing Center Journal* 34, no. 1 (Fall/Winter): 45–64.
Özmen, Kemal Sinan. 2011. "Acting and Teacher Education: Being Model for Identity Development." *Turkish Online Journal of Qualitative Inquiry* 2 (2): 36–49.
Ryan, Leigh, and Lisa Zimmerelli. 2010. *The Bedford Guide for Writing Tutors*. Boston: Bedford / St. Martins.
Shamoon, Linda K., and Deborah H. Burns. 1995. "A Critique of Pure Tutoring." *The Writing Center Journal* 15, no. 2 (Spring): 134–51.
Stanislavski, Constantin. (1957) 1961. *Creating a Role*. Translated by Elizabeth Reynolds Hapgood. London: Methuen.
Stanislavski, Constantin. (1936) 1980. *An Actor Prepares*. Translated by Elizabeth Reynolds Hapgood. London: Methuen.
Stanislavski, Constantin. (1948) 2010. *Building a Character*. Translated by Elizabeth Reynolds Hapgood. London: Methuen.
Stanislavski, Konstantin. 1988. *Stanislavsky on the Art of the Stage*. Translated by David Magarshack. London: Faber and Faber.
Trimbur, John. 1987. "Peer Tutoring: A Contradiction in Terms?" *The Writing Center Journal* 7 (2): 21–28.

5
PROFESSIONAL TUTORS, SHIFTING IDENTITIES
Narratives from the Center

Kimberly Fahle Peck, Lisa Nicole Tyson, Amanda Gomez, and Steffani Dambruch

Categorical titles can sometimes help us understand the identity of those who will fill those roles. For instance, a peer tutor generally refers to an undergraduate student, a graduate tutor to a graduate student, and a faculty tutor to an instructor at the institution. But what does it mean to be a *professional* tutor? Despite the fact that according to the National Census of Writing, 24 percent of four-year institutions and 55 percent of two-year institutions employ professional tutors (Gladstein and Fralix 2015), very little work has focused on this population. Steven Strang notes the ambiguity of the title "professional tutor," suggesting, "Even a definition of professional tutor can be problematic, because anyone paid to perform a task can, in the loosest sense of the term, be a 'professional'" (2006, 292). Strang goes on to offer the definition of the position for his center and uses his definition to demonstrate why professional tutors best fit the needs of his center. Our chapter does not seek to present a specific definition of professional writing tutors, because we recognize that the criteria and job expectations of this position will vary based on institutional context. Nor do we attempt to make a case for the use of professional tutors over other types of tutors in writing center work. Instead, this chapter aims to elucidate a shared characteristic we believe many professional tutors in writing centers hold: their identities as "plural careerists."

Brianna Braker Caza, Sherry Moss, and Heather Vough (2018) offer the following definition of plural careerists: "People who choose to simultaneously hold and identify with multiple jobs" (703). Their study sought to understand how individuals create a harmonized personal identity and a sense of authenticity amid multiple professional identities. While this label may be inaccurate for a minority of professional tutors who serve in these roles as part of full-time employment, many professional tutoring positions are part time, so those individuals in these positions often hold other professional positions as well, making them plural careerists. Therefore, we suggest that the theories of professional identity coming from organizational psychology provides a helpful framework to understand the experiences of professional tutors that builds on current conversations in writing centers focused on peer tutors and transfer.

Much of the previous discussions related to writing tutors and transfer has focused on what peer tutors learn and are able to transfer from their experiences as tutors into their future careers. *The Bedford Guide for Writing Tutors* states of undergraduate tutors, "Many former tutors report that their work tutoring writing prepared them well for their future professional positions" (Ryan and Zimmerelli 2016, 4). The Peer Tutor Writing Tutor Alumni Project is grounded in the question of what tutors "take with them" (Hughes, Gillespie, and Kael 2010), focusing on a unidirectional trajectory of tutoring experiences to future careers. In this way, considerations of writing tutors and transfer have primarily focused on what G. N. Perkins and Gavriel Salomon (1988) categorize as forward-reaching transfer, which describes when people learn and are able to abstract and use what they learned in future situations. One might be tempted to think, then, that when considering professional tutors, it is more accurate to think about backward-reaching transfer, or the ability to draw on previous experiences to determine appropriate actions, since these tutors ostensibly have more professional experiences from which to draw. Yet, we contend that in the case of professional tutors who are plural careerists, this relationship between tutoring and other professional experiences is cyclical due to the fact that professional tutors often hold multiple professional positions simultaneously. We suggest that the concurrently held professional positions of many professional tutors prepare, shape, and enrich their work tutoring writing, and their tutoring work simultaneously informs their other professional identities. This interrelationship is sometimes complementary and sometimes complicated.

To explore this multidirectional transfer and the role it plays in professional tutor identity, we draw on Caza, Moss, and Vough's (2018) categories of identity struggles for plural careerists. From interviews with almost fifty plural careerists, Caza, Moss, and Vough presented three main themes related to their participants' struggles with identity, which they labeled "being me," "feeling me," and "seeming me." Being me responses came from those who valued multiplicity within themselves and saw holding multiple careers as allowing them to engage with multiple aspects of themselves instead of being limited to a single focus. "Feeling me" responses expressed confusion about who they were supposed to be when enacting different roles, and "seeming me" responses identified struggles related to how others perceived them due to their multiple roles. Our chapter draws on these three categories of plural careerist identity struggles as a framework to understand the lived experience of professional writing tutors and how they negotiate their identity in their work. We argue that professional tutors, and the administrators that support them, need to intentionally reflect on the interrelationship of the multiple professional identities professional tutors hold not only as ways to support both professional development and individual career growth, but also to acknowledge how the professional tutor as plural careerist is part of a larger trend toward contingent labor in higher education.

To support our argument, we include three stories from professional tutors, who along with their work in the writing center also held other professional identities, including hairstylist, creative writer, and adjunct instructor, respectively. These stories point to the ways other professional identities can help define what it means to be a professional tutor, the ways being a professional writing tutor can impact other professional identities, and times when professional identities can feel in tension. At the end of each narrative, each writer offers questions for other professional tutors to consider as they work through their own identity as plural careerists as a heuristic to promote the identity transfer work we are advocating in this chapter. Following the narratives, we consider the economic realities facing some part-time professional tutors that, while not always explicitly invoked in the individual stories included here, are an important part of the story of professional tutors for the field to consider. We conclude with considerations for directors to best support professional tutors in light of both these economic realities as well as our larger argument about identity and knowledge transfer for plural careerists.

OUR STORIES

Lisa Nicole Tyson: Helping Others Find Their Style

> *This narrative describes my journey of discovering how to meld the identities of writing tutor and hairstylist. My experience exemplifies Caza, Moss, and Vough's identity category, being me, as I found the connection between two seemingly different identities.*

Starting out as a professional tutor, I thought my time as a teacher would be the only experience I could draw on. I quickly realized that many of the skills I acquired from my years as a hairstylist could be applied to tutoring sessions. I was a professional tutor for a semester before simultaneously working as a professional tutor and graduate assistant tutor while completing my studies. The most difficult part of being connected to so many different institutions was that I did not feel that I was a real part of any of them. As a professional tutor, graduate assistant, and later an adjunct instructor, I felt pulled in multiple directions without being able to participate in the community, such as attending university events. I simply did not have the time in my schedule, since I was commuting between three different schools and also working as a hairstylist. My experience relates to Caza, Moss, and Vough's "being me" identity struggle. I was not then, and still am not, willing to give up doing hair as a profession entirely. Being an academic is important to me but so is being a hairstylist. All of these roles are me and help me to feel true to myself. I eventually came to consider them to not be as disparate identities as I first imagined.

Many are loath to refer to customer service skills in tutoring, but it relates to ideas of professionalism. When I started as a graduate assistant tutor, working with fellow graduate students, it was quickly obvious which tutors had a background in service industries (food, retail, etc.), as they were able to transfer the skills they had acquired in those roles to the role of writing tutor. After all, although the commerce side is generally not present in tutoring centers, we are still providing a service as tutors. Being able to frame my own experience as a tutor by considering its similarities with the hair consultations I have with clients is what first revealed to me how my multiple careers relate to each other. I was able to cyclically improve my consultation strategies as both tutor and stylist.

The aim of any hair consultation is to decide collaboratively on a style that the stylist will help create but that will also work for the client. In tutoring, it is similar with a few clear distinctions. While in tutoring, the student is the one doing the creating, it is still a similar cooperation to decide on the finished product. Students or clients are coming to us for our expertise, though ultimately they have to walk out and own their writing or hairstyle. We as tutors can provide assistance but not magically make something without the involvement of the client or student. It can sometimes be difficult for people to let go of that control when working with others, but I had had years of experience doing it before I ever started tutoring.

Collaborating on a road map for the session and setting the tone during this consultation phase is crucial for stylists to maximize the time allotted to appointments. Many tutors intuitively have developed something of a consultation without necessarily framing it that way. A conversation at the beginning of the session to assess needs and goals of the student is just a given. I suggest tutors pause for real reflection on what that beginning time accomplishes. Especially for new tutors, it can be beneficial to follow some kind of framework or guidelines for how to start a session from other professional experiences. As they gain experience, they will adapt it to their own style, but to start, it can be rather overwhelming. I know when I first began tutoring, once I was in the middle of the session, I felt quite comfortable and in my element. However, until I realized the connection between hair appointments and tutoring appointments, I admit I was always rather unsure how to begin with students.

Stylists have to figure out how clients relate to their hair and often how they feel about life in general, in addition to how comfortable they are with the process of styling their own hair. While tutoring, we often have to educate students about how writing works, just as stylists educate clients on the technicalities of hair when those clients have unrealistic expectations. As tutors, we want to know where the student is in the writing process. However, knowing how the student is feeling about the assignment or the class or the semester, or writing in general, can be so beneficial for deciding on how to proceed. If there is some apprehension, taking a few minutes to provide some reassurance is not wasted time. It can build rapport and also make the student more open to suggestions and more willing to engage in the session and provide input. The forging of relationships is the aspect of tutoring and styling hair that hooked me from the beginning.

While some of the advice here is similar to what can be found in tutor guidebooks, for me, an understanding of how to collaborate with students really came from my work as a stylist, and this framework has enriched my writing center work. Although both professions have creative and technical aspects to them, being a writing tutor allowed me to feel like a part of the academic world and assist people in creating, and being a hairstylist allowed me to be the one doing the creative part; I'm grateful I've found ways to express both of these aspects of my identity.

Questions for Self-Reflection, Disparate Identities:
- What parts of yourself does being a writing tutor allow you to express? What parts of yourself do your other professional identities allow you to express?
- What skills and knowledge that you've gained from outside professional roles can support your work as a writing tutor?

- What skills and knowledge that you've gained from being a writing tutor can support your work in other professional roles?
- What are your long-term goals? How does both your work as a tutor and in other professional roles support these goals?

Amanda Gomez: Writer? Tutor? Advocate.

> This narrative discusses my experience trying to make sense of how my identities of creative writer and professional tutor connect. My initial struggle to synthesize these identities reflect Caza, Moss, and Vaugh's feeling me category of identity struggle.

Imposter syndrome was not something I anticipated as a professional writing tutor. Upon my hire, I felt assured in my abilities to assist students with their papers. I had worked as a graduate writing tutor at a previous institution, and I had already worked as a writing and creative writing instructor in many nontraditional settings: a jail, a literary center, and local nonprofits. Still, despite my work history, I felt disconnected from this new writing center. Working as a professional writing tutor instilled this fear in me of being uncovered as an intellectual fraud. What I had associated as a strength, my identity as a creative writer, I began to associate as a weakness. I felt inferior to my fellow professional tutors, with whom I associated more pedagogical training based on their fields and concentrations. I felt inadequate to address students' needs.

As a creative writer, my writer-tutor identity did not seem feasible in this context. I embodied the institutional divide that has often polarized creative writing departments and rhetoric and composition departments in academia; creative writing dismissed for its whims and fancies, and composition lauded for its solid footing in research and pedagogy. I struggled with both compartmentalizing the writer and accessing the tutor within me, with how to negotiate the space of each tutoring session. In other words, I lacked a clear understanding of what was expected from me and how to create a merged and integrated identity, echoing Caza, Moss, and Vough's "feeling me" struggle with identity.

There is a distancing effect that encompasses the title of "professional writing tutor." I am not a peer in the students' eyes. Instead, I am a professional, a so-called expert in all matters related to writing. Furthermore, the use of the word "professional" is imbibed with the connotations that I am outside of the university. I am a separate entity brought in to help the student. There's no connection of me to the student or to the university. As a professional writing tutor, then, I am concerned with not only my role but my authority as well. In her article "The Writing Teacher Who Writes: Creative Writing, Ancient Rhetoric, and Composition Instruction," Mary Hedengren (2016) posits that both the fields of creative writing and composition also struggle with this fact, whether authority comes from a solid grounding in writing pedagogy or whether authority comes from a proven history in writing established through publications, what she describes as an "ethos as a practitioner."

Besides my experience as a writing practitioner, most of my other experience revolves around writing instruction in nontraditional settings; thus, one of my primary concerns has always been student motivation. There are no grades, so I am constantly navigating factors that encourage or discourage students to revise their writing. When I first began teaching, I always began with writing mistakes to avoid. As a writer, I knew the pitfalls of beginning writers, and concerned with my students' success, I believed I was helping them before they even started their papers. However, over time, I became weary with this process. In the jail, I was reinforcing an incarcerated state with more rules, and outside the jail, my students, especially my creative writing students, felt their imagination fenced in. Often, they argued with me and were eventually put off, and my ability to reach these students extinguished.

My resolve was to develop a pedagogy of empathy, and teaching was a way to empower students. Knowledge was not just something that was disseminated from the top down, but it was something more collaborative, a key idea in writing centers. Whenever I created an assignment, I also participated, as if I were a student. I emphasized my writer identity and wrote alongside students to show even instructors do not write well in their first drafts. I can remember one class at the jail in which I had simply forgotten my worksheets for how to do peer reviews, so I had to improvise. I introduced the concept of peer reviews to the class, and I asked the students to determine the guidelines and expectations for how the class should run for the day. While I don't remember everything they said or wrote on the board, I do remember one rule: "We can't share what we wrote once we leave." Perhaps, for some teachers reading this, this is something basic or evident, but it reminded me of something I think we easily forget; students may often have an idea of what is right for their papers more than we may know. Had I not asked the students to collaborate at the jail that morning, I would not have learned an essential lesson of trusting our work with others.

In the writing center, it is hard not to read a student's paper and simply see that whatever their intentions, the message they intended to deliver is not on the paper. However, starting with what is wrong with a paper can increase the distance that already exists between the professional writing tutor and the student. As these outside "professionals," it is our responsibility to place the agency back in the students' hands, to remind them the paper is their own; we are simply there to help interpret what it is they want to say in a way that meets their goals. Perhaps our role as outsiders is an asset. If we are interpreted as agents existing outside of the university, then the student feels empowered against the cloistering effect of academia, which does not always provide students access to their own language.

Working as an instructor in nontraditional settings helped me understand the importance of dismantling the myth that only instructors, or writing tutors, possess knowledge worthy of being shared. Students can also provide valuable input, and our job is drawing it out of them to the best of our abilities. This idea is not new and is at the heart of discussions of non-directive tutoring. However, it was through emphasizing my identity as a writer and sharing my own struggles that I fully came to realize the value of these methods and merged my identities as both writer and tutor, becoming neither writer-tutor nor tutor-writer, but moving from "professional writing tutor" to "writing advocate."

For many, this approach could be too idealistic. To pretend as if a power dynamic does not exist between tutors, especially professional tutors, and students could be foolish and impractical, and many students may not desire this approach because they just want their paper "fixed," but I think the role of writer advocate can be for the student and for the writing process. Working as a professional writing tutor taught me that we not only help students write, but are there to help students understand that bad writing is more than just mechanical errors. Bad writing is writing in which we fail to surprise ourselves, and if students are not allowed to participate in this process of self-discovery, then they miss out. Similarly, bad teaching and tutoring are when we fail to *be* ourselves and draw on our strengths and experiences to reach students.

Questions for Self-Reflection, Writer-Tutors:
- How does your own writing practice inform your tutoring pedagogy?
- What writing techniques or practices have you learned or developed that can enhance or help your students' writing?
- How is creative writing (workshop) feedback dis/similar to providing tutoring feedback?
- What are your long-term goals as a writer? How do these goals align with your professional tutor responsibilities?

Steffani Dambruch: Tutor-Teacher-Trickster

> *In this narrative I detail the negotiation of Caza, Moss, and Vough's identify formation of seeming me in my daily work as both an instructor and professional tutor. My occupation of both of these roles, despite sometimes conflicting perceptions and expectations of me by students and colleagues, often creates workplace serendipity.*

When students arrive in the writing center with marked-up drafts from their instructors, writing tutors must do what Muriel Harris terms the double-work of interpretation and translation to transform "teacher language into student language" (1995, 37). Yet in exiting the classroom and entering the writing center, Harris's double work for me becomes an exercise in either hiding or asserting my teacher authority in the tutorial (see Shiell in chapter 3 in this volume for guidance on training for this shift). I serve as both an adjunct instructor and professional writing tutor, often tutoring students in different sections of the course I teach. Instructor authority means I often no longer navigate tutoring as an act of translation; I know what the first-year composition competencies are for my institution. Yet expressivist writing tutor pedagogy encourages me to modulate this authority to meet the students' needs as a facilitator sans red pen. I am a "tutor-teacher," who, so baptized by Clyde Moneyhun and Patti Hanlon-Baker, both shares the desk and stands behind it, shifting constantly between upholding disciplinary authority in the classroom and deferring to student authority in the writing tutorial (2012). Yet, what is the professional impact of such a constant and liminal navigation of authority and identity? In addition, is occupying the plural careerist role of the tutor-teacher detrimental to workplace visibility, particularly in light of university discussions of contingent labor and promotion?

Positioned in between the two roles, the tutor-teacher is reflected in the Caza, Moss, and Vough's plural careerist paradigm as struggling with "seeming me," or the complex desire of the "perception that others see them as they see themselves" (2018, 716). Neither all tutor nor all teacher, I cling to no categorical workplace identity. The factors of "seeming" are further complicated in our writing center's slippery spatial rhetoric. Because we coexist in a learning center staffed with undergraduate peer tutors, we often blend in, tutoring just desks away from peer math tutors, business tutors, psychology tutors, and so on. Many tutees are surprised that I also teach; this generally prompts them to downshift to a more deferential discourse. For example, a sophomore literature student became a frequent tutee after he discovered

I was faculty, addressed me as "professor" instead of by my first name used in the center, and emailed me for office hours beyond tutoring. It struck me that I had moved from tutor to supplemental instructor for the course in his mind and certainly unbeknownst to his instructor. This prompted an outline of the writing center's policies; my role was to facilitate, not direct, his own process. Just before submitting his final paper, however, he angled to hear how I would grade his essay, demonstrating his continued expectation of evaluation (see Matthew Sharkey-Smith's discussion in chapter 7 this collection for the context of online tutoring). In this instance the me I "seemed" to the student was my very real role as faculty, yet it superseded the "tutor me" that guided him in the writing center.

As a tutor-teacher, adopting a healthy perception of "seeming me" comes down to an awareness of the cyclical relationship between the feedback I give in the classroom versus the tutorial. I remain mindful of my feedback in tutorials by asking good questions, which is a direct transfer from my classroom mode of Socratic questioning. This happy interrogation leads to the idea of spontaneous "trickster moments" in which a student makes a self-discovery about her own writing process, according to the authors of *The Everyday Writing Center* (Geller et al. 2007, 17–8, qtd. in Moneyhun and Hanlon-Baker 2012, 4). Discoveries that empower beginning writers to articulate their processes are the gold standard of tutoring and teaching. Tutor-teachers occupying the liminal space of "seeming" faculty and "seeming" tutor by default are rewarded with many opportunities to bear witness to student trickster epiphanies.

While the teaching and tutoring transfer is interconnected, the unique pluralism of the tutor-teacher goes beyond the classroom and the writing center to the workplace at large. Upon the discovery I had dissected his assignment instructions to tutor his student on her revisions, a full-time faculty colleague exclaimed: "It just occurred to me that you can see all of my feedback. Was it helpful? Was it too much? Did the student 'get' it?" We proceeded to compare feedback techniques and prompt design. His trickster moment about my insider view of his course's mechanics made me realize that perhaps the best metaphor for the shifting professional identity of the tutor-teacher as plural careerist, the me I "seem," is just that—the trickster, capable of shape-shifting to reflect, inspire, or guide the needs of all.

Yet the professional trickster, who through joyful antagonism reveals truths to others, is hardly free from hard truths. As dialogue of contingent faculty labor continues, the precarious existence of the tutor-teacher should be acknowledged as having one foot in an English department and another in student support services. Does working in multiple departments show the tutor-teacher to be seen as not a peer of faculty or administrators, but a wayfaring trickster with no permanent residence—or hope for full-time pay? Should not a serious academic relinquish identities in excess? At minimum, writing center directors should acknowledge the precariousness of tutor-teachers and let them know they are what they hope to seem: impactful and visible. Hired by many, promoted by few, the tutor-teacher seems to exist at the nexus of all contingent writing instruction: on the outside but with a valuable view in.

Questions for Self-Reflection, Tutor-Teachers:
- What is unique about your writing pedagogy that has informed your tutoring?
- Which tutoring techniques have enhanced your teaching and vice versa?
- How is student feedback different in teaching versus tutoring?
- How do you hope to "seem" as a teacher versus a tutor? Are these workplace identities the same or different?
- What are the professional benefits of both teaching and tutoring at the same time? How are these benefits in line with your long-term goals in the profession?

ECONOMIC REALITIES AND HOLISTIC DEVELOPMENT
Kim Fahle Peck's Considerations for Administrators

The narrative snapshots included above highlight the interplay between identities these professional tutors experience, but do not necessarily engage with why they have these multiple professional identities in the first place. While I think the tutors whose stories are told here took on writing center work because they saw value in this work personally and professionally, it would be disingenuous not to mention the economic realities impacting decisions for many to become professional tutors. At the center where we all worked together (since beginning work on this chapter, most of us have moved on to different positions inside and outside of writing center studies), professional tutoring positions are part time, so most professional tutors hold this position as well as other positions—sometimes at as many as three or four different organizations—simultaneously (which, as Miriam E. Laufer mentions in chapter 1 this collection, is also the situation of many adjunct faculty tutors). Many of the tutors I supervised became tutors to complement other professional activities, including serving as adjunct instructors, such as Lisa and Steffani, or writing and teaching opportunities outside of traditional academic institutions, such as Amanda. Some professional tutors may seek this complementary position because other positions they hold are also part time and may not provide sufficient funds for them to comfortably live without seeking additional employment. Also, these other positions might be inconsistent, particularly for those serving as adjuncts, who may never be sure how many sections they would be able to teach semester to semester and who sometimes experienced the frustration of classes they were scheduled to teach being cancelled at the last minute. What can a writing center administrator do in light of this precariousness?

I had been a plural careerist before securing a full-time position as the coordinator of a writing center. I simultaneously worked part time as a professional tutor, an adjunct instructor, and an administrative assistant in a registrar's office. I was acutely aware of the reality of piecemeal, unguaranteed employment, and this shaped my approach as an administrator responsible for professional tutors. Because of budgetary constraints, tutors could work around ten hours per week in my center, but I strove to keep the number of hours tutors were scheduled, though modest, at least consistent semester to semester so at least this part of the financial equation for tutors would be consistent. Tutors were also encouraged to share their availability for tutoring *after* scheduling other commitments, in an attempt to be as flexible as possible in creating the schedule each semester to balance our coverage needs with their unpredictable schedules. I also made it a habit to keep an ear to the ground about employment opportunities, both part time and full time, that my tutors might be interested in and qualified for, passing along position announcements whenever they were appropriate. None of these actions are revolutionary, but they were grounded in an attempt to assuage some financial anxiety for my colleagues. Administrators working with part-time, professional tutors need to have an awareness of the precarious situation some professional tutors might be in because of larger systemic issues related to contingent labor practices in academia. Our field has shown interest in the issue of contingent writing center workers, but has largely focused on administrators (Caswell, McKinney, and Jackson 2014) or administrators and peer tutors (Fels et al. 2016). We hope our chapter reminds the writing center field to also consider part-time professionals when engaging with research into the labor conditions and practices in our field.

Individual administrators, unfortunately, are rarely in a position to make direct interventions related to institutional labor practices. I suggest, therefore, that writing center administrators focus on supporting individual tutors to achieve their personal and professional goals. To do this, they must first understand the multiple professional identities their tutors hold and help them consider the ways these identities mutually inform each other. This type of reflective work supports not only the tutors themselves, helping them to harmonize their identities and potentially identify future opportunities, but also supports the writing center because tutors who successfully transfer the skills and knowledge they have gained from other professional identities bring unique expertise and knowledge to their work with writers.

Administrators should understand their tutors' personal and professional goals. Are they looking for additional part-time opportunities to complement their identities or allow them to express different aspects of their identities? Are they looking to secure full-time employment? Having this knowledge about their tutors allows administrators to both share opportunities that might be of interest to them and help administrators consider what types of professional development or leadership opportunities they might offer for professional tutors to help them achieve their goals.

I am happy to say that all of the tutors who shared their stories in this chapter have since obtained full-time positions, some teaching and others in administrative roles. Some have continued to do part-time tutor work even after securing a full-time position, and others have not. I make no claim to their successes in their professional trajectory; I can only say this was ultimately the outcome I hoped for them. As Anne Shiell notes in chapter 3, writing centers employing professional tutors often find themselves in the contradictory position of wanting to both train and retain tutors to support the quality of their center but also wanting to support professionals in obtaining new employment opportunities that match their professional goals. I would argue that administrators supporting professional tutors need to embrace this contradiction. Ted Baker and Howard E. Aldrich explored identity in people in what they called "boundaryless careers" (1996). These differ from plural careerists because it describes individuals who work for different employers in succession as opposed to simultaneously. However, the conclusions they draw on how these individuals can be successful is relevant for plural careerists and those that support them. They claimed that for people to construct successful "boundaryless careers," "they must express and build their identity across several employers. They must achieve a sense of authenticity and self-efficacy through the structuring and evolution of the path from one employer to another . . . as well as through the individual jobs that make up work histories" (Baker and Aldrich 1996, 142–43). I suggest that part of the job of administrators supervising or mentoring plural careerist professional tutors is to support their development of a harmonized sense of identity so they can "be me," "feel me," or "seem me" and can clarify how their various professional roles redefine what it means to be a professional tutor and how serving as a professional tutor might support or redefine their professional trajectory.

Questions for Reflection, Administrators:
- How can you help professional tutors to feel a sense of belonging in the writing center?
- How can you encourage professional tutors to reflect on the overlap in their roles?
- How can you assist professional tutors in conceiving of the skills they are transferring *in* to the writing center?
- How can you assist professional tutors in conceiving of the skills they are transferring *from* the writing center to their other roles?
- How can you help support professional tutors' future goals?
- If any of your professional tutors are experiencing identity struggles related to Caza, Moss, and Vough's "being me," "feeling me," "seeming me" categories, how can you help them embrace their roles and develop a singular or synchronous professional identity, dependent on their future goals?

REFERENCES

Baker, Ted, and Howard E. Aldrich. 1996. "Prometheus Stretches: Building Identity and Cumulative Knowledge in Multiemployer Careers." In *The Boundaryless Career: A New Employment Principle for a New Organizational Era*, edited by Michael B. Arthur and Denise M. Rousseau, 132–49. New York: Oxford University Press.

Caswell, Nicole I., Jackie Grutsch McKinney, and Rebecca Jackson. 2014. "A Glimpse into the Working Lives of New Writing Center Directors." *Forum: Issues about Part-Time and Contingent Faculty* 18 (1) [insert in *College Composition and Communication* 66 (1)]: A3–A7.

Caza, Brianna Barker, Sherry Moss, and Heather Vough. 2018. "From Synchronizing to Harmonizing: The Process of Authenticating Multiple Work Identities." *Administrative Science Quarterly* 63 (4): 703–45.

Fels, Dawn, Clint Gardner, Maggie M. Herb, and Liliana M. Naydan. 2016. "Toward an Investigation into the Working Conditions of Non-tenure Line, Contingent Writing Center Workers." *Forum: Issues about Part-Time and Contingent Faculty* 20 (1) [insert in *College Composition and Communication* 68, no.1]: A10–A16.

Gladstein, Jill M., and Brandon Fralix. 2015. "National Census of Writing." http://writingcensus.swarthmore.edu.

Harris, Muriel. 1995. "Talking in the Middle: Why Writers Need Writing Tutors." *College English* 57 (1): 27–42.

Hedengren, Mary. 2016. "The Writing Teacher Who Writes: Creative Writing, Ancient Rhetoric, and Composition Instruction." *Pedagogy* 16 (2): 191–206.

Hughes, Bradley, Paula Gillespie, and Harvey Kael. 2010. "What They Take with Them: Findings from the Peer Writing Tutor Alumni Research Project." *Writing Center Journal* 30 (2): 12–46.

Moneyhun, Clyde, and Patti Hanlon-Baker. 2012. "Tutoring Teachers." *Writing Lab Newsletter* 36 (9–10): 1–5.

Perkins, D. N., and Gavriel Salomon. 1988. "Teaching for Transfer." *Educational Leadership* 46 (1): 22–32.

Ryan, Leigh, and Lisa Zimmerelli. 2016. *The Bedford Guide for Writing Tutors*. 6th ed. Boston: Bedford / St. Martin's.

Strang, Steven. 2006. "Staffing a Writing Center with Professional Tutors." In *The Writing Center Director's Resource Book*, edited by Christina Murphy and Byron L. Stay, 291–99. Mahwah, NJ: Lawrence Erlbaum Associates, Publishers.

6
TEACHERS VERSUS TUTORS
Is There a Place for Faculty Tutors in a University Writing Center?

Arundhati Sanyal and Kelly A. Shea

Historically, there has never been a time when tutoring has not involved faculty tutors. In the Oxford and Cambridge Universities system, the practice of inducting brilliant young scholars as "tutors" who would be paired with a single or selected group of students to meet with them individually began at least a hundred years ago with a more recent trend toward peer tutoring. This faculty tutoring model has continued to this date, with much variation, and been extended to online tutoring, as referred to by John Morgan (2013). Although for not quite as long a period of time, the history of tutoring at Seton Hall University (SHU) has followed a similar trajectory in terms of the movement from faculty tutors to peer tutors and from face-to-face faculty tutors to online faculty tutoring.

For nearly forty years, the Writing Center at Seton Hall has functioned with undergraduate, graduate, faculty, and professional tutors. While it began as part of a basic skills program for freshmen in the early 1980s, the center has increasingly served more than first-year writers, moving to tutoring students at both the undergraduate and graduate levels as well as setting up an email-based online writing lab (OWL), which serves upper-level and graduate students. In the late 1990s, when the first-year composition program added English department faculty associates, part-time writing faculty, and graduate student teaching assistants who were also officially assigned tutoring duties as part of their teaching loads, a more formal tutor-training program was implemented, though neither faculty nor graduate tutors were required to participate (Grieco 2018; Wilkowski 2018). Indeed, Seton Hall's faculty tutors are not trained, per se. This is the case despite the fact that twenty-plus years ago, with the hiring of a rhetoric/composition faculty writing center director, we embraced the notion of tutoring pedagogy as student centered, based on Kenneth Bruffee's work in "disrupting . . . traditional

DOI: 10.7330/9781646420858.c006

teacher-centered activities" and validating "collaborative learning practices" (1984, qtd. in Gillam 1994, 39). And while we have maintained the faculty tutor model to serve the growing and varied needs of students, how well this works at SHU has not been assessed in systematic fashion except for a 2006 study on OWL tutoring, which determined that faculty tutors are more effective, substantive online tutors than undergraduate tutors who, despite their training, tended to focus more on mechanics in the OWL interaction (Shea 2011, 9).

Despite this finding, we (and, we presume, other writing administrators) are conflicted by the role that faculty tutors play in our center. Some are strong tutors; some do the bare minimum. Some are willing; some are not. Some have come through our undergraduate and graduate programs and have thus been trained as tutors; some have not. We have long wondered whether there is a place for faculty tutors in our, or any, writing center. Still, there are typically about fifteen faculty tutors engaged in active tutoring at the SHU Writing Center; they are needed partly due to a large population of graduate students who bring their dissertations at various stages of composition. The faculty tutors range in position: they are full professors, term faculty, adjunct faculty members, graduate teaching assistants, and professional tutors (typically former faculty members), and they represent a variety of disciplines and professions (including medievalists and attorneys). For any writing center administrator, therefore, it is essential to study the nature and impact of faculty tutoring at the center. (NB: for the purposes of this chapter, when the term "faculty tutors" is used, we are referring to all the categories. In the data section, at certain points we also specify particular types of faculty tutors.)

In 2018, we administered a faculty tutor survey that attempted, in our context, to explore the fine lines and power dynamics, which exist in any writing center, among authority and collaboration, teaching and tutoring, professional and academic relations, and proofreading and suggestive commenting. But we chose not to rely on a purely quantitative survey; instead, we drew from the advice of writing center scholars Lauren Fitzgerald and Melissa Ianetta, who point out that "while surveys currently might be the most common method of empirical research in the tutoring of writing, discourse analysis is among those research methods most directly connected to the work of a writing tutor" (Fitzgerald and Ianetta 2016, 257). And so we did both—we've administered a survey that gathered not only quantitative data but also qualitative verbatim comments from current and former faculty tutors. The results of this project have helped us to assess faculty tutoring in the writing center to ensure an enriching experience for tutees and to find challenging niches for faculty tutors—to work, perhaps, within a developing writing-across-the-curriculum program—and to examine labor issues for these tutors.

What we found is that, in general, faculty tutors (of all stripes) tend to be more focused on their faculty persona than taking on a tutor persona in the writing center conference. This seems to stem from a lack of training *as tutors* as well as a clear recognition that they are simply not, nor can they be, *literal* peer tutors. There is also a general sense that since faculty tutors have been trained as teachers, they know what they need to know to tutor. Even those faculty who might be interested in tutor training are, perhaps, not as inclined to participate, possibly due to time or financial constraints—or, indeed, resistance. Further, since a good number of faculty tutors are "required" to tutor, they might not think they *should* take more time to be trained. In other words, while not a direct quote, the sentiment might run something like this: "If they're going to require me to tutor, then they must think I can do it." And yet the concern is that without training, faculty will be too directive and "teacherly" in the writing center conference instead of being more non-directive and "peer-like." The question for SHU and, indeed, any writing center, is whether we should sacrifice the peer-centered model or non-directive tutoring in response to the need for tutors. This is the balancing act that any center with faculty tutors must attempt and what we had in mind when we undertook our faculty tutor survey.

REVIEW OF RELEVANT LITERATURE

Before we look at the data, we consider scholarship that has explored the concept of "faculty tutor." John Morgan (2013) revisits the much-hallowed institution of the tutorial at Oxford University in his article. According to Morgan, the tutor is usually an advanced scholar and teacher who meets with the student regularly and reads papers that are written by the student expressly for such tutorials. In distinctive ways this tutorial encourages an active and self-directed course of reading and writing. The tutor occupies an influential place in the overall intellectual life of the student, thus marrying the roles of the instructor in class with the peer tutor who is the avid listener and intellectual confidante of the student. Morgan refers to a tutor of St. John's College, Dr. Will Moore, who suggests that "the root of the tutorial method is skeptical, a method that inquires, probes, scrutinizes" (Moore 1968, qtd. in Morgan 2013, 525). This process of questioning assumptions models for the student the attitude she should bring to any work that she writes in response to her readings and lectures in college. Paradoxically then, the role of the tutor is participatory: "The role of the tutor in working with a student is to serve as a provocateur and responder to the student's insights and observations relative to the textual materials being considered in the encounter" (Morgan 2013, 528).

The writing that students bring to the writing center has been studied in depth by Linda Flower et al. in *Reading-to-Write: Exploring a Cognitive and Social Process* (1990). Building on the work of Mina Shaughnessy and David Bartholomae, Flower and her colleagues note that entering the academic discourse community requires new textual conventions, expectations, and habits of mind. Her argument centers on how writing teachers have to develop a "metacognitive" awareness of their own processes and strategies as they read and write. This process is facilitated by not just classroom instruction but reiterating the necessity and ubiquitous value of this metacognition in the tutoring setting of the writing center as well. Writing center theorists such as Muriel Harris agree that constant practice and rehearsing of such strategies are facilitated by tutors trained in conversing, demonstrating, and modeling such metacognition: "Strategies are easy to learn in an environment when the person next to the writer can answer questions as the writer proceeds and can offer some midstream correction or encouragement when something is not going well" (1995, 34). While the instructor cannot fulfill such intimacy and close attention in the classroom, the faculty tutors might be able to marry their experience with metacognition to the camaraderie of one-on-one tutoring and can enhance the students' own metacognitive development more effectively than the peer tutors alone can.

Harris presents the tutor as an intermediary figure who inhabits a middle space between classroom instruction and the student's private world (Harris 1995, 27). The strength of tutoring, according to her article, is the ability of the tutor to eschew classroom authority and the necessity of grading or judging the student-writers' every work (28). By implication, then, the writing center community is effective precisely because it is the "other" to the classroom environment. The authority of the instructor figure is replaced by the dynamic communication between the tutor and tutee in such an environment. The question for the faculty tutors is how at ease they might be with discarding authority for their tutoring personae at the center. As our survey results reveal, the notion of the provocateur who has the Socratic stance of questioning without appearing to be knowledgeable can be a tricky expectation from the faculty tutor.

In researching and examining the triadic relationship among tutor, tutee, and the instructor in the American writing center experience, Terese Thonus (2001) realigns the tutor's role as negotiated directives bestowed either from the instructor's end or the tutee's. Her study follows through from the conception of the writing center as a site that fosters the "unobtrusive" coaches that Stephen North had laid forth in 1984 and one that he subsequently revised in 1994 by admitting that such complete lack of authoritative affect in tutoring is near impossible given how much tutoring remains "enmeshed in a system or systems—educational, political, economic, social, and so on" (qtd. in Thonus 2001, 59). Based on her findings, Thonus argues that "writing center tutors teach and construct themselves as teachers, and by evaluating tutees' writing and suggesting changes in both content and form, they fulfill a more 'teacherly' than 'peer' role" (Thonus 2001, 61).

Another approach to the triadic relationship is to explore the question of who constructs the definition of the tutors' roles. Ben Rafoth (2000) focuses on how significant it is for the tutor to be a peer and a "real audience" for the tutee. He suggests that tutees might focus on a peer tutor's ideas in ways they might not with a faculty tutor's (82). There is a perceived "difference" between the classroom instruction and tutoring, so much so that the latter is privileged by students as allowing them to think independently even as they are being guided, unlike in the classroom. Paula Gillespie and Neal Lerner (2000) underscore how this question could be completely dependent on context and situation: "At times writers will position you as proxies for their instructors, expecting an evaluation of their writing. At others, they will put you in the role of co-conspirator, especially when they admit plagiarizing or simply not caring about what they're writing" (22). Here the tutee is shown to be deciding how she wishes to perceive the tutor's role. So the trainee tutor is cautioned to understand the underlying manipulation that might be taking place between the roles of the tutor-as-instructor and the tutor-as-peer. Undeniably, within the conception of the American writing center, the role of the course instructor is significant. In the words of Thonus, "While what the instructor 'wants' becomes the agenda of the tutorial session, and what the tutee produces becomes the object of the instructor's evaluation, the instructor is not present. Nevertheless, his or her tacit participation strongly impacts the tutee's and the tutor's definition of the tutor's role" (Thonus 2001, 61). And this creates the simultaneous presence of the "instructor-like tutor" as well as the "peer tutor" in the writing center with the tacit approval of both course instructors and tutees, respectively.

Thonus identifies three mechanisms that underlie tutor-tutee relations: "directives, pronouns, and talk-off-task or 'small talk'" (2001, 63). "Being directive" appears to be the ultimate lapse within peer tutoring as it "provides a powerful means of communicating a homogenous set of social expectations for behavior" (qtd. by Thonus 2001, 64). Such behavior entails too close of an involvement in the student's work. Ideally, however, the tutor avoids appropriating the persona of the instructor in conversing with the tutee. This begs the question of whether the instructor-like tutor or the faculty tutor is a hindrance or a benefit within the writing center structure. The first-person plural "we" when used in the context of the tutoring session might be indicative of similarity of academic status and solidarity within peer tutoring, while the first-person singular from the instructor-tutor along with directives lends a distance between tutor and tutee. The issue of "small-talk" is seen as an added value of the peer-tutor model in ways that facilitates the notion of the writing center as a space for conversation about writing.

What do instructors think of their students' tutors? How much of an instructor role are they willing to concede to the tutors of writing centers? Thonus provides an array of expectations on the part of instructors that lends considerable credence to the role of faculty tutors. Some course instructors perceive the tutor as a surrogate of the instructor in the writing center and remain quite satisfied with that function with or without supervision. Others feel that the faculty tutor is poised to "teach" the student in the writing center in ways that is near impossible for the instructor to fulfill in class. Interestingly, Thonus's study found that tenured faculty and those with no firsthand experience of tutoring at the center tend to have greater expectations from faculty tutors and also "anticipate that [such] tutors act with greater authority than their training warrants or permits" (Thonus 2001, 65–66). Other instructors feel that the faculty and tutor perform separate functions, yet, once within the writing center, they register positive experiences precisely because of the distinctive roles of each (66).

So how does a tutor translate into practical operation this nuanced role? Dave Healy (1993) argues for an innate difference between the roles of instructor and tutor in terms of assuming and repudiating authority, respectively: "The advantage tutors have over teachers in this enterprise is that even if students try to invest tutors with authority, tutors can resist that role, while teachers, as long as they give grades, have a harder time shedding their image as authority figures" (21). Clearly, the faculty tutor has to acquire this expertise of resisting the expectation of authority once she occupies the writing center space and steps out of her classroom and office. Elizabeth Chilbert (2008) personalizes this experience of teaching composition courses and tutoring at the writing center by narrating the personality divide that this process calls forth, which involves accepting wholeheartedly the dualism involved and living up to the innate nature of each role as, and when, it is called forth, only to switch back to the opposite role once that becomes necessary: "Thus, my teaching self will always be a self that acts with authority over a group of writers while my consulting self will always try to resist having authority directly over writers" (2). Clearly there is a skill level that is transferrable from a composition instructor to a writing tutor, even though the process might eschew the directive mode. Helon Howell Raines (1994) points out that as a composition instructor who is also a writing tutor, she sees that the move from one role to the other parallels the move from one writer and situation to the next and, therefore, should be organic to the professional functions of instructor and tutor alike (159). Perhaps the operative word here is "should."

Recent studies on the "constructedness" of tutor and writer identities are also worth mentioning. Here, identity is all-encompassing and includes race, sex, gender, age, language background, physical and learning ability, and cultural identity. Fitzgerald and Ianetta (2016) identify the writing center as a site of conversation that facilitates the writing process through a one-on-one negotiation of the student-writer's specific writing needs mediated through their identities and the tutor's specific introduction of academic discourse.

So where does the faculty tutor fit in this conversation? How can the faculty tutor fine-tune such spatial identity creation through tutoring writing? What are the ways in which a writing center's institutional history reflects the changes in both student demographics and writing center pedagogies? What do these trajectories suggest about our writer centers' concepts of "student," "tutor," and/or "writing"?

SURVEY RESULTS

To answer these questions and more, we administered a survey to our faculty tutor colleagues and received seventeen responses, though not all questions were answered by all respondents. Probably the most surprising and notable responses came from the following three questions: Please describe the role of the Writing Center tutor. Do you see much difference between a faculty tutor and a peer tutor? If yes (14 out of 15 respondents said "yes"); please describe the difference between a faculty tutor and a peer tutor. In addition, the questions about the training needed for undergraduate peer tutors versus faculty tutors and whether the respondents' expectations of tutoring changed since they became faculty tutors also garnered some intriguing responses.

Please describe the role of the Writing Center tutor.
It seems clear the faculty tutors believe that the role of a writing center tutor is to help students with particular writing assignments, to focus on the assignment at hand, rather than, as one respondent put it, to help students "become better writers beyond the assignment." This reflects Thonus's analysis that the instructor's preferences, or the assignment, and the tutee's writing product toward that goal are the focus of the tutor's role (2001, 61). In fact, while four responses seem to acknowledge the idea that giving feedback and/or working on the "development of the writer" are as important as the "current school work," most clearly focus on the assignment as the holy grail: the phrases "writing assignments," the "goals" of the assignment, "feedback from the student's professor," "their essay," "the paper," "a piece of writing," and even helping students with "editing" come up in the majority of the responses, while the idea of helping students "fully realize their potential as writers" only come up in a few. One respondent even points out that s/he was "cautious not to step beyond the expectations of the professor/assignment." And even those few who acknowledge the writing process also speak to the current "writing project" as the focus of the tutor's role. There are mentions of providing "guidance and support," acknowledging that "the tutor does not teach" or help "students grapple with the macro-level issues," but there are also mentions of "chip[ping]-in with writing a thesis or conclusion to an essay" or helping with editing or grammar.

There is an apparent, though perhaps unconscious, conflict in many faculty tutors' approaches to tutoring: they understand the need to help the whole student think about writing in general and improve their work "beyond the assignment," but they also feel strongly the need to help students with the task at hand—the outline, draft, or final product (the assignment that has to be turned into the professor) before them. We would also suggest that some of these responses are a direct result of the requests that the tutees make in their Writing Center sessions. As pointed out in the SHU OWL tutoring study, "what do the words 'proofreading' or 'editing' really mean to tutors and tutees?" (Shea 2011, 7). When faculty tutors mention that they help students with these tasks, could it be because those are the terms that the students use when they express "what specifically they would like help with on the essay"?

Certainly, the paradox of the tutoring situation is very real for faculty tutors as well, though it may be more focused on some faculty members' and tutees' concerns about the professor for whom the tutee is writing, rather than on the tutor as faculty. Perhaps this concern contributes to the tendency to work on grammar and citation guidelines in tutoring sessions. These situations also speak to Healy's and Chilbert's points above that there is, possibly, a duality of roles that faculty tutors need to consider in their work in the writing center, including considering Thonus's idea of directive tutoring versus conversational tutorials.

Do you see much difference between a faculty tutor and a peer tutor? If yes, please describe. If no, please describe.
Of the 17 faculty tutors who responded to most of the questions, 15 answered this question. But the majority sentiment was clear: 14 out of the 15 said that they did see a difference between a faculty tutor and a peer tutor. And we can see from the responses of the 14 that they do not see themselves as "just" tutors. They see themselves as much more, possibly more like instructors, but, also, perhaps, like a "better" version of a tutor. The operative words in these responses are "more," "experience" or "experienced," "better," "expertise," "authority," "effective," "reliable," and "enhanced understanding." Not only did these faculty tutors feel that their experience, expertise, credentials, and even age gave them an edge, but in a few cases they are actually rather critical of peer tutors (more on this attitude below).

As for how these faculty tutors see themselves as different from peer tutors, for several respondents it seems to stem from the fact that they are compositionists and thus "know how to actually teach students to write." Another way of looking at this stance is stated as follows: "Faculty tutors bring a certain level of expertise to the session, not because they are better trained, but simply because they're better acquainted with what a successful paper looks like from grading full classes with similar assignments." Others add that because faculty tutors are used to writing assignments and to teaching the classes many of the tutees are taking, it puts them in a better position to help students interpret the material and the assignments. This approach invokes the idea of the tutor as teacher, which harkens back to the "instructor-like tutor" mentioned above in the discussion of Thonus's case studies. Thonus's point also gets at the issue of whether faculty tutors want to be there in the first place. To be fair, however, most faculty are cognizant of the benefits of peer tutors, even as they harbor some hesitation. Another faculty member suggests that "the peer tutor may be able to relate better to the tutee, especially if they're not far apart in age, but the faculty tutor should have the benefit of having helped many students in a variety of writing situations . . . this gives them the ability to ask better questions, to anticipate problems, and to propose a wider range of possible solutions."

Here is where we begin to see both veiled and explicit critiques of the peer tutors. One faculty tutor indicates that the difference between peer and faculty tutors "is in the tutee's/student's perception of the tutor . . . faculty tutors are viewed as more reliable and knowledgeable . . . I have had many tutees . . . say 'I signed up for you because you're a professor.' Larger communities of tutees (graduate students and faculty, for example) do not trust peer tutors." This gets to issues of authority, which Thonus, Healy, and Chilbert all address. It would seem that issues of authority might also come from the students' own faculty, so this might be a matter of faculty perception—that is, those faculty sending students to the writing center might perceive and communicate that a faculty tutor is best for certain students. And this idea begs the question: who tutors whom? Perhaps a graduate tutee is better assigned to a graduate tutor or a faculty tutor—that would essentially be "peer tutoring" for the graduate tutee. Another faculty tutor suggests that faculty tutors are "better writers and have more authority to convince students that given advice will help them."

Finally, there are the faculty tutors who try to see both sides of the story, as it were, suggesting that peer tutors had an easier time relating to the tutees, which could be helpful or detrimental, depending on the case; this person also acknowledges that "the students seemed better at the administrative and management side of the job." Another faculty tutor, who has also trained undergraduate tutors, points out that "given that I always learn a great deal from the peer tutors even as I am training them . . . , I would emphasize the learning current flows in both directions."

Respondents see faculty tutors (themselves) as being of higher intellect and abilities and find problems with peer tutoring for many reasons; some of these reasons might indicate that faculty tutors misunderstand the idea of student-centered tutoring, while others are genuinely convinced that the more knowledge, experience, and authority one has, the better one is able to tutor students. This seems like an area for training, as well. It may be that faculty tutors don't completely understand that, as one faculty tutor did say, "a tutor does not teach" (see above). Or maybe it is a matter that, the way it is described by Thonus (2001, 77), faculty tutors function in this role as "writing instructors of a different sort."

Do undergraduate tutors need training? Do faculty tutors need training? Yes/No and Why/Why Not?

Faculty tutor respondents indicate that undergraduate tutors do need training. The only respondents who did not answer with a resounding "Yes" are two: one said that "Some might," while another said that "I am not sure because I was not an undergraduate tutor." Perhaps the question was not clear. But most seemed to understand the question as asking for their opinion on the strengths and weakness of peer tutors. In fact, four of the seventeen respondents, anticipating the next question, point out that "all tutors need some training" or "even faculty need training" or "anyone who does tutoring needs training, not just undergrads," which seems to acknowledge that tutoring is not intuitive, and that students, as one faculty tutor says, "need further development themselves as writers and editors." Another adds, "too often, undergraduates think tutoring is correcting, editing, and proofreading." Interestingly, some faculty tutors worry that other faculty tutors are also too focused on those aspects; in answer to the question about whether faculty need training, one faculty tutor says that tutoring is not intuitive for faculty and that, in an eerie echo of the undergrad tutor critique above, "too often, faculty tutors think tutoring is correcting, editing, and proofreading. They also sometimes mistake tutoring for teaching." This is where tutor training and introduction to tutoring pedagogy may improve the content of discourse and thinking about tutoring for faculty tutors.

As for the other faculty tutors, most acknowledge that faculty tutors need training, but three of them say they feel that separate training is not necessary, mostly because they know what they need to know "if they tutored before and also teach" and "if you are qualified to teach students and have been trained by the university, the skill intrinsic to tutoring should be present." Others, however, seem to think that "faculty tutors need help at times in not becoming the teacher of the student, respecting the difference in roles" and that "all tutors ideally need training to stay sharp by which I mean attuned to the best possible techniques for eliciting a student's work instead of doing it for the student" and that "tutoring is not intuitive and not an inherent skill. It needs work." Another faculty tutor puts it quite concisely: "[faculty tutors] too could benefit from a review of best practices." Two of the respondents indicate that training might place an additional burden on faculty, so they should be paid for this time; as undergraduates are paid for training time at our center, this makes sense.

But as for the types of training that faculty (and undergraduate tutors) need, there are differing opinions here, too. Several faculty tutors seem to feel that undergraduates need help with "scenarios," "situations," and "mock tutoring sessions" as well as training in "editing," "grammatical rules," and "proofreading marks." In fact, of the fifteen respondents to this question, five not only mention but focus on editing or grammar as primary, which is antithetical to the way most peer tutors are trained. Others discuss "minimalist tutoring" and "nondirective, tutee-led tutoring." In terms of their own training, the fifteen respondents' replies ranged from "I'm not sure" to "protocol of the job" to anything that focuses on best practices, writing center scholarship, and the same issues in which undergraduate tutors are trained. One faculty tutor provides an interesting observation about this latter notion: "Faculty tutors should have similar training to peer tutors, if in a more concise way. Faculty tutors are sometimes even more stubborn in their tutoring styles, so I think it is healthy for them to see how other colleagues approach tutoring." Another faculty tutor suggests that "anything that puts them in communication with the undergrad tutors . . . so that everyone is on the same page" is advisable. Clearly, as with the role of the tutor, faculty tutors have different ideas about training, but these suggestions beg the question of whether and how we can offer faculty tutor training. Interestingly, and perhaps not surprisingly, it seems likely that faculty tutors' expectations of themselves mirror what they expect of the people who tutor their own students.

What are your expectations of the people who tutor your students?

These answers also range from "edit and revise" to "tutor (not teach)" to "guide," provide "feedback," offer "encouragement," respect and understand the goals of "my assignments," and follow "my comments and suggestions for my students." Others focus on the need to help their students to become better writers beyond the assignment, to understand their writing processes and to help them gain confidence. When asked if they expect more from the faculty tutors than undergraduate tutors, though, most (twelve) said they do not.

Have your expectations of tutoring changed since you became a faculty tutor?

An equal number of respondents say their expectations have (7) or have not (7) changed, while 3 say they aren't sure. The commentary ranges from "always room for improvement" to "I had a better sense of how hard it is to tutor well" and "I now expect to stimulate my tutees to think critically by engaging in questioning rather than suggesting solutions to their writing issues." As ever, the responses vary widely, and all the responses lead to the need for thoughtful analysis of the role of the faculty tutor and the place of faculty tutor training.

DISCUSSION

While a tricky proposition, faculty tutor training can certainly make those tutors aware of their options in terms of scaling back their teacherly selves without compromising on skills and expertise. Training to reflect on tutoring and communications can tune tutors in to their own strengths and style, which can, in turn, help them hone and recognize their best practices. We might start by sharing with the faculty some writing center scholarship on peer tutoring and discussing with them what this might look like from a faculty tutor perspective. Faculty tutors, indeed, are not peer tutors, except when they work with other faculty members or, perhaps, graduate students. Thonus's ideas of asking faculty to think of themselves, when they tutor, as "writing instructors of a different sort" (Thonus 2001, 77) are germane here. Perhaps the goals and practices of peer tutors would not work for faculty tutors, not only from the tutors' perspective but from the tutees' perspective.

In the open-ended comment section of the survey, one tutor says s/he would like to know about "the other training that occurs beyond the one that I [conduct]." In fact, faculty tutors could be more actively encouraged to attend each other's training sessions—and, possibly, be paid to do so, as the undergraduate tutors are paid to attend training. This is a labor/compensation issue that must be addressed if the faculty are to be asked to participate in tutor training. In addition, a beginning-of-the-year roundtable, followed by shorter, topic-based sessions through the semester, could enhance conversation and self-awareness of faculty tutors. Writing short journals on tutoring experiences or writing "tutoring plans" for sessions with permanent appointments with graduate students, international students, and students with second-language writing needs also would be useful.

While the survey shows that a majority of respondents (thirteen out of seventeen) are somewhat to very familiar with writing center pedagogy, research, and scholarship, it appears that we might still need to take a more systematic approach to providing access to the latest information. Faculty tutors may be more confident in creating their own vocabularies commensurate with their tasks of tutoring in a more holistic sense and examining the larger mechanisms of organization and conception rather than mechanics alone. Faculty tutors in tandem with writing center administrators could begin training graduate tutees and, possibly, get involved with a burgeoning writing-across-the-curriculum/writing-in-the-disciplines initiative. The OWL research results—the takeaway was that faculty tutors are better equipped to provide online responses, especially since more of the OWL tutees are now graduate students—perhaps point to a direction for all faculty tutoring.

CONCLUSION

In the end, the short answer to the question, Is there a place for faculty tutors in a university writing center? is "Yes." The long answer, contained in this analysis, is "Yes, and we need to figure out what that 'place' is." To be accurate, faculty tutors are not (typically) peer tutors, and perhaps we should not be asking them to try to take on that role. As non-directive and hands off as they might be, their tutees will have a certain expectation of such tutors once they know or perceive that they are also faculty members. And yet there are growing groups of clients—nontraditional students, international students, graduate students, even faculty colleagues who seek writing support—who could be well served by faculty tutors. These are all growing populations at SHU and, we imagine, at other institutions.

At the same time, it is not too much to ask faculty tutors to participate in some tutor training, which will help them as tutors no matter which tutees they are tutoring. The critical issue is to create an environment in which faculty will appreciate and embrace tutor training; perhaps it should be more appropriately called "professional development."

We fully expect that this reflection will continue to open up the SHU Writing Center, on both a short- and long-term basis, to the ways that faculty can best provide their own thoughtful and reflective tutoring expertise to the university community. Some ideas for us to consider include the following:

1. Moving away from "required" faculty tutoring to the normalization of the appointment and hiring of faculty tutors: solicit those interested by advertising within the university employment system and setting up an interview and subsequent training process.
2. Paying faculty tutors for the work they do either through course release (as is currently the case) or hourly professional rates.
3. Developing faculty tutor training, professional development, and best practices seminars or meetings that could be shared spaces for peer and faculty tutors to converse. The excellent ideas offered by our colleague Miriam E. Laufer in this volume's chapter 1, "Redefining Training for Faculty Tutors," would be a solid place to start.

4. Looking at growing categories of clients, particularly the international graduate community, to investigate their use of our services and how the faculty tutor fits in to provide an optimal contact zone for faculty tutors.

These ideas are critical for us at SHU to consider, and we urge our colleagues at other institutions with similar situations to undertake their own appropriate studies.

REFERENCES

Bruffee, Kenneth A. 1984. "Peer Tutoring and the 'Conversation of Mankind.'" In *Writing Centers: Theory and Administration*, edited by Gary A. Olson, 3–15. Urbana, IL: National Council of Teachers of English.

Chilbert, Elizabeth. 2008. "When Roles Collide: On Being a Writing Center Tutor and Composition Instructor." *Praxis: A Writing Center Journal* 5 (2).

Fitzgerald, Lauren, and Melissa Ianetta. 2016. *The Oxford Guide for Writing Tutors: Practice and Research*. New York: Oxford UP.

Flower, Linda, Victoria Stein, John Ackerman, Margaret J. Kantz, Kathleen McCormick, and Wayne C. Peck, eds. 1990. *Reading-to-Write: Exploring a Cognitive and Social Process*. New York: Oxford UP.

Gillam, Alice M. 1994. "Collaborative Learning Theory and Peer Tutoring Practice." *Intersections: Theory-Practice in the Writing Center*, edited by Joan Mullin and Ray Wallace, 39–53. Champain, IL: NCTE.

Gillespie, Paula, and Neal Lerner. 2000. *The Allyn and Bacon Guide to Peer Tutoring*. Boston: Allyn and Bacon.

Grieco, Chrysanthy. 2018. "A Little Information." September 17. Email message to Kelly A. Shea.

Harris, Muriel. 1995. "Talking in the Middle: Why Writers Need Writing Tutors." *College English* 57 (1): 27–42.

Healy, Dave. 1993. "A Defense of Dualism: The Writing Center and the Classroom." In *The Writing Center Journal* 14 (1): 16–29.

Morgan, John H. 2013. "Re-inventing the Tutorial in an Internet World: An Enhancement of an Old English Tradition." In *Journal of Alternative Perspectives in the Social Sciences* 5 (3): 522–32.

Moore, Will G. 1968. *The Tutorial System and Its Future*. New York: Pergamon.

North, Stephen M. 1984. "The Idea of a Writing Center." In *College English* 46 (5): 443–46.

North, Stephen. 1994. "Revisiting 'The Idea of a Writing Center.'" In *The Writing Center Journal* 15 (1): 7–19.

Raines, Helon Howell. 1994. "Tutoring and Teaching: Continuum, Dichotomy, or Dialectic?" In *The Writing Center Journal* 14 (2): 150–62.

Rafoth, Ben. 2000. "Helping Writers to Write Analytically." In *A Tutor's Guide: Helping Writers One to One*, edited by Ben Rafoth, 76–84. Portsmouth, NH: Boynton/Cook.

Shea, Kelly A. 2011. "Through the Eyes of the OWL: Assessing Faculty vs. Peer Tutoring in an Online Setting." In *Writing Lab Newsletter* 35 (69): 7–9.

Thonus, Terese. 2001. "Triangulation in the Writing Center: Tutor, Tutee, and Instructor Perceptions of the Tutor's Role" *Writing Center Journal* 22 (1) (Fall/Winter): 59–82.

Wilkowski, Bernadette. 2018. "A Little Information." September 17. Email message to Kelly A. Shea.

7
BETWEEN DEFINITIONS
Negotiating the Role of Professional Writing Consultants Online

Matthew Sharkey-Smith

When I got my first job in a writing center, I didn't know what to expect: in graduate school, I was trained to teach composition in a traditional, four-year college environment—we only cursorily discussed writing center work. Many of my peers and I sought jobs teaching composition, and some of them made a living by stitching together income from adjunct positions at several universities. Holding several positions at once has become something of a rite of passage in the teaching of writing, and one I also wanted to complete as a first step toward a faculty career, but those adjunct jobs were difficult to get despite their low pay and instability. I instead found a job as a writing tutor in the Walden University Writing Center (WUWC). Walden is a for-profit, fully online, public-benefit university focused primarily on graduate education for working adults, and when I began my job it was most similar to that of a peer writing consultant in a traditional college environment. I reviewed students' papers and provided feedback on their writing. I was paid hourly and worked full time, though some of our staff chose to work part time. We were all attracted to the flexibility of this position. By virtue of working at an online university, we were, and are, able to work from any location with an Internet connection and, for the most part, set our own schedules—ideal circumstances for graduate students or anyone else needing to make a living while pursuing a fledgling career in another field.

Accordingly, my colleagues and I tended to think of this job as a bridge to the next phase in our professional lives, something we would do for a few years and then leave once we had outgrown it. Curiously, though, many of us have stayed for several years (I just completed my eighth), because our jobs and the WUWC overall have matured to a degree none of us predicted when we were hired. That maturation has

DOI: 10.7330/9781646420858.c007

centered on a continual redefinition of our work as educators and professionals in the writing center field.

Negotiating these definitions has often been challenging, requiring us to occupy a tenuous space between the roles of faculty and peer tutors while leaving us at times without a clear understanding of our powers and responsibilities. However, I argue that this process has also yielded unique pedagogical and professional opportunities. This is only my experience at only one institution, but my hope is that this account can help other professional writing consultants more fully establish themselves in their institutions and in the writing center field. While there are many dimensions to the work as a professional consultant, here I focus on a few that in the WUWC have shifted significantly in my time there: our sense of authority and power, our teaching practices, and our status both in our institution and in the writing center discipline. By charting our center's locations along these axes, I argue for an approach that professional consultants in other settings could adopt to better define their own roles.

INSTRUCTIONAL AUTHORITY

Unlike the students at a traditional four-year university, the students we tend to see in the WUWC are financially independent adults pursuing education to further their careers. Often, they haven't written an academic paper in years, and when they come to our center they present a huge variety of instructional needs. Many have strengths in some aspects of writing, such as maintaining a scholarly tone and supporting claims with evidence, but need guidance in others such as thesis development, organization, and synthesis. And many only want information about the rules of APA style. Many only need the confidence to recognize the skills they possess, while others need a thorough grounding in the process and practices of scholarly writing. Like any student body, our students are complex and defy easy generalization. They do, however, have a set of persistent tendencies, and over time this uniqueness has shaped our sense of instructional authority and the resulting pedagogy we use in our consultations.

When students first come to the WUWC, they often regard my colleagues and me as authority figures, and they tend to expect feedback similar to what they receive from their faculty rather than the collaborative approach articulated in classic writing-center pedagogy (Carino 2011; Jewell and Cheatle 2016). While adult-learning theorists champion instruction that recognizes adult students' self-directedness and openness to cooperation with their teachers (Kenner and Weinerman 2011), our students rarely exhibit the fellow-traveler spirit that students in traditional writing centers can share with their peer tutors. We in the WUWC are typically seen, to some degree, as the teacher by our students (a dynamic also described by Kimberly Fahle Peck, Lisa Nicole Tyson, Steffani Dambruch, and Amanda Gomez in "Professional Tutors, Shifting Identities: Narratives from the Center," chapter 5).

Yet, we are not faculty. We have no classrooms, virtual or otherwise, and we give no grades. In accordance with seminal writing-center theory, we strive to maintain the writer's sense of agency in their own work and avoid framing writing issues as having "correct" answers (Brooks 1991; Corbett 2008; North 1984). Often the only information we have about a student's assignment comes from the student, and even when the student offers us their assignment prompt or rubric, we still lack a full understanding of their course and their instructor's preferences. Because we work online and mainly asynchronously, we often know little, if anything, about a student that they don't volunteer in their appointment form—for example, we have no body language, tone of voice, or other nonverbal cues to work with—and must take their writing at face value. In practice, these factors don't necessarily limit the value of our consultations, but they do orient our work toward a different purpose than that of course faculty.

In our work as professional writing consultants, we occupy a role between that of peer and faculty. Students know we are part of the instructional apparatus available to them and often expect us to simply provide edits on their work to make it acceptable to their faculty, and consequently we cannot be the ideal, non-directive peer advocating only for the student; we cannot help but bear some level of institutional authority. Similarly, we cannot structure students' learning over time and compel them through it with the motivation of a grade as faculty do in writing courses.

This in-between-ness has its advantages. We can draw upon our expertise and experience when needed, allowing us to function similar to an academic advisor, guiding students toward a set of rhetorical choices that are likely to be fruitful and away from ones that are not. When I give a PhD student feedback on their prospectus, for example, I can ask critical questions about their research design or suggest that they move information about their research problem's significance to a different section because, despite the fact that I have no formal training in their field, I have read many prospectus drafts, understand how they will be evaluated, and know the most common challenges these students face.

Despite being pulled toward (and, at the same time, pushed away from) these other roles, we still endeavor, as Stephen North (1984) articulated in his canonical "The Idea of a Writing Center," to "produce better writers, not better writing" (438). Like faculty, we help students satisfy institutional or curricular expectations in their writing, but like peer tutors our central purpose is to help students grow as writers. We never intended to be seen as quasi-faculty, but since our students perceive us as having authority, regardless of our attempts to not be perceived that way, we have tried to use it to their benefit.

PEDAGOGY

Along with our sense of instructional authority, our team of professional consultants has developed a unique pedagogy. We have grounded our work in scholarship as much as possible, but, compared to classical writing-center pedagogy or composition theory, relatively little scholarship exists for online writing-center consultations (Prince et al. 2018). Over time, our pedagogy has become a synthesis of seminal writing center ideas, conventions borrowed from instruction in online writing courses, and practical experiences gained from our setting and our students.

Writing center consultations have traditionally been understood as face-to-face interactions held on a physical campus. As part of an online university, we have no physical space, so the many environmental considerations face-to-face centers must make aren't applicable to us. Furthermore, we primarily use an asynchronous approach, a mode of instructional discourse that is widely used but not uniformly articulated or understood (Denton 2017; Prince et al. 2018). We offer some synchronous services, and we often pilot new offerings, but our students tend to prefer the flexibility of asynchronous feedback. The vast majority of them are adults with responsibilities to their families and careers, and asynchronous consultations fit into their schedules better than face-to-face ones held at particular times. Asynchronous feedback also persists once the appointment is done, so our students can review our comments at any time.

Asynchronous consulting is a common offering in writing centers offering online services (Prince et al. 2018), but, until we developed our own training guide for this form of consulting, we had few resources available to train new hires with or to study for professional development (for additional information on training consultants in the WUWC, see Shiell, "Examining Assumptions about Training and Development for Writing Center Professional Consultants," and for information on training faculty consultants, see Miriam E. Laufer, "Redefining Training for Faculty Tutors," chapters 3 and 1, respectively). For example, consultants in face-to-face writing centers tend to follow a non-directive pedagogy, in some cases even refraining from touching the student's paper at all (Brooks 1991; Corbett 2008; Shamoon and Burns 1995). Asynchronous feedback, however, cannot be purely non-directive, as we have no live discussion with the student—Socratic questioning doesn't work if the consultant cannot guide the student toward a new understanding of their writing via a series of quick, back-and-forth exchanges. As much as we value dialogue with our students and encourage it as much as we can, the minimalist approach advocated for in foundational writing-center scholarship is infeasible in our setting.

Lacking a set of established practices for giving asynchronous online feedback in a writing center context, we imported some aspects of our pedagogy from the composition field. We have relied most heavily on Beth Hewett's (2010) *The Online Writing Conference*, a manual for instructors teaching writing courses online. In contrast to the non-directive approach common in face-to-face writing centers, Hewett (2010) advocates for a hands-on, directive approach, arguing that explicitly telling students what to do to revise their writing is the only practical way, in an asynchronous mode, for them to develop their skills.

Perhaps owing to its intended use in classroom instruction, this approach requires a stable notion of efficacy: in any consultation there are problems in the student's writing, and by applying the consultant's feedback the student can fix them and, more important, develop a skill model that she can draw upon in future writing tasks. In the WUWC, we consider this efficacy in the context of the student's goals and define it using a mix of sources—the student's assignment, consultants' assessments of the student's strengths and challenges in their writing, and, for formal issues, APA style. Students often say they appreciate the clarity and efficiency of this directive approach, and, anecdotally, I have seen it work well when coupled with the empathy and individual attention prized in traditional writing-center pedagogy.

I find Hewett's (2010) point about the need for clarity in asynchronous feedback unassailable. In the WUWC, we have seen, and still occasionally see, how an instructor's well-intentioned Socratic questioning can be easily misinterpreted and how, without a live back-and-forth with the student, those misinterpretations can be challenging to address. That said, I and many of my colleagues have long been uncomfortable with a purely directive approach in our consultations. Such an approach can subordinate the student's rhetorical agency to the consultant's, which does the student a disservice and oversimplifies the complex and contingent decision-making inherent in writing. In the writing center field, proponents of directive feedback argue that it allows a student to benefit from their consultant's expertise and progress more efficiently and definitively in their writing (Corbett 2008; Shamoon and Burns 1995), which in my experience can be true, but if not tempered with nondirectivity it does little to equip students to make their own rhetorical choices and produce creative work in any discipline.

In practice, most of the consultants in the WUWC use a blend of directivity and nondirectivity in our consultations. Generally speaking, we take a more directive approach for rule-based concerns such a grammar and APA style—issues that have clearer definitions of correctness in our setting—and a more nondirective one for the fuzzier categories of argument development, organization, and voice. We also encourage our consultants to experiment with and individualize their pedagogies. We recognize that we are professionals and, as with our students, we should have the freedom to make our own choices in our work.

While our methods differ significantly from those used historically in writing centers, they allow us to achieve similar goals. As in face-to-face writing centers, some of our students make just one or two appointments and never come back, while others make many appointments, some even returning weekly throughout their degree program. Working remotely and without a live dialogue complicates but does not preclude our students' skill growth or our ability to develop a rapport with them. The process is slower and requires of both parties more effort and, at times, guesswork about their feelings and reactions to comments, but at its best working in this way proceeds like an extended correspondence between characters in an epistolary novel, each side contributing to an exchange that grows richer and more meaningful over time.

INSTITUTIONAL STATUS

In our university, the writing center plays a unique role, one that, like our role as consultants, situates us between a traditional writing center and a faculty department. All of Walden's degree programs are grounded in the social sciences; it has no English or composition department to serve as the institution's authority on writing instruction. In the absence of such a department, we in the WUWC have become the de facto "writing people" at Walden. In addition to working directly with students, we support a writing-across-the-curriculum program, serving on curriculum committees and offering advice, writing resources, and holding webinars to faculty to help them more effectively teach writing in their courses. Having a professional staff means that like our students, others in the university increasingly see authority in us that we did not have in the earlier days of the WUWC, when it most resembled a writing center staffed by peers.

Despite that added authority, we do not have the same status as faculty. Occasionally, in our consultations with students, we see feedback they have received from their faculty that is problematic for one reason or another. In such situations, we generally avoid contradicting the feedback unless it is factually incorrect. Instead, we tend to offer an additional perspective on the issue at hand, and often we make the same point differently, providing more detail and offering the student concrete revision steps they could take. Sometimes students want us to adjudicate disputes with their faculty about the quality of their writing, which we treat similarly: unless the issue has a clear definition of correctness (e.g., a grammatical or APA style rule), we reframe it as a conversation the student should have with their faculty and try to equip them, as best we can, with accurate information. Rather than engaging, like faculty, in quantitative assessments of students' writing, we see ourselves as a test audience for our students so that they can learn new strategies and retire ineffective ones. Crucially, we don't function like graduate teaching assistants—our objectives complement those of faculty but are not subordinate to them. Over the years, our professional consultants have been called writing tutors, writing consultants, and now writing instructors, a series of titles that reflects the change in our center's understanding of itself and our university's understanding of us. Now, having established a firmer institutional footing for ourselves, we operate in parallel to faculty. We are free to draw our own conclusions about what students need to work on, even if those conclusions have little impact on the papers they are currently writing.

Like faculty positions, our jobs are more stable and have had more potential for growth than those of peer consultants. We engage in a variety of professional development exercises to help us make thoughtful and deliberate instructional decisions and ground ourselves as much as possible in scholarship (for examples, see Shiell, "Examining Assumptions about Training and Development for Professional Writing Center Consultants," chapter 3). We also spend time on projects and research to develop and expand our services alongside our consultations. We offer a few synchronous services, namely, webinars on a variety of writing topics and live chat so students can converse with consultants. Our website has a wide range of text and video content covering all aspects of writing, and it has become comprehensive enough that it serves as a kind of textbook or reference manual for all of our instruction. We visit many of Walden's online classrooms to promote the WUWC, answer student questions, and offer writing suggestions similar to course visits many face-to-face writing centers conduct on their campuses. We have self-paced, interactive modules to help students learn foundational skills in areas such as grammar, paraphrasing, and scholarly voice. We also have an active social-media presence, and we maintain a blog where our consultants address writing topics in a more personalized and nuanced way than we can on our website. All of these activities and services enrich our asynchronous consultations with our students, and they allow our staff to learn new skills and vary their day-to-day work.

As we have expanded our reach within Walden, we have grown significantly. The WUWC nearly doubled in size three years ago in an effort to meet demand for our services. We now have a staff of twenty full-time, salaried, professional consultants, and we regularly hire graduate assistants to help us do our jobs more effectively and to give these students experience in our field. The consultant team in the WUWC isn't a faculty department, but it is now the size of a composition or English department at many other universities, reflecting the institutional support we receive and our usefulness to our students.

SCHOLARSHIP

As part of our recent growth and ongoing professionalization, we in the WUWC have increasingly participated in and contributed to writing center scholarship and discourse. Each year some of our consultants attend local and national conferences, which have included the Conference on College Composition and Communication, the Association of Writers and Writing Programs conference, and the International Writing Centers Association conference.

At those conferences, we often encounter staff at other writing centers who are interested in providing online consultations, but they have found relatively little scholarship that they can use to guide the development of such services. The information that exists tends to focus on synchronous consultations, perhaps out of a belief that rather than embracing the unique characteristics of distance learning, online consulting should as much as possible replicate the experience of a face-to-face consultation (Denton 2017). The merits of that debate are beyond my purposes here, but regardless of which mode is better, or whether there is an agreed-upon definition of better to make such a distinction meaningful, writing center discourse tends to view online work from the perspective of traditional face-to-face centers, which has resulted in a lack of scholarship specifically for asynchronous online consultations (Denton 2017; Prince et al. 2018).

In an effort to fill this vacuum, some of my colleagues have collaborated with others in our field to create the Online Writing Centers Community (http://onlinewritingcenters.org/), an organization intended to support scholarship specifically for online writing centers. Several consultants have written for publication as well; a few of us published an article recently in *WLN: A Journal of Writing Center Scholarship* (Prince et al. 2018). All of this has been done, and funded, in the name of student need and our institution's emphasis on providing support services.

Before we had these opportunities, several of us in the WUWC felt a bit like outcasts from the writing center community. Its scholarship often required significant adaptation to be meaningful in our setting, and the topics we were most interested in were rarely addressed in its journals and conference presentations. As a result, we have attempted to fill this gap ourselves, starting conversations and building communities with others doing similar work to, we hope, advance the field overall.

IN-BETWEEN-NESS AS A SITE OF OPPORTUNITY

If our experience in the WUWC is any example, professional consultants at other universities may face issues of definition similar to ours. Their institutional dynamics will be different—perhaps they work entirely face to face or perhaps they operate alongside a composition department that bears responsibility for writing instruction at their university—but they will likely need to make similar considerations. How do they relate to faculty? To peer consultants? How might they find a balance between traditional writing-center pedagogy and the authority students confer on them due to their professional status? Which approach, or set of approaches, will best serve their students? How might these professional consultants grow in their roles and broaden the scope of their centers' work in their institutions?

Because their circumstances will likely be different from ours, their answers to these questions will almost certainly differ from ours as well. Although I did not consider this when I began working as a writing consultant, I now believe, looking back on the process of self-definition our writing center has undergone, that our staff and students have all tended to benefit whenever we in the WUWC have embraced our uniqueness. We are neither faculty nor peer consultants, yet we satisfy an otherwise unmet demand. Rather than downplaying what distinguishes our role from those more traditional ones, we have used those differences to expand the writing center model and meet our students' needs.

For as long as the definitions of a professional consultant remain in flux, I would encourage other professional consultants, with whatever methods they have available and within whatever institutional limitations placed upon them, to similarly regard their own in-between-ness as a site of opportunity. This role has emerged because students need writing support they haven't been getting elsewhere, and this new space may afford significant growth and innovation.

REFERENCES

Brooks, Jeff. 1991. "Minimalist Tutoring: Making the Student Do All the Work." *Writing Lab Newsletter* 15 (6): 1–4.

Carino, Peter. 2011. "Power and Authority in Peer Tutoring." In *The St. Martin's Sourcebook for Writing Tutors*, edited by Christina Murphy and Steve Sherwood, 112–27. Boston: Bedford/St. Martin's.

Corbett, Steven J. 2008. "Tutoring Style, Tutoring Ethics: The Continuing Relevance of the Directive/Nondirective Instructional Debate." *Praxis: A Writing Center Journal* 5 (2).

Denton, Kathryn. 2017. "Beyond the Lore: A Case for Asynchronous Online Tutoring Research." *Writing Center Journal* 36 (2): 175–203.

Hewett, Beth L. 2010. *The Online Writing Conference*. Portsmouth, NH: Boynton/Cook.

Jewell, Megan Swihart, and Joseph Cheatle. 2016. "Toward a Professional Consultant's Handbook: Researching Support and Training Methods." *WLN: A Journal of Writing Center Scholarship* 41 (3–4): 10–17.

Kenner, Cari, and Jason Weinerman. 2011. "Adult Learning Theory: Applications to Nontraditional College Students." *Journal of College Reading and Learning* 41 (2): 87–96. https://doi.org/10.1080/10790195.2011.10850344.

North, Stephen. 1984. "The Idea of a Writing Center." *College English* 46 (5): 433–46. https://doi.org/10.2307/377047.

Prince, Sarah, Rachel Willard, Ellen Zamarripa, and Matt Sharkey-Smith. 2018. "Peripheral (Re)Visions: Moving Online Writing Centers from Margin to Center." *WLN: A Journal of Writing Center Scholarship* 42 (5–6): 10–17.

Shamoon, Linda K., and Deborah H. Burns. 1995. "A Critique of Pure Tutoring." *Writing Center Journal* 15 (2): 134–51.

8
FACULTY AND PROFESSIONAL CONSULTANTS, THE WRITING CENTER, AND STEM

Catherine Siemann

It is a commonplace that the twenty-first century university places an increasing emphasis on science, technology, engineering, and mathematics (STEM) (Jaschik 2014). As STEM programs move ever further to the forefront of higher education, writing centers are not immune to the effects of shifting student populations and curricular emphasis. At many STEM-focused universities, faculty and professional writing consultants play an important role in the writing center, and as colleges and universities in general intensify their focus on STEM, a professional or mixed peer-professional tutoring model becomes increasingly valuable.

The wealth of experience faculty and professional tutoring staff brings to the writing center makes these individuals exceptionally valuable for working with the sometimes complicated tutoring situations that are typical of STEM programs and STEM students: writing done for STEM classes and research projects, which may be difficult for the uninitiated peer tutor to understand, and working with STEM students, who often self-identify as weak writers. Neither peers nor professionals may have relevant content knowledge of STEM subjects, but professionals have advantages in working around that. Certainly, extra caution must be exercised by professional writing center staff not to simply replicate a student/teacher dynamic. But in many ways, faculty and professional consultants are ideally placed to serve as expert outsiders, who are "an interested, rhetorically savvy audience wanting to better understand [specialist subject] knowledge" (Nowacek and Hughes 2015, 181).

WHY PROFESSIONAL TUTORING STAFF?

Why are professional and faculty tutors particularly well suited to work with STEM subjects and STEM students? If trained properly and self-aware about the potential pitfalls of the dynamic, faculty and professional tutors can bring a confidence to working with writing outside their own academic field that comes from the breadth and depth of their experience with student writing. Professional tutors at the New Jersey Institute of Technology (NJIT), where I direct the writing center, are often instructors in our own First Year Writing Program. NJIT's First Year Writing sequence is tailored for our unique student body. The second course in the sequence, HUM102, centers on a semester-long research project, very often in the student's own field of study. Accordingly, many of our professional tutoring staff are already accustomed to working with students on science and engineering-related subjects, at least at the introductory level.

Most of our professional staff have MAs or PhDs in composition and rhetoric/writing studies, or in literary studies, while still others have MFAs in creative writing. Since NJIT has no graduate programs in the humanities, we sometimes hire graduate or law students in English from area universities. A large percentage of the staff have extensive classroom teaching experience, and a considerable number have worked at writing centers at their graduate or undergraduate institutions, which exposes us to a variety of methods and practices from other writing centers, which we may adopt for our own.

While the strengths of professional and faculty tutors are undoubted, it's also a fact that at STEM-centered institutions, peer tutors are often difficult to come by. As STEM enrollments increase across the board, this trend is likely to increase in colleges and universities generally. Undergraduates with heavy STEM course loads, labs, and internships, are unlikely to have room for tutor-training classes in their overcrowded schedules. Even finding the time for paid work as peer tutors can be problematic, with all the competing demands on their time. Graduate students in science and technology are funded to do laboratory-based research, with little reason to seek additional campus employment. Steven Strang, the longtime writing center director at MIT, considers the reasons why peer tutoring has been unsuccessful there in his article "Staffing a Writing Center with Professional Tutors" (2010 292). Without English majors, he writes, "we don't have a built-in pool of students for whom service in a writing center would be an important addition to their resumes" and, additionally, "the prestige of being selected to work in the center paled against the desire to do well in physics classes" (292). Math and science grades are the pathway for these students to achieve their academic and professional goals.

Strang's experience mirrors my own. The Cooper Union, a small engineering and fine arts school where I first tutored, used only professional staff. From there, I went on to become writing center director at NJIT, a medium-sized public research university that has recently achieved R1 status.

When I arrived here in fall 2014, there were no student writing tutors at all, only professionals. We have since instituted a small cohort of peer tutors from our Honors College, for whom we are one of many choices to fulfill a community service requirement. But, as Strang says, the students' academics always come first, especially in an intensively test-based culture. Peer consultants start later in the semester than our professional staff, and tutor for only two to three 45-minute sessions per week, providing no more than 15–20 percent of our tutoring hours in any given semester. They are valuable in sharing a student perspective on assignments and, in particular, familiarizing us with classroom practices and genre expectations. For this reason, a mixed model incorporating both professional and peer tutoring staff is ideal in a writing center that deals with STEM subjects and STEM students.

Our position as a primarily professional staff is not as unusual as writing center scholarship seems to suggest. While the majority of writing center discourse presumes peer tutors, a substantial minority of four-year institutions (and a narrow majority of two-year colleges) employ professional tutors as Kimberly Fahle Peck, Lisa Nicole Tyson, Steffani Dambruch, and Amanda Gomez point out in chapter 5. Experienced writing instructors come into the writing center with solid grounding in the basics. Some training in writing center pedagogy, with its "different goals and outcomes," is still important for successful writing center work, of course. But as Miriam E. Laufer points out in chapter 1, by looking specifically at faculty and professional tutors we can even further explore enduring tutoring topics, delving deeper into issues that arise in our particular centers. Since many of our professional tutoring staff return semester after semester, there is an opportunity to build an extraordinary depth of experience.

EXPERT OUTSIDERS AND COLLABORATION IN THE WRITING CENTER

Rebecca Nowacek and Bradley Hughes's concept of the "expert outsider," though conceived in connection with peer tutor training, proves equally useful for professional and faculty consultants working with students on STEM subjects. Research in the field has suggested that tutors with subject expertise may be especially effective, yet writing tutors with expertise in science and technology are not widely available, certainly not in the numbers in which they are needed. In their study, Nowacek and Bradley focus on the threshold concept of the expert outsider, "*experienced, effective conversational partners for writers*" as key to tutor education (Nowacek and Hughes 2015, 181; emphasis in original). Further, "tutors draw on knowledge of writing processes and genres, as well as the affective, institutional, and ideological contexts for writing to inform their conversations with writers" (181). Who is better informed of such processes and contexts than faculty and professional tutors with specialized knowledge as teachers or practitioners of writing? Genre and rhetorical knowledge can guide writing center staff to useful positioning with regard to lab reports, personal statements, and papers in scientific and technical fields, even if it is not a genre of writing they themselves perform.

Nowacek and Hughes write of tutors as being reluctant to give up their "teacherly role" (2015, 182). Why, then, would I suggest that professional consultants, many of whom are also writing instructors, be able to do so, when the more usual role for many of them is literally that of teacher? A combination of pedagogical experience and a theoretical understanding of rhetorical roles allows them to inhabit multiple positions with an ease that is far greater than for peer tutors, who have had less time to work through their understanding of those roles.

Certain approaches are particularly beneficial for professional tutors. For example, Jeff Brooks' classic "Minimalist Tutoring" essay has a very different valence when assigned to a professional tutoring staff than it does with peer tutors. Peter Carino, among others, has raised valid concerns about Brooks's non-directive approach. Peer tutors may too easily cede authority to those whom they are tutoring, and render themselves ineffective (Carino 2003, 96–97). However, Brooks's notion of non-directive tutoring becomes a valuable corrective for writing center staff who are used to the position of authority in the front of the classroom. It reminds them to step back and let the clients use their voices.

A clear division of roles also helps to maintain the distinction between teacher and tutor. At the writing centers where I have worked, NJIT and Cooper Union, it is established policy that writing consultants who are also instructors do not work with their own students in their role as writing tutors. The collaborative nature of what happens in a writing center session is distinct from the more authoritative role these same individuals may enact in their office hours with students whose assignments they have created and whose work they will grade. There is also a first-name policy, to emphasize the collaborative nature, though students not infrequently resist this and want to refer to the professional staff as "professor." Brooks's admonitions to "make the student the primary agent" is thus a useful reminder to those seen as authority figures (1991, 2). "I want to hear your voice less, and their voices more," is the occasional corrective I have to make with NJIT's professional tutoring staff, but it is surprisingly infrequent.

Andrea Lunsford's now-classic notion of the Burkean Parlor emphasizes shared power and control, and the negotiations of collaboration (1991, 8). This may be more difficult to achieve with the power imbalance of a professional tutor on one side of the table, but a thoughtful and conscious effort on the part of deeply committed and experienced writing center staff, used to drawing out and affirming student writing, performs this collaboration effectively. Muriel Harris describes the writing center tutor as "a hybrid creation—neither a teacher nor a peer," which seems to suggest that peer tutors must take on some of the qualities of instructors, while instructors likewise take on some of the attributes of peers (1992 371). This is where the notion of cross-mentoring between peer and professional tutors can be of great value; we will return to this subsequently.

SUBJECT EXPERTISE VERSUS THE EXPERT OUTSIDER

Nowacek and Hughes's "expert outsider" position revisits the notion of the "ignorant" versus the "knowledgeable" tutor dynamic, which Susan M. Hubbuch explores in an influential 1988 article in *Writing Center Journal*. Hubbuch contends that the ignorant tutor serves the student writer more effectively, situating the student as the expert in the subject matter and conventions, as well as in drawing the student out as the responsible party for "developing his/her own ideas" (29). One of the prime arguments against professional tutors is that as authority figures, students are less likely to develop collaborative relationships with them. Hubbuch's position may be extended to suggest, however, that a professional tutor without subject matter expertise may more readily overcome the perceived power differential.

Subsequent work, by Kiedaisch and Dinitz, Shamoon and Burns, and others has questioned the assumption that non-directive tutoring is always preferable and raised concerns about the importance of understanding discipline-specific rhetorics in tutoring writing (Kiedaisch and Dinitz 1993; Shamoon and Burns 1995). Sue Dinitz and Susanmarie Harrington argue that tutors with greater disciplinary expertise conduct more productive sessions, "in part because it allows them to be more directive in ways that enhance collaboration" (2014, 74). However, they acknowledge that "trying to regularly match students with tutors in their discipline would bring on a logistical nightmare" (94). They believe that tutor confidence is one of the biggest problems for those lacking specific expertise, and this is an issue rarely found among faculty and professional tutors.

Nowacek and Hughes address the generalist-versus-specialist debate by suggesting that the tutors do hold disciplinary expertise, specifically in tutoring writing (2015, 182). While "tutors cannot possibly hope to be content experts for every writer and draft they encounter, they can instead capitalize on lack of content knowledge to position the writer as bringing in a different type of knowledge and the tutor as an interested, rhetorically savvy audience wanting to better understand that knowledge" (181). This lack of content knowledge would seem to return them to Hubbuch's original position, as "ignorant" tutors, but in Nowacek and Hughes' conception, there is instead a meeting of two experts—the student as subject expert and the tutor as the possessor of a sophisticated awareness of genre and rhetoric. This is a natural positioning for a professional consultant and a STEM student.

Work with graduate students in STEM can be fruitful for professional consultants in the position of expert outsiders. Despite lack of buy-in from some faculty advisors, who seem reluctant to let their graduate students out of the lab, or doubt us because of our lack of subject-matter expertise, we have seen at NJIT that graduate students in STEM work effectively with our expert outsiders on their dissertations and articles. In my own experience tutoring our doctoral candidates, many of whom are international students concerned with clarity, I do not find it necessary to understand every term used in order to see whether a coherent sentence or argument is being set forth. Further, the students find it of value to explain their work in layperson's terms.

Although consultants who have written their own master's thesis or doctoral dissertation may not share advanced subject knowledge of a science, technology, or math field, they will understand the conventions and purpose of a graduate writing project, as well as the need for a clear argument, with supporting research and data. Strang at MIT has made the same point (2010, 292). The commonality of the dissertation process between tutor and student is a bonding point. One of our professional consultants, who was himself completing his dissertation in American literature at another university, made common cause with a regular tutee revising her dissertation in biology. In addition to helping her in developing the organization, support, and clarity of her own project, the tutor enlisted her as a colleague of sorts. They empathized with regard to the process of writing the parallel works that were to be the entry point for them both into their chosen professions. In doing so, the consultant empowered the student, who had been given a conditional pass, pending revisions, in her dissertation defense, and gave her back her confidence in her own project.

PEER-PROFESSIONAL CROSS-MENTORING AND OTHER TRAINING

As previously stated, professional tutors bring to the writing center an already well-developed awareness of rhetorical and genre considerations. In addition to writing center best practices, training can focus more specifically on the specific needs of our STEM students, both in their coursework and in other capacities. Because of the complex schedules of the adjunct faculty, who often teach on multiple campuses, and graduate students at other universities who make up the bulk of our professional tutoring staff, we are rarely able to hold staff meetings. Miriam E. Laufer raises a similar issue in chapter 1; on her campus, presemester training and a virtual discussion board are utilized. At NJIT, without funding for presemester training, we have focused on providing training materials and holding individual or small-group discussions with the director. A discussion board on Canvas supplements and brings the larger group together. Focused training regarding genres of writing, as well as on working with the student body of a STEM-centered institution or program, are of inestimable benefit to these consultants and to the writing center where they work.

Kristin Walker has written about the importance of genre theory in preparing tutors to work with specific populations. She worked in a discipline-specific writing center, at a large research university, designed for the use of students in the Electrical and Computer Engineering (ECE) Department. Despite the narrowly focused scope of the tutoring center, it was staffed primarily by graduate students in composition and rhetoric and English, with the addition of one undergraduate specialist in the discipline (Walker 1998, 29–30). As the tutors often found themselves struggling to understand the engineering-centered writing they were asked to work with, they created their own ways of gaining expertise. They interviewed professors in the discipline, held staff meetings designed to focus on the genres of writing with which they were working, and developed models for the tutors to use (35–37). By raising their own level of expertise with the genres of writing surrounding the ECE discipline, even if they had not become experts in the subject matter itself, they were able to create their own form of expert outsiderhood.

Walker's experience was unusual in that the majority of writing centers are not confined to a single academic department, and the ability to create the very specific type of training that Walker discusses is simply not available in most cases. Even at a STEM institution such as NJIT, we are asked to deal with students and projects from a much wider range of disciplines, each of which has its own conventions and which of course includes humanities classes. Certainly, a writing center at a STEM-based institution must be aware of best practices for working with engineering genres, or lab reports, or premed personal statements. Examples of and standards for these genres are made available via a website or Canvas page, and through self-guided PowerPoint training units.

Among the recommendations that Jo Mackiewicz makes are learning to differentiate between "engineering writing that is intended to inform and engineering writing that is intended to persuade" and to consider rhetorical moves such as audience, purpose, and visual elements, as well as specific conventions of engineering writing (2004, 327). While much of this would seem to be basic rhetorical awareness translated to a specialized field, she also suggests, more concretely, that "perhaps the best way to help tutors understand engineering writing is by asking them to write a set of instructions for a simple procedure or a technical description of a simple mechanism" (327). This exercise could be easily implemented with professional staff, even outside the context of formal training sessions.

A recent study by Robert S. Weissbach and Ruth C. Pflueger builds on Mackiewicz's work and found the most effective way of working with nonspecialist peer tutors was to build on one particular assignment and provide intensive training for the tutors (Weissbach and Pflueger 2018, 208). This thoughtful and thorough approach proved highly effective but would be extremely time consuming and limited in how many such classes and assignments the writing center could thus assist. Weissbach and Pflueger found that more generalized training was ineffective. However, they are working with peer tutors without technical backgrounds, noting that despite active recruitment from all majors, the writing center has "been able to recruit only one engineering student to tutor writing in the past 15 years" (219). At NJIT, members of our peer tutor contingent do frequently come from STEM majors, particularly engineering, biology, and computer science, while the professional majority are true expert outsiders, focused on writing. These two groups, with their differing but significant expertise, work effectively in helping to train each other.

Since the peer tutors' rigorous engineering and science curricula do not leave room for semester-long tutor-training classes, we have developed a program of cross-mentoring, a collaborative process that benefits both peer and professional consultants. The peer tutors at NJIT do a series of orientation meetings with the director, with carefully chosen readings to introduce them to writing center best practices, as well as to spark questions and discussion about the tutoring process. They sign up to shadow our professional staff for two to three weeks, observing sessions by a number of different consultants, to give them a sense of varied tutoring styles. As part of this process, they do mock tutoring sessions, both as tutor and tutee, which gives the professional staff the opportunity to provide guidance and to evaluate the peer tutors' readiness to take sessions on their own. The peer tutors write reflections and meet with the director to discuss what they have observed and experienced.

The professional writing consultants, meanwhile, learn from our peer tutors, who share their subject knowledge and understanding of science writing conventions. In addition, they provide insight into their experiences as students at a STEM-centered university, which differs from our professional staff's experiences, coming not only from the humanities but often from more academically diverse institutions. Aisha Khan, a master's student in biomedical engineering who was our center's first graduate consultant, had a peer-tutoring background from her undergraduate institution. She observed that she and our peer tutors were able to bring their hands-on experience with writing for science courses into play, particularly with regard to documents such as lab reports and to "usages specific to our discourse communities, like the use of passive voice." Aisha and our undergraduate STEM peer tutors were able to work with our professional staff to share these experiences but also found that our professionals provided them with significant learning opportunities as to approaches and methods.

Peer tutors, engaged in their own scientific and technical studies, have sometimes also provided a bridge between the science or engineering expertise of the tutees and expertise in rhetoric and writing of the professional consultants. Working with graduate students is often intimidating to undergraduate peer tutors, and the graduate students work best with consultants who have themselves written on the master's or doctoral level, as Strang suggests (2010, 292). However, on occasion, the pairing of peer tutors (particularly those involved in undergraduate research) and professional consultants on these projects has enabled our staff to work together to blend their strengths to provide exceptional assistance combining both writing and subject matter assistance.

A future goal is to formalize the already-existing cross-mentoring by pairing peer tutors with professional writing consultants in official mentor-mentee relationships. While there are logistical difficulties in the matching process, this can be overcome by a mix of in-person and online connections. This collaboration will supplement the mentoring that the peers are both receiving and also giving during their regular sessions, and strengthen centerwide collaboration even further.

FACULTY AND PROFESSIONAL TUTORS AND STEM STUDENTS

The self-selected group who work alongside our consulting staff as peer tutors are skilled writers themselves. However, at a STEM-focused university, our professional staff often face challenges in working with students whose primary orientation is toward math and science. It is not infrequent to hear among our students, "I'm no good at writing; why do you think I'm here?" They often come to us for help with subjects outside of their primary focus, such as first-year writing, history, literature, philosophy, and business classes, as well as for personal statements for graduate and professional programs. Working with a population of STEM students requires an understanding of the place our students are coming from.

Faculty and professional tutors should be aware of STEM students' approach to writing projects, which may be very different from their own or that of students in other disciplines. Richard M. Felder and Rebecca Brent, in their manual on STEM education, point out that employers of STEM graduates rank such skills as "oral communication, teamwork, written communication, critical thinking, analytical reasoning, complex problem solving, information literacy, and innovation and creativity substantially higher than technological skills and quantitative reasoning," which they term professional skills (2016, 217). But "many STEM students are . . . hostile to professional skill instruction, viewing it as a distraction from the *real* science, math, and engineering that they came to college to learn" (218). In addition to feeling that a concentration on writing is a waste of their time, students in the STEM fields very often share a belief that their inclinations toward math and the sciences somehow preclude them from being effective at written communication. Here, as Amanda Gomez has suggested, our consultants can act as types of writer advocates, helping to empower student writers (Fahle Peck, Tyson, Dambruch, and Gomez, chapter 5 in this book).

At NJIT, we have been engaged with several studies that focus on our students and their literacy habits, one centering on digital reading practices and the other on self-efficacy in student writing. The latter is more specific to the writing center, so I will discuss it briefly.

Numerous studies have centered on self-efficacy: students' beliefs about their capabilities as writers determine writing outcomes (Bandura et al. 1996). Inspired by the emphasis on data-driven research universitywide at NJIT, John Wolf and I developed a study looking at the self-perceptions of student writers in our STEM university population, with the goal of developing collaborative methods to be used by the writing center staff and First Year Writing instructors that would address those self-perceptions. With the aid of a Faculty SEED Grant, we carried out a pilot study in academic year 2016–17. A substantial proportion of our students self-identify as weak writers or as not being engaged with or interested in the writing process. Using a pre-post design, we investigated the impact of a writing center outreach program, which was administered in participating first-year writing courses. With this data, we have begun to expand the work of the Writing Center on NJIT's campus by educating instructors and administrators as to additional contributions we can make throughout the university.

Our pilot quantitative study measured the extent to which supplemental instruction affects first-year composition students' writing self-efficacy. It centered on a collaboration between writing center and writing instructors to address the needs of the students at NJIT, where many students believe that their math and science orientation means that they are inherently poor writers. A series of three in-class workshops by writing center personnel was paired with three mandatory writing center sessions. Workshops focused on brainstorming, revision, and a third topic of the instructor's choosing; the sessions were intended to reinforce the ideas in one-on-one practice. We found that participation in the program impacted first-year writing students' opinions about the writing as well as their self-reported writing anxiety in a statistically significant way. Over the course of the semester, students in both the treatment and control groups demonstrated increases in writing self-efficacy, but gains were nearly twice as large for those in the treatment group. Preliminary data also demonstrated that participation in the writing center outreach program impacted first-year writing students' opinions about writing as well as their self-reported writing anxiety.

CONCLUSION

While NJIT's writing center focuses on aiding a student population made up almost entirely of those studying scientific and technical-related subjects, STEM is growing in popularity throughout universities worldwide. The experiences of our professional writing consultants, coming from liberal arts backgrounds themselves, will be more and more the case in both specialized and nonspecialized institutions. Training writing center staff to work with growing population of STEM-oriented students is a subject of increasing significance in writing center work, but in the role of expert outsiders, it can have a significant impact.

REFERENCES

Bandura, Albert, C. Barbaranelli, G. V. Caprara, and C. Pastorelli. 1996. "Multifaceted Impact of Self-Efficacy Beliefs on Academic Functioning." *Child Development* 67 (3): 1206–22.

Brooks, Jeff, 1991. "Minimalist Tutoring: Making the Student Do All the Work." *Writing Lab Newsletter* 15 (6): 1–4.

Carino, Peter. 2003. "Power and Authority in Peer Tutoring" in *The Center Will Hold: Critical Perspectives on Writing Center Scholarship*, edited by Michael A. Pemberton and Joyce Kinkead, 96–113. Logan: Utah State University Press.

Dinitz, Sue, and Susanmarie Harrington. 2014. "The Role of Disciplinary Expertise in Shaping Writing Tutorials." *Writing Center Journal* 33 (2): 3–13.

Felder, Richard, and Rebecca Brent. 2016. *Teaching and Learning STEM: A Practical Guide*. San Francisco: Jossey-Bass.

Harris, Muriel. 1992. "Collaboration Is Not Collaboration: Writing Center Tutorial vs. Peer-Response Groups." *College Composition and Communication* 43 (3): 369–83.

Hubbuch, Susan M. 1998. "A Tutor Needs to Know the Subject Matter to Help a Student with a Paper:—Agree—Disagree—Not Sure." *Writing Center Journal* 8 (2): 23–30.

Jaschik, Scott. 2014. "The STEM Enrollment Boom." *Inside Higher Education*. April 7, 2014.

Kiedaisch, Jean, and Sue Dinitz. 1993. "Look Back and Say 'So What': The Limitations of the Generalist Tutor." *Writing Center Journal* 14 (1): 63–74.

Lunsford, Andrea. 1991. "Collaboration, Control, and the Idea of a Writing Center." *Writing Center Journal* 12 (1): 3–10.

Mackiewicz, Jo. 2004. "The Effects of Tutor Expertise in Engineering Writing: A Linguistic Analysis of Writing Tutors' Comments." *IEEE Transactions in Professional Communication* 47 (4): 316–28.

Nowacek, Rebecca S., and Bradley Hughes. 2015. "Threshold Concepts in the Writing Center: Scaffolding the Development of Tutor Expertise." In *Naming What We Know: Threshold Concepts of Writing Studies*, edited by Linda Adler-Kassner and Elizabeth Wardle, 171–85. Logan: Utah State University Press.

Shamoon, Linda, and Deborah Burns. 1995. "A Critique of Pure Tutoring." *Writing Center Journal* 15 (2): 134–51.

Strang, Steven. 2010. "Staffing a Writing Center with Professional Tutors." In *A Writing Center Director's Resource Book*, edited by Christina Murphy and Byron L. Stay, 291–300. New York: Routledge.

Walker, Kristin. 1998. "The Debate over Generalist and Specialist Tutors: Genre Theory's Contribution." *Writing Center Journal* 18 (2): 27–46.

Weissbach, Robert S., and Ruth C. Pflueger. 2018. "Collaborating with Writing Centers on Interdisciplinary Peer Tutor Training to Improve Writing Support for Engineering Students." *IEEE Transactions on Professional Communication* 61 (2): 206–20.

PART 2

Graduate Student Consultants

9
WHEN IS A PEER NOT A PEER?
Negotiating Authority and Expertise in Graduate Student Writing Consultations

Marcus Weakley and Mark Pedretti

The normative tutoring situation presumed by a large swath of writing center scholarship is the undergraduate peer-to-peer consultation (e.g., Bruffee 1984; Harris 1986; Ryan and Zimmerelli 2010; Ianetta and Fitzgerald 2012; Vanderberg 1999). As noted throughout this collection, the peer-to-peer model presents asymmetries of power and authority (Lunsford 1991; Bokser 2001) and raises important questions about the nature of "peerness" in peer-based, undergraduate tutoring (Carino 2003)—especially when compared to an ideal of collaboration and reciprocity often referred to in writing center literature (Bruffee 1984; Hawkins 1980). Nonetheless, in the undergraduate context, power dynamics are predominately related to the tutorial situation itself—that is, to the teaching of writing, and the expertise of the tutor in writing pedagogy and practice (Carino 2003)—and not determined in advance by the relative status, rank, or discipline of tutor and student. Peer-to-peer undergraduate tutorials are not likely to entail predetermined discrepancies in authority, status, or expertise: a sophomore tutoring a senior will rarely be challenged on their legitimacy due to class rank alone, and a senior tutoring a sophomore cannot claim a privileged knowledge on the basis of theirs. This exclusivity, however, is not the case at the graduate level.

The dynamics of authority and expertise change significantly—and often in ways even further from the ideal of "peerness"—in graduate-to-graduate writing center tutoring. On the one hand, rank *does* matter in graduate school: doctoral students are asked to engage in more complex writing and research tasks than master's students, and this experiential gap can limit the tutor's ability to work from a position of familiarity with a more advanced student. Differences in rank thus have the potential to *appear* as irremediable gaps in the depth and quality of knowledge. Because graduate students are ostensibly being socialized into professional fields (Weidman and Stein 2003), and thus learning to participate in highly specialized discourse communities (Swales 1990), fluency with particular academic languages takes on special importance over general argumentation, and the lines between "content" and rhetorical knowledge become harder to discern. Protestations of "that's not how we do it in my field" are not uncommon in the graduate writing center—a fact acknowledged by the field-specific contingency of much advice in graduate writing textbooks (e.g., Swales and Feak 2012). The specialization and gradation of graduate education create sites of incommensurability depending on the tutorial participants.

In order to better understand the negotiation of differential authority and expertise in a way that provides solution-based insights for other graduate consultants and centers in similar situations, we designed and distributed a survey of predominantly open-ended questions to past and present writing consultants at a graduate-only institution. This evidence-based approach (Babcock and Thonus 2012; Denton 2017) focused on three different types of power dynamics: difference of degree (MA vs. PhD), difference of field (e.g., English vs. economics), and difference of seniority within the same field (e.g., first vs. fifth year in English). By focusing on these three types of dynamics, we sought to provide a framework through which our findings would be applicable to other graduate-level consultation scenarios. We also sought to continue to develop our understanding of what graduate "peerness" might uniquely entail.

An analysis of our findings shows that even though consultants experience power dynamics based on all three relationships, the difference in field is the most common and significant obstacle toward a session's goals. This finding provides the opportunity for specific changes in consultant training and session approach, such as the formalization of session interventions to provide explanation of graduate-level, genre-based writing pedagogy for tutees. Responding consultants also consistently reported a self-assessed lack of authority, a finding that implies the benefit of intentionally developing comfort with differences in content knowledge. Both of these suggestions we establish and discuss in more detail as additional tools in a praxis of graduate tutoring applicable across a wide range of graduate-level tutoring scenarios.

The format of this chapter—in keeping with a standard for evidence-based studies—moves next to a review of relevant literature on the topic before an explanation of the study's method: the constant comparative method (Boeije 2002). From there, we report the results of the survey. Then, we analyze the themes and provide practical changes based on analysis in the discussion section.

LITERATURE REVIEW

Scholarly discussions of power or authority asymmetries in writing tutorials have predominantly focused on those dynamics as they inhere in the tutorial situation itself. That is, explorations such as Peter Carino's "Power and Authority in Peer Tutoring" (2003), John Trimbur's "Peer Tutoring: A Contradiction in Terms?" (1987), or Linda Shamoon and Deborah Burns's "A Critique of Pure Tutoring" (1995) primarily see disparities between tutor and student as a function of their roles *as* tutor and student—differences in knowledge, authority, or agency inherent in the tutorial situation itself. Carino (2003), for instance, argues:

> Tutorials . . . depend on authority and power, authority about the nature of the writing and the power to proceed from or resist what that authority says. Either tutor and student must share authority, producing a pleasant but rare collaborative peer situation as in the tutorial on the lab report, or one or the other must have it, and in writing centers the one with it is more often the tutor, as is the case in the second tutorial on the play review. (107)

Differential authority is created by the respective roles of tutor and student, and the differential knowledge *about writing* that each role entails. Trimbur (1987), as his title suggests, sees a structural contradiction in the notion of peer tutoring that begins once a student is selected to become a tutor: "The tutors' success as undergraduates and their strengths as writers single them out and accentuate the differences between them and their tutees—thereby, in effect, undercutting the peer relationship" (23). Shamoon and Burns (1995), by contrast, are willing to advocate for a tutorial paradigm that would acknowledge a hierarchy of knowledge in a manner similar to a master class in music, where the expertise of the master is its raison d'être, but the relevant skill here is writing itself; the tutor takes up the position of the "expert music teacher" and the student that of learner, "from novice to near expert" (140). When we talk about differences of power and authority, we typically confine that dynamic to the field of writing, not those that tutor and student bring to the tutorial situation from the rest of their academic lives.

Meanwhile, a substantial body of literature has explored the role that expertise plays in writing tutorials, in the form of the specialist-versus-generalist tutor debate: should writing tutors be knowledgeable about specific disciplinary conventions, or is their ignorance a virtue that forces the student to explain them? The operative dynamic here, however, is principally one sided—it is solely the *tutor's* expertise that is at issue. Susan Hubbuch (1988) raises the concern that a tutor's shared field-specific knowledge would override the non-directive tutorial model, and the tutor would end up imparting that wisdom to the tutee instead of focusing on argumentation. Since then, Sue Dinitz and Susanmarie Harrington (2014) have demonstrated, to the contrary, that disciplinary expertise is an asset to tutors in working with students from their shared disciplines and that "with expertise, tutors were able to implement the core lessons from their tutor training" (92)—in other words, disciplinary knowledge enabled better deployment of the practices of generalist tutoring. Dinitz and Harrington found little evidence of Hubbuch's feared "appropriation" in the sessions they studied and suspect that very specific content knowledge, rather than just disciplinary affinity, may be the underlying culprit of interference; tutor and student can have a more productive session if both are studying history but not if both are writing a paper about Abraham Lincoln. Much of this discussion has taken place equally in the area of embedded tutoring or writing fellows programs, with staunch advocates for both generalist and disciplinary approaches (Soven 2001; Soliday 2005; Severino and Trachsel 2008).

It is worth emphasizing that the bulk of this research is based on, and thus applies directly to, undergraduate tutoring situations and that only the tutor's disciplinary knowledge is treated as the independent variable. The student is generally figured as inert and somehow discipline free—after all, if the student were a skilled user of disciplinary discourse, they would not be at the writing center in the first place. As we have suggested, the dynamics of a graduate writing tutorial are markedly different from that of an undergraduate one (Powers 1995; Summers 2016), and graduate students arrive at the center already equipped with operative disciplinary knowledge at the levels of both subject mastery and awareness of discursive conventions. It is not solely the tutor's expertise in writing that is in play here; rather, that expertise functions in relation to the field-specific knowledge, the degree being pursued, and the amount of time spent in graduate school of the tutee. Only Sarah Summers's (2016) recent study of graduate tutors at UCLA recognizes the "fluid and relational" (128) role that disciplinary expertise plays for *both* tutor and student in the graduate context. While Summers addresses tutors' degree program and progress in passing, she treats them as additional facets of expertise, rather than separate, and potentially causal factors. We seek to extend Summers's analysis of the bidirectional interplay of expertise, while also studying these other potential zones of asymmetry—degree program and time in degree program—in the current research.

METHODS

Participants

Twenty former and current tutors (11 women and 9 men, age range: 22–40) of a writing center at a graduate-only university in Southern California were asked to complete a survey about their experiences with power dynamics in tutorials. They represented a wide range of disciplines, including English, history, philosophy, psychology, political science, religion, and information systems and technology. Out of these 20 requests, 9 anonymous responses were collected.

Procedure

The survey was designed to address the three power disparities we have identified: degree, field, and seniority. Survey questions were designed to establish the prevalence of awareness of such power dynamics in the survey group, obtain details about the participants' experiences, learn how the tutor responded, see if the tutor would have acted differently after reflection, and elicit advice for others in similar scenarios. For each disparity, the survey asked:

1. Have you ever had an experience where (degree, field, seniority) affected a tutoring session's ability to meet its goals?
2. Please describe the situation in as much detail as possible.
3. What did you do to address the situation?
4. Upon reflection, what would you do differently?
5. What advice would you give to other graduate tutors in the same scenario?

We employed the constant comparative method of qualitative analysis in the grounded theory approach (Glaser and Strauss 1967; Boeije 2002) to identify recurring themes in respondents' answers. Given that we received responses from nine participants, the open-ended nature of the questions combined with a dedicated set for each disparity gave us ample material to analyze and thematize. Over numerous readings, each participant's responses were first compared singularly for consistency and themes; then, participants' responses were compared to each other as thematized wholes. Finally, after fragments of responses were thematized, these were compared across similar groupings numerous times. This iterative and inductive process produced core themes based on both scenarios in sessions and consultant responses. The study's limitations are the same as others of similar size and method: small sample size, difficulty generalizing results given the type of response and institutional characteristics, and coding inconsistencies (Kolb 2012; Fram 2013). However, we believe the study's results offer insights for developing tutor pedagogy and training.

FINDINGS

Because responses to Question 1 were determinative for identifying scenarios where disparities were evident, we focused on those responses which responded affirmatively to that question. Across the three power dynamics for 9 respondents, we received 15 affirmative responses out of the possible 27 (8 of 9 in field, 3 of 9 in degree, 3 of 9 in seniority). Clearly, differences in field were most prevalent, but we draw on all 15 affirmative responses to develop meaningful patterns of power discrepancies in tutorial sessions. Participant comments show that power dynamics were expressed explicitly and implicitly in sessions and originated both from tutors (about themselves) and from tutees. Within these contexts, the most significant scenarios were when (1) the tutor is explicitly undermined in the session, (2) the tutee explicitly or implicitly sees out the tutor due to knowledge discrepancy, and (3) the tutor perceives a lack of authority in himself or herself. Tutor responses followed predictable lines, given tutors' rhetorical and writing center pedagogical training, but still suggest strategies for training and session approach that incorporate the explicit discussion of writing center pedagogy and targeted forms of questioning. We now cover each of these topics in more detail with examples of participant responses.

Common Scenarios

Tutor Explicitly Questioned or Undermined in Session

Numerous respondents indicated that they had been told explicitly by tutees that their comments were not applicable or helpful; however, these instances were predominantly reported in terms of an incommensurability between disciplines—the "that's not how we do it in my field" defense. For example, one respondent wrote, "If I recall correctly, I was working with either a math or science student. We came to a point in their writing where the main concepts and sequencing logic between paragraphs was deteriorating. When I pointed this out, the client swatted away my critique with the standard defense, 'That's just how we do it in my field.'" Given the fact that the disciplines of tutor and tutee will often vary in writing center sessions and that tutors are not expected to be experts about every kind of graduate-level disciplinary writing, this reported occurrence was expected. Also, questioning techniques utilized by tutors that place the burden of explanation on the tutee may understandably be misunderstood as a lack of authority.

In most cases, however, the session involved a tutee from a natural, technical, or social science and a (presumed) tutor from the humanities or social sciences; the familiar divide between the "hard" and "soft" fields was used by tutees to explain rhetorical strategies or lack thereof. This explanation is evident particularly around discussions of coherence, clarity, and other higher-order topics. While working with a student from mathematics, one tutor wrote, "The crux of his 'contribution' in the piece, though, was just a set of arithmetic operations—there was no commentary justifying his method, nor any explanation of why his work was filling some gap in the extant research. But when I pushed him on it, he began by waving it off as if I just didn't understand the math (or why the math was important)." In one instance, a student challenged the tutor in terms of *both* their discipline *and* their degree program. They explained how

> a male, international student had come in with a dissertation chapter in economics (I was a consultant in my last year of my MA in English). . . . He then inquired what year I was in my program and in what field (I told him). He redirected the conversation to his sentence-level concerns and wanted to go through the chapter line by line. He told me that because I'm not in his field, I might not understand his idea.

Tutee Explicitly or Implicitly Pursues Tutor Due to Knowledge Discrepancy

The disparity in power also worked the other way around, where students would purposely seek out certain tutors because they were further along in the same degree program. While disparity of field was used by students to justify ignoring tutors' comments, seniority within the same discipline was actively sought after by some students, presumably on the premise that tutors' similar content knowledge would be helpful in ways that generalist tutoring would not be. For example, one respondent wrote, "Students in the same program usually want to know more than just an assignment. . . . Furthermore, they seek you out JUST because you are the 'expert' on the issue, which sometimes hampers the readability of the paper." Another added, "Because we had been meeting for weeks, she knew that I was further along in my MA program than she was. . . . Over time, though, I noticed that the student had been overreliant on my suggestions and were [*sic*] not challenging them or giving them a second thought. She would implement the changes immediately and ask questions like 'Is this OK?'" In both of these cases, the tutor was asked to use their advanced status in a degree program to supply information beyond rhetorical or structural topics.

Tutor Perceives Lack of Qualification or Authority in Self

Another typical instance in which a power dynamic affected the outcome of a session was when tutors self-assessed a disparity on their own end—that is, when they perceived themselves as insufficiently familiar with the student's field to effectively guide their writing. This phenomenon has been documented by both Summers (2016) and Dinitz and Harrington (2014), when tutors felt "the need to convey expertise—and cover insecurity—during appointments" (Summers 2016, 130) based on being new tutors, or early on in their own degree programs. In our survey, such insecurities were mainly documented in terms of a disparity of field. For example, one respondent conveyed:

> The person in the session is part of a music/religious studies class and thinks about research and argument/evidence in a different way than I do. Part of the problem has been that he is unclear about the goals of his project and the paper. But part of the problem has been that it was hard to get him to recognize how he was thinking differently than the professor when he wanted to be operating at a more formalized academic level to match people in his field. I don't know his field that well so there is no specific answer I can give him.

In this case, the tutor felt that their understanding of rhetoric and paper structure, combined with a student's indecision, inhibited progress.

Insecurities were also expressed in terms of a disparity of seniority within the same field. For example:

> A student in the PhD program in English came to the Writing Center to work on a seminar paper that involved a lot of theory. She was further along in the program than I was (I was in my last semester of my MA and about to begin my PhD). She wanted feedback on her interpretation and discussion of a literary theory. . . . During the session, I felt like I was not asking the "right" questions to help her develop her ideas . . . I was self-conscious about how little I knew about her topic and felt that I wouldn't be able to help her.

Nonetheless, in either form, the disparity was not explicitly or implicitly brought up by the student; the tutor regulated their own behavior on the basis of a self-perceived lack of competence. This power dynamic provides a different challenge for tutor-training or session approach from a difference of field inhibiting graduate-level writing instruction. Nonetheless, consultants' responses to these scenarios provide important insights on shifts in praxis for specific graduate-level power dynamics, which we will elucidate below.

Consultant Responses

In addition to these prominent session types, where one or another disparity appeared regularly, tutors articulated common themes in relation to both how they viewed those situations at the time, and what they would do differently in hindsight. Across all three scenarios, respondents reported using strategies of explicit discussion of rhetorical or writing center theory and strategic questioning to move sessions forward. At the graduate level, both of these practices appear to take on primary roles in responding to inhibitory power dynamics.

Explicit Discussion of Rhetorical Devices, Writing Conventions, and/or Writing Center Pedagogy

Several tutors negotiated the types of sessions described above by explicitly discussing aspects of rhetoric or writing center pedagogy that they felt applied in the scenario. For example, one tutor wrote, "I argued that in any field clarity was important, especially when dealing with highly complex concepts. By the end of the session, the client found a way to communicate in a more clear and direct manner." Another conveyed that they "actually mentioned that not knowing their field might make me a better tutor with which to work. I told them that writing should stand independent of prior knowledge—the paper should provide any background knowledge necessary. Also, effective writing is clear even without knowledge of the subject matter. Structure stands out." Both of these are important elements of writing instruction, and making them explicit to the tutee served an important pedagogical function.

Respondents conveyed the same sort of ideas when reflecting about what they would have done and what they would like to do next time, after reflection. One consultant explained it as "I might ask what it meant to help someone with their writing. I would hopefully help the student to realize what many of us need is a non-expert (on our subject matter) to provide feedback on the independence of our discussion of our subject and the clarity with which we discussed the subject." Another responded, "I think I could actually secure more 'authority' by telling the student that, if s/he considers that 'field' matters in writing, then every consultant here (including me) are all experts in the field of 'writing.' Sometimes it helps to let the student know that writing is itself a field that should not simply be dismissed as an auxiliary skill that comes second to their discipline." In all of these cases, consultants considered that the power dynamic might be altered, ameliorated, or circumvented by applying explicit discussion of pedagogical theory as a session's praxis.

Employ Some Form of Questioning

The other technique consistently reported by respondents was the use of questioning—again, an important part of writing center pedagogy—to navigate these situations. However, respondents also indicated that they had to take on a role in which they could ask clarification questions in order to minimize confrontation. One example: "I started by playing dumb, asking him to lead me through the math. Once he explained and justified it, I asked why he hadn't done so in the text of the paper and we worked out ways to present his work as thought out and important." Or, as another consultant explained,

> Instead of presenting these suggestions as direct comments to the student, I tried to play along with my role of "the ignorant" and framed my feedback as questions by asking the student questions that make them stop and think about the parts/paragraphs/sections that may be problematic. Sometimes in answering my questions, the student would be able to notice the problem (without my directly telling the individual that this could be a problem).

In this specific application, consultants alleviate or negotiate a power dynamic to refocus the session on its pedagogical goals.

DISCUSSION

Our findings show that power dynamics are important in graduate-to-graduate writing center tutoring and that the relative locations of tutor and tutee sometimes set up circumstances that inhibit session goals. However, this is not a one-way street; both tutee and tutor play an important role in this dialectical process. Tutors' own perceived knowledge, familiarity, or confidence with the conventions of fields other than their own are significant. Further, even though all three types of power dynamics investigated—degree, field, and seniority—were reported by tutors, the responses show that disparity of field is the primary context in which such asymmetries assert themselves. While our analysis yields insights for graduate-level writing centers in relation to all five themes reported above, the remainder of this chapter will focus on developing praxis in cases of difference of field and the importance of overall approach in graduate peer tutoring.

Even though the sample size of this study is too small to demonstrate statistically valid correlations, it does offer heuristic insights (Arnould and Epp 2006) for developing tutor pedagogy and training to address these disparities. When confronted with situations whereby disparity of field was impeding a session, a number of tutors explicitly turned to rhetoric and other Writing Across the Curriculum strategies employed in this writing center that inform both desired goals for sessions and best practices for successful peer-based cross-disciplinary graduate tutoring. This was an often-mentioned strategy in consultant responses. One representative piece of consultant advice was that graduate-level consultants should "try to remind students (and themselves) that though there are challenges to not knowing discipline-specific content during sessions, our expertise in composition and rhetoric does have significant weight when it comes to sessions with students from fields different from ours." While we might expect graduate students to be more attuned to the disciplinary construction of discourse, reminding them of how the rhetorical situation—along with other rhetorical elements common to writing center pedagogy—can improve disciplinary writing in a multidisciplinary tutoring session provides valuable context. By understanding the theoretical framework in which writing center pedagogy takes place, both tutor and tutee can understand session practices as an intentional praxis.

Moreover, our research suggests that the explicit intentionality suggested above can be combined with other established writing center pedagogies to form a broader praxis. Formalizing an early or presession intervention in instances where disparities are more likely to be present—especially as part of a set of practices to address this issue—is a potentially preventative measure. This formalizing could range from information on a website, to information on a session sign-up form, to an example at the beginning of a first session. Summers (2016) recommends this general strategy as part of graduate writing tutors' "toolkit" under the category of "managing expectations" (136). The presession, early session, and intrasession approaches of providing theoretical context for applied practice all work to shift the perceived framework and goals of writing centers and improve the success of sessions and can be applied widely across a variety of writing centers' institutional contexts.

Evidence from respondent experiences about power disparities in sessions also points to a misunderstanding of assumed goals. A student in a technical field that goes to the writing center to ensure that their grammar is correct may be surprised that a tutor makes suggestions on clarity, structure, audience, or coherence; the tutor, on the other hand, is assuming that the goal of the session is to work on higher-order issues and that sentence-level issues are appropriate but to a lesser degree. In our research, few tutors discussed either goal-setting or expectation-establishing discussions at the beginning of sessions as a way to address this power dynamic. For example, one respondent advised consultants to "try to identify how much of the problem is due to a difference in field (assumptions, processes, habits of mind in that field) and how much of the problem is due to miscommunication at the individual level between you and the person you are tutoring (assumptions, habits of mind, personality and communication styles)." This tutor felt that such a discussion sets up a framework to recontextualize a session for a tutee who enters with an assumption different from the direction the session takes. This same respondent further noted, "the process of stating the expectations and assumptions of our separate fields in a more explicit way was more useful than I would have thought when I first started working at the [writing center]. Exploring what is a personal choice vs what is normal in the field is useful for addressing habits that are no longer helping a student in their writing/communication." This practice is already a part of the pedagogy at our writing center, to some extent, but an overt formalization into practice would most likely work to preempt some possible instances of this disparity in graduate centers generally.

The incidence of perceived disparities on the part of the tutors—not just the tutees—is worth addressing. Tutors can and will adjust their sense of field expertise through more experience with graduate-level sessions. However, there is also something to be said for encouraging consultants to expect—indeed, to accept—such asymmetries as a part of the graduate-level tutor experience. Along these lines, one respondent suggests, "I would also advise graduate student tutors to work on being comfortable with this disparity and to find ways in their sessions to connect to the student and the work—especially if you approach it from a place of curiosity." Curiosity, in turn, helps deepen Socratic questioning, a well-established form of working with structure and argumentation without content knowledge. Such Socratic questioning may represent an intensification of what Summers (2016) calls the "discussion-based strategies that are likely familiar to writing teachers and common in writing center consultations" (132)—not simply engaging in dialogic discussion about the student's text but actively and intentionally shifting into a maieutic mode to draw out underlying premises from the student through systematic interrogation. Or, if curiosity is too much to ask, simple acceptance of this dilemma as an intrinsic and a processual part of writing center instruction may help a tutor employ rhetorical strategies, even when faced with scenarios such as those discussed in this study.

Finally, our research recommends strategies for modifying training and ongoing professional development. Training should be given to consultants on specific genres—especially scientific and technical ones, according to our research—to fill perceived gaps between writing center practices and the subsection of tutees who most often bring up the "not in my field" excuse. These changes can set tutors up to more overtly address differences in ways that limit the impact of the discrepancy of field. One direction for increasing our understanding of power disparities in graduate-level sessions would be, in future research, to more closely track discipline on the side of both tutor and tutee to yield data that would help deepen our understanding of particular dynamics (and how to train for them). Additionally, more extensive training about Writing Across the Curriculum and genre theories, and how to talk about them with tutees, will give consultants tools to help situate a session's pedagogical goals and methods for unfamiliar students. Both session interventions and consultant training can have strong impacts on navigating power dynamics in the graduate writing center and be easily applied by consultants and/or centers.

REFERENCES

Arnould, Eric J., and Amber Epp. 2006. "Deep Engagement with Consumer Experience: Listening and Learning with Qualitative Data." In *The Handbook of Marketing Research: Uses, Misuses, and Future Advances*, edited by Rajiv Grover and Marco Vriens, 51–82. Thousand Oaks, CA: SAGE Publications.

Babcock, Rebecca, and Terese Thonus. 2012. *Researching the Writing Center: Towards an Evidence-Based Practice*. New York: Peter Lang.

Boeije, Hennie. 2002. "A Purposeful Approach to the Constant Comparative Method in the Analysis of Qualitative Interviews." *Quality and Quantity* 36 (4): 391–409.

Bokser, Julie A. 2001. "Peer Tutoring and Gorgias: Acknowledging Aggression in the Writing Center." *Writing Center Journal* 21 (2): 21–34.

Bruffee, Kenneth A. 1984. "Peer Tutoring and the 'Conversation of Mankind.'" *Writing Centers: Theory and Administration*, edited by Gary A. Olson, 3–15. Urbana, IL: NCTE.

Carino, Peter. 2003. "Power and Authority in Peer Tutoring." In *The Center Will Hold*, edited by Michael A. Pemberton and Joyce Kinkead, 96–113. Boulder: University Press of Colorado.

Denton, Kathryn. 2017. "Beyond the Lore: A Case for Asynchronous Online Tutoring Research." *Writing Center Journal* 36 (2): 175–203.

Dinitz, Sue, and Susanmarie Harrington. 2014. "The Role of Disciplinary Expertise in Shaping Writing Tutorials." *Writing Center Journal* 33 (2): 73–98.

Fram, Shelia M. 2013. "The Constant Comparative Analysis Method Outside of Grounded Theory." *The Qualitative Report* 18 (1): 1–25. http://nsuworks.nova.edu/tqr/vol18/iss1/1. Accessed February 14, 2021.

Glaser, Barney, and Strauss, Anselm. 1967. *The Discovery of Grounded Theory: Strategies for Qualitative Research*. Chicago: Adline.

Harris, Muriel. 1986. *Teaching One-to-One: The Writing Conference*. Urbana, IL: National Council of Teachers of English.

Hawkins, Thom. 1980. "Intimacy and Audience: The Relationship between Revision and the Social Dimension of Peer Tutoring." *College English* 42 (1): 64–68.

Hubbuch, Susan M. 1988. "A Tutor Needs to Know the Subject Matter to Help a Student with a Paper: __Agree __Disagree __Not Sure." *Writing Center Journal* 8 (2): 23–30.

Ianetta, Melissa, and Lauren Fitzgerald. 2012. "Peer Tutors and the Conversation of Writing Center Studies." *Writing Center Journal* 32 (1): 9–13.

Kolb, Sharon M. 2012. "Grounded Theory and the Constant Comparative Method." *Journal of Emerging Trends in Educational Research and Policy Studies* 3 (1): 83–86.

Lunsford, Andrea. 1991. "Collaboration, Control, and the Idea of a Writing Center." *Writing Center Journal* 12 (1): 3–10.

Powers, J. K. 1995. "Assisting the Graduate Thesis Writer through Faculty and Writing Center Collaboration." *Writing Lab Newsletter* 20 (2): 13–16.

Ryan, Leigh, and Lisa Zimmerelli. 2010. *The Bedford Guide for Writing Tutors*. 5th ed. New York: Bedford / St. Martin's.

Severino, Carol, and Mary Trachsel. 2008. "Theories of Specialized Discourses and Writing Fellows Programs." *Across the Disciplines* 5 (2).

Shamoon, Linda K., and Deborah H. Burns. 1995. "A Critique of Pure Tutoring." *Writing Center Journal* 15 (2): 134–51.

Soliday, Mary. 2005. "General Readers and Classroom Tutors across the Curriculum." In *On Location: Theory and Practice in Classroom-Based Writing Tutoring*, edited by Candace Spigelman and Laurie Grobman, 11–43. Logan: Utah State University Press.

Soven, Margot. 2001. "Curriculum-Based Peer Tutors and WAC." In *WAC for the New Millennium*, edited by Susan H. McLeod, 200–32. Urbana, IL: NCTE.

Summers, Sarah. 2016. "Building Expertise: The Toolkit in UCLA's Graduate Writing Center." *Writing Center Journal* 35 (2): 117–45.

Swales, John M. 1990. *Genre Analysis: English in Academic and Research Settings*. Cambridge: Cambridge University Press.

Swales, John M., and Christine Feak. 2012. *Academic Writing for Graduate Students*. 3rd ed. Ann Arbor: University of Michigan Press.

Trimbur, John. 1987. "Peer Tutoring: A Contradiction in Terms?" *Writing Center Journal* 7 (2): 21–28.

Vanderberg, Peter. 1999. "Lessons of Inscription: Tutor Training and the 'Professional Conversation.'" *Writing Center Journal* 19 (2): 59–83.

Weidman, J. C., and E. L. Stein. 2003. "Socialization of Doctoral Students to Academic Norms." *Research in Higher Education* 44 (6): 641–56.

10
INTEGRATING GRADUATE STUDENT CONSULTANTS
Community Building in Writing Centers through Onboarding and Mentorship

Genie Giaimo and Joseph Cheatle

Establishing communities of practice are beneficial to educational and occupational settings. Defined as "groups of people who share a concern, a set of problems, or a passion about a topic, and who deepen their knowledge and expertise in this area by interacting on an ongoing basis," communities of practice are both formal and informal spaces in which tacit knowledge is developed and shared (Wenger, McDermott, and Snyder 2002, 4–5). Communities of practice sometimes develop organically, but, more often, they must be nurtured by administrators in order to remain successful (85). According to Etienne Wenger (1998), communities of practice are defined by three elements: a collective understanding of the accountability and a commitment to that accountability, a community built by members through mutual engagement that establishes norms, and the development of communal resources (language, routines, artifacts, documents, stories, styles, etc.). And writing centers, as Anne Ellen Geller et al. (2007) point out in their work *Everyday Writing Center*, are communities of practice that, as complex organizations, comprise administrators, staff, and consultants.

Although we frequently talk about community building and collaboration in writing center scholarship (Harris 1992), we lack evidence-based research on how—or if—communities form in writing centers, particularly among graduate consultant cohorts. We advocate, in this chapter, for establishing clear onboarding and mentorship programs in order to build successful communities of practice in writing centers and to connect graduate consultants to the broader culture of a writing center. Because graduate consultants often have different training and writing center education from their undergraduate peers, it is imperative that writing center administrators foster an identity, community, and mission among their staff members. Required training helps establish a shared common language among all consultants—for those who enroll in a peer tutor–training class (frequently undergraduate students), as well as for those who are trained outside of formal educational settings (frequently graduate students). In this work, we look more closely at two practices, onboarding and peer mentoring, that help build community and establish a community of practice.

While we are both working at new institutions, this chapter was written when we were writing center administrators at the Ohio State University (OSU) and Michigan State University (MSU); however, we believe that there is a need for onboarding and mentorship at any writing center that employs graduate student consultants (and could be extended to undergraduate, faculty, and professional consultants). The Ohio State University and Michigan State University are large public Research 1 institutions located in the Big Ten Academic Conference. Both writing centers have a mixed undergraduate and graduate staff—a model common to many large research university writing centers (among many others). Both run multiple on-campus sites as well as robust online writing centers. And, although MSU's center has a larger staff size than that of OSU, both serve writers of all levels across campus. Both programs also have similar hiring and recruitment models in which undergraduates are hired through a peer tutor–training course while graduate students are hired from across the disciplines and with varying levels of prior writing center experience. A course is not required for graduate consultant employment with either writing center. Both writing centers offer a mentorship program; however, OSU's model is a formalized and blended (graduate and undergraduate consultants together) small group model with weekly training and knowledge-sharing activities. Michigan State's, on the other hand, is a graduate-only mentorship program in which consultants meet to debrief about sessions, go have coffee, take a walk, or just socialize. Onboarding and mentoring help us speak to the concerns and diversity of experience among our graduate staff populations, and through evaluation and assessment, these programs can improve in the future. We believe that writing centers already establish fairly strong communities of practice and benefit from the tacit knowledge that consultants share among themselves; however, more intentional onboarding and mentoring of graduate consultants may help them, in particular, to acclimate into writing center culture more quickly and seamlessly.

ONBOARDING

One way to establish writing center culture and community among graduate consultants is through a deliberate onboarding program. Onboarding is an integral part of creating community for a broad variety of corporations and organizations; it is also a way to nurture communities of practice through "building a case for membership" (Wenger, McDermott, and Snyder 2002, 85). In other words, onboarding helps to "launch the community" while also providing a platform to share "ideas, insights, and practices as they [participants] discover what knowledge is most important and valuable" to writing center work (86–89). Different from employee orientation, onboarding "begins when a new employee is offered a position and ends when the employee is considered fully functional. It covers an employee's first year, incorporates various offices and functions, addresses the whole range of employee needs (equipment, accounts, training, networking), and is strategic in focus" (Graybill et al. 2013, 201). Onboarding, then, is an ongoing wraparound support model for employees that includes legal and policy compliance training, duty clarification, organizational culture training, and networking or connection opportunities (Caldwell and Peters 2018, 28).

During onboarding, lines of communication ought to be established, and information about the organization ought to be meted out in "small doses that allow for the employee to internalize and apply to his or her work assignments" (Graybill et al. 2013, 202). Cam Caldwell and Ray Peters (2018) note that onboarding "often provides employees with a volume of information that is overwhelming, impractical, and impossible for new employees to incorporate within a short period" (28). Organizations either include too much or too little information for their new employees, thus either overwhelming them with too much information or underpreparing them for their new positions (28). Effective onboarding processes "improve performance, inoculate against turnover, and increase job satisfaction" (28).

Although onboarding employees can be challenging due to the changing landscape of employment, including employee mobility and staff downsizing (Graybill et al. 2013, 202), writing centers have confronted their own challenges of high employee turnover, fluctuating employee numbers, varying levels of institutional support, and a mobile workforce since their inception. Therefore, writing centers face similar onboarding challenges to other organizations, including high rates of staff turnover—as Megan Boeshart Burelle and Meagan Thompson note in chapter 18; however, because many writing centers are staffed by part-time student labor, they also face novel challenges, including underpreparation, and staff resistance to center enculturation. So much information accumulates within writing centers, yet with high rates of turnover, knowledge management becomes a critical factor in staff onboarding and professionalization. Jolie Graybill et al. note that onboarding is often a year-long process (2013, 201); however, writing centers frequently have the additional challenge of an even shorter timeline in which consultants are hired, trained, and exit the center. Sometimes, this cycle of hiring and leaving occurs in a year, or even a semester! Therefore, considering strategic onboarding for staff—such that it might even start, as it does for OSU, prior to consulting—helps to lengthen the onboarding timeline and prepare graduate consultants for their jobs more quickly and effectively. It also helps to move writing centers into closer alignment with onboarding best practices, which include policy and duty clarification, information management, networking opportunities, and, importantly, organizational enculturation. Writing centers, such as OSU's and MSU's, are uniquely poised to offer innovative onboarding solutions to graduate staff members that create a positive and effective workplace culture and attendant community. For other examples in this collection of onboarding, please see Vicki Behrens and Alex Funt's chapter on writing center training at the University of North Carolina at Chapel Hill, chapter 15, as well as chapter 12, Rebecca Nowacek et al.'s essay describing an onboarding process at Marquette University.

To date, there exists little empirical evidence on the efficacy of training or onboarding of graduate consultants in writing centers, perhaps because of a lack of standard operating procedure across writing centers. Currently, we are assessing consultant enculturation into the writing center at OSU, including onboarding efficacy, through hand-coding randomly selected session notes written by graduate and undergraduate consultants, across multiple semesters, and coding them for variables such as collaboration, flexibility, and directiveness. Our assessment has found that graduate and undergraduate consultants enter into their work with different skill sets and implicit knowledge, perhaps because of the different training and support that they are given prior to working in the center. Graduate consultants initially demonstrate far higher levels of collaboration than undergraduate consultants, while undergraduate consultants demonstrate more flexibility in their consulting strategies than their graduate counterparts. Yet, when one institution established a presemester onboarding program explicitly for graduate consultants, they reported higher levels of consulting flexibility than previous graduate consultant cohorts. Receiving tacit knowledge from external experiences (such as teacher training or the undergraduate consulting course), then, plays an important role in the ways in which graduate and undergraduate consultants carry out their consulting practice. Therefore, training is not the only indicator of consulting performance in the writing center; workplace culture also heavily impacts consulting practice. Culture, then, is an important factor that writing centers ought to account for in onboarding of staff because it can be more powerful than even robust intersemester training programs in terms of the effect on consultant behavior and affect.

Although it is popular in writing centers to run multiday presemester orientations, this model is not necessarily the most effective because it lumps far too much information into a relatively short period of time with little thought to audience or context. Following best practices for onboarding seen in industry, OSU recently amended its onboarding from a lumped multiday model to one that starts prior to the first semester of employment and runs throughout the year. New graduate consultants are given ample time to reflect upon their tutoring practices and to think about their work within the constellation of the writing center organization, which is multifaceted and multitudinous. Similarly, there are roundtable discussions at the presemester workshop about leadership and conducting research in the writing center. Offering a number of professional development opportunities helps to bring new consultants into community-oriented practices and to develop their skills early on in their writing center work. The graduate consultant onboarding program at OSU begins with a hybrid online/in-person model that includes roughly ten hours of activities, learning modules, and quizzes. Newly hired graduate consultants participate in the hybrid model during the summer, prior to the generalized all-staff workshop, at the start of the term. The presemester onboarding attempts to familiarize new graduate consultants with writing center policies and procedures through assigned ethnographic tasks as well as quizzes; it also teaches new consultants common and shared tutoring practices (such as agenda setting and concept mapping). For those who are already trained in writing center work at a previous institution, this material is a refresher on tutoring best practices, as well as the first engagement with OSU's culture and priorities (not to mention, policies). For those who are new to writing center work, onboarding is critical in establishing how writing center work differs from teaching work and from editorial work; it also engages new graduate consultants in carrying out reflective practices common to the center. While onboarding is a process that occurs throughout the first year of employment (through training, knowledge sharing, and networking opportunities), the presemester onboarding sets the tenor for the culture of the writing center for new graduate student employees.

Except for the summer graduate consultant onboarding, and a "newbie" consultant training during the presemester workshop at the start of the fall term, there is no split between undergraduate and graduate consultant training and community building. New graduate consultants attend hour-long mentorship group meetings, as well as 4 one-hour all-staff meetings, alongside their undergraduate peer consultants, throughout each semester. Through these mentorship group meetings, we believe that undergraduate consultants are uniquely poised to support and educate new graduate consultants and that shared training and networking opportunities facilitate knowledge sharing and community building; therefore, a blended training model is imperative to enculturating new graduate consultants to our writing center. Overall, our assessment of different cohorts of consultants has verified the positive effect that cross-collaboration among consultants of different groups has on consulting practice, including consultant flexibility and collaboration levels.

Because the process of onboarding new graduate consultants is ongoing, we suggest a number of best practices, including the following:

1. Avoid overloading new consultants with information by prioritizing critical over noncritical information.
2. Provide new consultants multiple opportunities for engaging with the policies and knowledge of the writing center.
3. Engage consultants early on with leadership and research opportunities.
4. Provide networking and community-building opportunities.
5. Incentivize participation in community activities, either through payment or flextime.
6. Assess onboarding programs and revise according to articulated need and other findings.

The onboarding program at OSU is new; therefore, it is imperative that it is continually assessed for its efficacy. Future assessment will include surveys on consultant onboarding experiences, as well as analysis of consultant exit surveys. Generally speaking, we are interested in understanding the different ways in which graduate and undergraduate consultants navigate the OSU writing center's workplace culture and expectations. Attendant questions may include how onboarding prepares different cohorts of consultants for work outside of the writing center, postgraduation, and how transfer of learning occurs with different information sharing mechanisms in the center. Developing an onboarding program and assessing its efficacy, over time, helps to demonstrate how writing centers are professionalization spaces that prepare consultants for work outside the institution.

MENTORSHIP

A second way of creating community for graduate students in writing centers is through formal peer-mentoring programs (for another view of mentoring see Anna Sicari, chapter 11). Graduate students are frequently a part of their own disciplinary community of practice outside of the writing center and focused on completing their own programs of study (there are, historically, very few programs that offer a degree in writing center studies at either the undergraduate or graduate level). As such, they often do not have time to complete long and extensive formal training that would integrate them into the center. Peer mentoring offers one way to introduce new graduate students into the writing center's community of practice in an effective and efficient way. While mentoring has always existed in writing centers (particularly informally and ad hoc), the focus of this work is on structured mentor programs with measurable outcomes and assessment. Mentoring (the process of pairing an experienced person with a less-experienced, or new, person) has long been viewed as an effective way of integrating new personnel into existing organizations. At its most basic, mentoring offers collegiality and networking (Beltman and Schaeben 2012); meanwhile, at its best, mentoring offers career and "psychosocial" support to mentees (Lunsford and Baker 2016). Additionally, mentor-mentee relationships often go beyond the impersonal to focus on personal and professional growth (Lunsford and Baker 2016).

Mentoring has long been a staple of academia, particularly for new graduate students (who are commonly paired with faculty members) and new faculty members (who are commonly paired with senior faculty members). According to Susan Beltman and Marcel Schaeben (2012), "Mentoring is a well-established, evidence-based social support strategy that can enhance academic, social, personal, and career outcomes of recipients" (34). While mentoring does have beneficial outcomes, traditional mentoring relationships can be problematic primarily because they frequently include people of different rank and, therefore, power. Because a traditional mentoring relationship is usually one directional from mentor to mentee, it can cause unequal power dynamics that may result in distrust (Bennion 2004). And, in their work, Brad Johnson and

Jennifer Huwe (2002) explore the numerous ways in which mentoring may go wrong, including bad matching, incompetence, conflict, mentor neglect, boundary violations, and more.

Peer mentoring, meanwhile, has numerous advantages that traditional mentoring relationships may lack. Foremost is that relationships can be developed in programs that lean into their structural advantages in order to decrease competition and foster camaraderie. A formal and structured peer-mentoring program is advised by Scott Bryant (2005) and others because they can be used to enhance the positive aspects of mentoring while decreasing any negative aspects. For example, Elizabeth Bennion (2004) notes that "when structured to avoid both hierarchy and competition, a peer-mentoring relationship can facilitate intellectual development as well as a better balance and integration between one's professional and personal lives" (112). These relationships are often more egalitarian because they are between peers rather than between people of different rank and status (Bennion 2004; Tollefson-Hall 2015). Peer mentoring has been shown to be particularly effective during transitional periods and as a form of social support for students (Beltman and Schaeben 2012; Tollefson-Hall 2015; Falchikov 2001; Harmon 2006; Heirdsfield et al. 2008; Terrion and Leonard 2007). And as Vincent Tinto (1987) notes, the process of pairing experienced students with incoming or new students is one that tasks continuing students with some degree of responsibility for incoming students, which results in increased retention for both groups of students but also an "enriched educational experience" (177). The transition experienced by first-year students, in many ways, also reflects the experience of transition graduate students feel.

Since peer mentoring is a reciprocal relationship, there are benefits for both mentees and mentors that participate in these structured relationships. Benefits for mentees include strategic knowledge, insights, and essential information (Bennion 2004, 111); furthermore, peer mentoring can foster a sense of community and belonging for mentees as well as social support (Tollefson-Hall 2015). There are also benefits for mentors who participate. While not as much research has been completed about mentor outcomes, in a first-year student mentor program in Australia (Beltman and Schaeben 2012), mentors reported positive outcomes in four main categories (in order of the most impactful): "Altruistic" (passing on knowledge and experience while receiving positive feedback), "Cognitive" (acquiring new skills or information), "Social" (interacting, and developing new friendships, with students), and "Personal Growth" (self and personal development). Additionally, mentors benefit from learning new views while also creating productive relationships with new potential collaborators and colleagues. There are also benefits from peer mentoring to the organization, including knowledge sharing, building intellectual capital, and socializing new employees (Bryant 2005). According to Scott Bryant, "Peer Mentoring provides an opportunity to externalize knowledge by turning tacit knowledge into explicit knowledge" (324). Often, knowledge within an organization or institution is developed over time and then becomes internalized; this can result in organization and institutional knowledge to be taken for granted. The process of mentoring requires that that knowledge be articulated and passed on to incoming personnel. Last, current mentees can become future mentors, thus creating a continuous cycle of support and knowledge sharing.

Mentoring programs can be a productive way to create community for incoming writing center graduate consultants. Recent research has shown that graduate students are six times more likely than the general population to struggle with depression and anxiety (Evans et al. 2018, 282). Work-related stress and lack of mentorship are contributors to this phenomena (282). In part, graduate students might be facing some of these challenges due to a smaller and more diffuse cohort and support network. In the writing center, undergraduate students take a required course to become consultants and, hence, come in as part of a cohort, while graduate students enter the center on their own and, often, without a support network. Mentoring may help to create a sense of a cohort while, more important, helping create a sense of community in the center. While there are a number of different models and permutations for mentoring (see OSU's model for mentoring as part of their onboarding process), one model is that used by the Writing Center at Michigan State University, which pairs experienced graduate consultants (mentors) with new graduate consultants (mentees); all new graduate consultants are required to participate in the mentoring program. Similar to many writing centers, graduate consultants in the MSU Writing Center are not required to complete a consultant training course (as undergraduates are required to do), and they come from a wide variety disciplines—this can result in a situation whereby graduate consultants may not have much writing center knowledge nor feel particularly attached to the center as they focus on their own studies.

While MSU has always encouraged informal mentoring, we recently began the process of codifying and formalizing a mentoring program in order to create more measurable outcomes and objectives while also increasing accountability (more information about the mentoring program at MSU can be found at writing.msu.edu). We recognized that this program affects both the mentor and the mentee and that the relationship is reciprocal; therefore, we developed a list of mentor and mentee outcomes.

Mentor Outcomes
- Gain mentorship experience.
- Professional development, resume/cv builder.
- Learn about complex issues consultants encounter outside their discipline.
- Build relationships with other graduate student consultants.

Mentee Outcomes
- Provide first-time writing center graduate consultants with mentorship, access to information, support, and community during their first year as a graduate consultant.
- Create a smooth transition into MSU's Writing Center culture.
- Grow into the many roles a writing center consultant will be tasked with and develop the necessary skills that they will need.
- Develop a sense of community.

All new graduate consultants are required to participate in the semester-long mentoring program while experienced graduate students can volunteer to be mentors, choose to be mentees, or opt to not be involved in the program at all. Both mentees and potential mentors complete an intake form in order to match interests and needs. The intake forms ask both mentees and mentors what they want to get out of the program, familiarity with campus, and writing center knowledge. We assume that even those who may have a significant amount of writing center knowledge (from previous institutions) can still benefit by other aspects of the program, particularly those directly associated with community building. The forms also provide a checklist of writing center, and other, issues that mentees and mentors may be interested in, including things such as client report forms, scheduling, mandatory reporting, community building, friendship, outreach, professional development, and more. As part of our attempt to make both parties as comfortable as possible with their match, we ask participants whether they want us to take identity markers (race, ethnicity, ability, sexual orientation, and others) into consideration during the matching process. In addition to the intake forms, we also require mentors and mentees to write a prereflection and postreflection in order to track how their expectations align with the results from the program. And then together each pairing creates and shares a document that details its collective plan for the semester. Pair members are also jointly required to develop a list of goals (social, consulting, professional development, friendship, community building, and more) to submit to a program coordinator at the beginning of the semester.

We track pairings through required meetings while suggesting activities that are designed to help create community and a sense of belonging. They are required to meet three times, each time for at least an hour, during the semester; since the center pays up to five hours of activities, pairings can choose two additional hour-long meetings. Suggested activities include a coffee outing, attending an event, going to a museum, studying together, following up after a consultation, and more. As part of the accountability and assessment of peer mentoring, a program coordinator tracks each pairing's activities, checks in with the pair throughout the semester, helps it meet its objectives, and conducts assessment of the program. The fact that the center funds this nonconsulting activity demonstrates how important it is to create a sense of community among graduate consultants as well as the importance of peer mentoring to the success of the center.

CONCLUSION

At the end of the day, however, it is often hard to establish a shared language and community of practice for graduate consultants because (1) graduate students are busy and overtaxed from their graduate programs and other obligations outside the writing center, and (2) practices in a large writing center of fifty-plus staff members often break down into niche or microcommunities, rather than a monolithic one. Therefore, it might be necessary to develop more extensive onboarding processes for graduate consultants if they are not required to take a peer tutor-training course. It might also be necessary to further scaffold onboarding and other training to prevent information overload. For graduate consultants, who lack a defined cohort upon entering into their writing center work, onboarding can help to establish a community of practice, which creates reflective and participatory opportunities and better prepares graduate students for tutoring work.

While onboarding prepares graduate consultants for tutoring work while creating a shared sense of community, peer mentoring benefits graduate consultants both inside and outside the center. Marvel Lang and Clinita Ford (1988) point out that mentor programs are proven effective in increasing retention rates, particularly for minority students. Peer mentoring is also beneficial for first-generation students (López 2014), graduate students of color (Bonilla, Pickron, and Tatum 1994), and women and ethnic minorities (Bennion 2004, 113). For these groups, during the transition into graduate school, mentoring can help them surmount obstacles that the mentor has either experienced or is aware of. And mentoring does not just help with information sharing, but it also builds a coalition by showing students from disadvantaged backgrounds that others from their communities have succeeded and that they are welcome in the institution. Onboarding, similarly, "improve[s] performance, inoculate[s] against turnover, and increase[s] job satisfaction" (Caldwell and Peters 2018, 28). While we do not think that writing centers need to follow the models that we have offered here for onboarding and mentoring, we encourage them to incorporate some form of both practices into their centers, with intention. And for writing centers who already utilize these programs, we encourage them to think about how to maximize the efficacy of their onboarding and peer-mentoring practices for the future.

REFERENCES

Beltman, Susan, and Marcel Schaeben. 2012. "Institution-Wide Peer Mentoring: Benefits for Mentors." *International Journal of the First Year in Higher Education* 3 (2): 33–44.

Bennion, Elizabeth. 2004. "The Importance of Peer Mentoring for Facilitating Professional and Personal Development." *PS: Political Science and Politics* 37 (1): 111–13.

Bonilla, James, Carlton Pickron, and Travis Tatum. 1994. "Peer Mentoring among Graduate Students of Color: Expanding the Mentoring Relationship." *New Directions for Teaching and Learning* 57 (Spring): 101–13.

Bryant, Scott E. 2005. "The Impact of Peer Mentoring on Organizational Knowledge Creation and Sharing: An Empirical Study in a Software Firm." *Group and Organization Management* 30 (3): 319–38.

Caldwell, Cam, and Ray Peters. 2018. "New Employee Onboarding: Psychological Contracts and Ethical Perspectives." *Journal of Management Development* 37 (1): 27–39.

Evans, Teresa M., Lindsay Bira, Jazmin Beltran Gastelum, L. Todd Weiss, and Nathan L. Vanderford. 2018. "Evidence for a Mental Health Crisis in Graduate Education." *Nature Biotechnology* 36 (3): 282–84.

Falchikov, Nancy. 2001. *Learning Together: Peer Tutoring in Higher Education*. London: Psychology Press.

Geller, Anne Ellen, Michele Eodice, Frankie Condon, Meg Carroll, and Elizabeth Boquet. 2007. *Everyday Writing Center: A Community of Practice*. Boulder: University Press of Colorado.

Graybill, Jolie O., Maria Taesil Hudson Carpenter, Jerome Offord Jr., Mary Piorun, and Gary Shaffer. 2013. "Employee Onboarding: Identification of Best Practices in ACRL Libraries." *Library Management* 34 (3): 200–218.

Harmon, Brad. 2006. "A Qualitative Study of the Learning Processes and Outcomes Associated with Students Who Serve as Peer Mentors." *Journal of the First-Year Experience and Students in Transition* 18 (2): 53–82.

Harris, Muriel. 1992. "Collaboration Is Not Collaboration Is Not Collaboration: Writing Center Tutorials vs. Peer-Response Groups." *College Composition and Communication* 43 (3): 369–83.

Heirdsfield, Ann M., Sue Walker, Kerryann Walsh, and Lynn Wilss. 2008. "Peer Mentoring for First-Year Teacher Education Students: The Mentors' Experience." *Mentoring and Tutoring: Partnership in Learning* 16 (2): 109–24.

Johnson, W. Brad, and Jennifer Huwe. 2002. "Toward a Typology of Mentorship Dysfunction in Graduate School." *Psychotherapy: Theory, Research, Practice, Training* 39 (1): 44–55.

Lang, Marvel, and Clinita Ford. 1988. *Black Student Retention in Higher Education.* Springfield, IL: Charles C. Thomas, Publisher.

López, Marissa. 2014. "On Mentoring First Generation and Graduate Students of Color." Race and Ethnicity: The Site of the Committee on the Literatures of People of Color in the United States and Canada. Modern Language Association. https://clpc.mla.hcommons.org/on-mentoring-first-generation-and-graduate-students-of-color/.

Lunsford, Laura Gail, and Vicki L. Baker. 2016 "Great Mentoring in Graduate School: A Quick Start Guide for Protégés." *Council of Graduate Schools, Occasional Paper Series* 4.

Terrion, Jenepher Lennox, and Dominique Leonard. 2007. "A Taxonomy of the Characteristics of Student Peer Mentors in Higher Education: Findings from a Literature Review." *Mentoring and Tutoring* 15 (2): 149–64.

Tinto, Vincent. 1987. *Leaving College: Rethinking the Causes and Cures of Student Attrition.* Chicago: University of Chicago Press.

Tollefson-Hall, Karin. 2015. "Building a Teaching Community through Peer Mentoring." *Art Education* 68 (4): 30–33.

Wenger, Etienne. 1998. *Communities of Practice: Learning, Meaning, and Identity.* Cambridge: Cambridge University Press.

Wenger, Etienne, Richard Arnold McDermott, and William Snyder. 2002. *Cultivating Communities of Practice: A Guide to Managing Knowledge.* Boston: Harvard Business Press.

11
CRITICAL MENTORSHIP IN THE WRITING CENTER
Teaching Intentional Kindness and Rhetoric of Respect in Staff Education

Anna Sicari

The lack of institutional support and mentorship for graduate students has recently received much attention in the field of writing studies (Martinez 2016; Madden and Eodice 2016; Madden and Stinnet 2016). A recent study in *Inside Higher Ed* discovered that graduate students are "six times as likely to experience depression and anxiety as compared to the general population" (Flaherty 2018). The findings on graduate students' experiences of isolation (Grasso, Barry, and Valentine 2007; Council of Graduate Schools 2018), their overall unhappiness, and the lack of institutional support for them represent a growing problem in higher education. Writing centers, similar to writing programs, very often employ graduate student tutors, as many of them are assigned to writing center work as part of their teaching assistant (TA) responsibilities, as discussed in Alex Wulff's "Making the Invisible Visible," chapter 14. It is probable, given the data, that the graduate students with whom we work are experiencing feelings of anxiety, depression, and isolation. As an employer of both graduate students and writing teachers, and as someone who values collaboration and support in the one-to-one context, I argue that writing center directors play a pivotal role in providing what I am calling critical mentorship for the graduate students who work in our spaces. The critical mentorship for which I am advocating is grounded in two main ideas already familiar to those of us in writing centers: intentional kindness, as advanced by Elizabeth Boquet, and a rhetoric of respect, from work done by Tiffany Rousculp. I believe that exploring frameworks of intentional kindness and the rhetoric of respect has been transformative for our staff, many of whom are graduate students who learn in our spaces for the first time about pedagogy and mentorship, as well as for the struggling writers (often

DOI: 10.7330/9781646420858.c011

graduate students) who seek our support. By reframing the way we think of mentorship—as a relationship based on kindness and reciprocal respect—we can teach this critical mentorship to our graduate students as they develop mentoring relationships with their cohort, the writers who seek their help in the center, and the future students with whom they will work.

As a writing center director who is committed to creating an inclusive and equitable center, I have grown increasingly interested in the scholarship of Boquet and Rousculp as a way to develop a pedagogical framework for the writing center staff. At a public Research 1 (R-1) University, I work with a large staff that consists of both graduate tutors, who have research assistant positions through the Writing Center, and undergraduate tutors. I have found that explicitly teaching intentional kindness and a rhetoric of respect to the staff has helped the graduate students in this space become stronger mentors and created organic systems of support that have moved beyond the center. In working and learning with my staff, I have found that I, too, have become a better mentor when thinking about ways to model kindness and respect as best practices in writing center work. In this chapter, I will develop and expand on the terms "intentional kindness" and "rhetoric of respect" as necessary components to critical mentorship, explore the obstacles to teaching and fostering this type of mentorship through a narrative, and discuss the implications this work on kindness and respect have for staff education and writing center work.

INTENTIONAL KINDNESS AND RHETORIC OF RESPECT AS FRAMEWORKS FOR CRITICAL MENTORSHIP

Elizabeth Boquet writes on intentional kindness in her keynote-turned-article, "'It's All Coming Together, Right before My Eyes': On Poetry, Peace, and Creative Placemaking in Writing Centers" (2015), and in her book *Nowhere near the Line: Pain and Possibility in Teaching and Writing* (2016). In both works, Boquet thinks about the increasing rise of gun violence in America, particularly in high schools, and the need to be teaching peace to our students and faculty. I see Boquet's theorizing of kindness as something to be taught in order to achieve peace. Peace, as I understand Boquet's work, is defined as antiviolence, and I later will put this concept in conversation with the recent social justice and antiracist work being explored by writing center scholars. Boquet writes, "Too often, we think of kindness as a quality someone either possesses or not.... We speak of kindness as a random act. Kindness, however, is really a habit, an orientation, something we practice, and indeed, can become better at." (2015, 26).

If writing center practitioners, or academics, are to rethink how we talk and think about kindness, to frame kindness as an orientation that can be taught and practiced, we might be able to resolve the foundational question Boquet asks, which is drawn from what Mary Rose O'Reilley poses, "Is it possible to teach English so that people stop killing each other?" (1998). While I do not mean to equate gun violence to the kind of academic violence that is perpetuated on a daily basis—and by this I mean the types of linguistic violence many students suffer from (Anzaldúa 1987; Denny 2010; Martinez 2016; Young and Condon 2017) and the academic hazing and bullying that it perpetuates—I do believe institutional violence comes from similar systemic issues that contribute to gun violence. As academics and as writing center professionals, as people who work with and mentor graduate students, we need to think about this question and examine our own acts of violence committed while working in the writing center, particularly with graduate students who suffer through an academic hazing that we often attribute to intellectual rigor and the realities of what graduate school looks like. Rather than accept the existing realities, and perpetuate them, intentional kindness provides a framework within which to examine these realities from the outside, to see them through a new perspective. How can we use kindness intentionally to change dangerous practices in working with graduate student writers? How do we teach this deliberate work on respect and what kind of resistance might we face in teaching it? This chapter argues for intentional kindness as a pedagogical method for staff education, as we work with graduate student writers who often do not associate kindness, or respect, with their work.

Boquet goes on to write, "kindness is something we practice in relation to community, and some kindnesses are not associated with any one individual but with a sense of collective purpose" (2015, 26). Kindness is relational and therefore an appropriate frame within which to rethink our institutional positionings in the academy and the way we respond to one another; as opposed to the competitive, individual mindset that so many academics adopt, behavior often learned in graduate school and carried into one's professional life, a sense of collective purpose allows us to frame our curriculum. Working with others involves developing relationships with people, and this is often difficult to do, particularly in the competitive context of higher education. To focus our attention to relations and relationships, I turn to Tiffany Rousculp's work, *Rhetoric of Respect* (2014), which draws on scholarship from ecocomposition as she puts forth rhetoric of respect in writing center work. Ecocomposition "provides a lens into relationships, places, and systems that both affect and are affected by discourse" and can "deepen our understanding of the forces that act on, and are changed by, writers interacting with one another through writing" (xv). In this text, Rousculp describes the community writing center she founded and how a "particular discursive ecology" evolved, which she calls "rhetoric of respect." Similar to Boquet's exploration of kindness, respect is more than just a feeling or the behavior of a particular individual: rather, it is always in relation to someone, and often it is used in the hopes of enacting change. Respect "entails recognition of multiple views, approaches, abilities, and importantly, limitations (especially our own). . . . Engaging within a rhetoric of respect draws attention to how we use language in relation with others" (Rousculp 2014, 25). Thinking of respect in this way, more specifically as rhetoric, helps in teaching and studying respect as a concept to be understood and applied in multiple contexts. Rhetoric of respect requires people to attempt to empathize with multiple and conflicting viewpoints in relation to your own beliefs and opinions, and think about how one communicates and responds to others—how one enters into a productive dialogue for some kind of understood mutual goal. Rhetoric of respect values reciprocity across differences and a valuing of the whole individual.

Teaching this rhetoric entails very difficult work and faces challenges, particularly when working with graduate students who are caught up in multiple webs of relations and power dynamics. It is, nonetheless, crucial work if writing center directors and professionals are to create the type of critical mentorship needed for any incremental change. The graduate students with whom we work in the center, and whom we mentor for academic success, are the direct and immediate future in academia. Rousculp argues for the importance of social action as she puts forth rhetoric of respect and discusses how understanding ideology is only one important aspect in an academic's work—and too often do we, as academics, remain in the "land of ideas." Of Rousculp's own disappointment in graduate school, she goes on to say, "I could not stay in the world of ideas, because I could not switch off the material world. . . . Critique must happen in conjunction with practical political activity if it is to be relevant at all to the democratic project" (2014, 34). As we mentor our graduate students and teach them ideologies on language and truth, writing center practitioners can teach them concepts of intentional kindness and rhetoric of respect so that the students can see how these ideologies can, and must, work with action in order for change.

Intentional kindness and rhetoric of respect go beyond the teaching of a "shared humanity" that Jonathan Alexander and Jacqueline Rhodes (2014) critique in their article "Flattening Effects: Composition's Multicultural Imperative and the Problem of Narrative Coherence." In this article, the authors discuss the need for embracing radical alterity and not knowing or fully understanding an/the other. They write, "We are called to respect one another precisely because we do not know one another" (450). While they discuss the need to rethink our assignments and storytelling in the writing classroom, and focus on the flattening effects of multiculturalism, their push for radical alterity and a focus on the respect of difference is in line with rhetoric of respect and intentional kindness. Rousculp writes that rhetoric of respect is a

> respect for the wholeness of the life each person brings to our relationships and for the relationships those individuals have with others. It is a respect for the importance of change, no matter how big or small, nor how it may be defined. Finally, it is a respect for the resources and limitations that we each bring to making change, acknowledging what we each can and cannot do and what our energies may create together. (2014, 154)

This definition and understanding of respect may encourage readers to rethink the way we talk about collaboration and mentorship in the writing center and how we can extend our principles and values to our graduate students. In doing this, rhetoric of respect requires us to teach one another to accept and learn from our own limitations and failures—to go beyond learning from our limitations and failures for future success but learning with our limitations and failures to see what can be created from shared energies. Through teaching and applying these frameworks of intentional kindness and rhetoric of respect, writing center directors can both mentor graduate students better and help graduate students become stronger and more critical mentors, for the writers they see in the writing center, for their peers and colleagues, and for their future students; in creating a network of critical mentorship, one based on kindness and respect, graduate students can gain more agency as they navigate their academic careers, and this practice can be started in the writing center.

INSTITUTIONAL OBSTACLES IN ACHIEVING AND SUSTAINING CRITICAL MENTORSHIP

As I have discussed, teaching and fostering this type of mentorship, one based on intentional kindness and respect, faces challenges and roadblocks. Here I will briefly narrate an experience that represents possible and very real obstacles to fostering this type of mentorship in writing centers. This narrative highlights how both the institutional positioning of the writing center, the "grand narratives" that still dominate the field, to cite Jackie Grutsch McKinney's *Peripheral Visions for Writing Centers* (2013), and the acquired academic behaviors of policing and regulating "nonexpert" bodies that dominate graduate mentoring practices, make teaching work on kindness and respect difficult.

Writing center work still remains on the margins of academia, as many academics continue to view writing centers as the kind of "fix it" shops that Boquet and Neal Lerner (2008), among many others, discussed more than a decade ago. McKinney (2013) argues that one of the grand narratives of writing center work is the field's marginalized position, and she discusses this in relation to the way writing centers are viewed institutionally. Very often, as Melissa Nicolas (2016) points out, writing centers are not seen as sites of research or scholarship. Instead, writing centers are feminized because they are seen as "nurturing, service-oriented places" (Nicolas 2004, 12). McKinney further problematizes Nicolas's argument: "Female directors who insist on cozy, inviting spaces may be unwittingly narrating their work as nonintellectual in the eyes of some" (2013, 26). This feminized narrative, or marginalized narrative, persists, though I agree with McKinney's pushback on this narrative, as it has created for many writing center scholars a continually progressive path, resulting in an uncomfortable feeling of fit in the academy.

While my writing center is relatively well funded, visible, and respected by administrators and faculty, I do find that the fix-it narrative still persists. Even well-meaning and good-intentioned colleagues will occasionally discuss how the writing center is a great starting place for the new English graduate students, until they go on to bigger and better things (such as teaching composition or an intro to literature course). This view, too, is not unique to my own writing center, and scholars such as Melissa Nicolas (2005) and Melissa Ianetta, Catherine Quick, and Michael McCamley (2007) have discussed the writing center's relationship to the composition classroom as it relates to graduate TAs. As the writing center at my institution is primarily housed in the English department, all first-year English graduate students with teaching assistantships are required to work in the writing center before they teach composition or introductory level courses. This rule often means I work with many students whose primary interests are not in rhetoric and composition, and I have found that the work on intentional kindness and respect has been especially helpful for me as I mentor students not necessarily invested in this work. Boquet asks, "What more is a university made of than its people?" (2016, 35) and I often find myself reminded of this question when I lack the patience in working with resistant graduate tutors. However, people are what make the writing center exist, and using a framework of kindness helps me find the patience to better understand their resistance. The writing center is made up of the consultants, even the reluctant ones—without them the space would not exist. I often find that most graduate tutors, when they recognize they are being heard, listen in return.

More difficult to overcome in the writing center is the daily academic hazing and the policing that graduate students experience and begin to model as they learn how to "make it" in the profession. Writing studies scholar Asao Inoue would characterize these exclusionary behaviors as part of the "white racial habitus" (2017) that both writing centers and graduate schools in general enact. Inoue describes how very often, graduate schools are indoctrinated into this white racial habitus, where "little emphasis is put on connected, relatedness, feeling, interconnection with others" (97). Instead, the focus is on the individual, and we teach graduate students how to learn academic hierarchy in order to succeed, often through inflicting pain on others. Writing centers are often implicated in such regulatory behavior (Grimm 1996; Inoue 2017), and graduate students in the writing center are often more ready to engage in this regulatory behavior, as they are exposed to academic hierarchy and exclusionary practices (hooks 1994; Ahmed 2017; Young and Condon 2017). Michele Eodice (2019) describes a particular difficult experience working with a graduate student in an upcoming chapter, and a graduate tutor's enjoyment of ostensibly having more expertise than undergraduates. I, too, have experienced and witnessed similar behavior, with graduate tutors not willing to collaborate with undergraduate tutors, as they do not see them as equals or peers. To them, mentorship is too often grounded in hierarchy: the advanced person knows; the novice learns. In conversations with graduate tutors who do not necessarily value their undergraduate peers, or who have not utilized kindness or respect in their sessions with struggling writers, I often ask Boquet's question: "What is a university made of than its people?" Interconnectedness is at the center of writing center work, and the only way to establish these relationships is through kindness.

While these narratives of marginalization and regulation are easier to combat in the center, as I have the ability to critically mentor the graduate students and discuss openly the importance of relationships and reciprocal respect as we work together to grow, they are more difficult to navigate with colleagues who remain "fixed" in their mindset regarding the writing center. In one particular experience, I remember the day I had to cancel workshops that the graduate students were excited to lead, as a colleague felt they were stepping on her expertise. Through listening to their undergraduate colleagues in the writing center, and recognizing the value in the peer-mentoring model, the graduate students created workshops to model to the participants how writing can be enjoyable. As Joseph Cheatle and Genie Giaimo discuss in chapter 10 in this volume, peer mentoring fosters relationships that "decrease competition and foster camaraderie." In understanding the importance of intentional kindness, the graduate students were beginning to think about themselves as critical mentors, recognizing "the scope of what is done [and can be done] in a writing center" (Boquet 2015, 27). These workshops were aimed to help create a sense of shared community among more junior writers learning a new type of discourse and more experienced writers in this field, similar to the idea of "leaderful learning" that Rebecca Nowacek et al. discuss in chapter 12; the goal was to support writers who were fearful of sharing their work in a noncompetitive, supportive environment, one focused on love and kindness and not necessarily the harsh critique they were used to receiving. The workshops aimed to celebrate all languages and honor differing voices through writing, and they came to these objectives through direct conversations with their undergraduate colleagues in the center. As they talked about their shared and mutual writing experiences in the academy, the graduate students wanted to offer these workshops as an attempt to create a dialogic experience with all participants, learning with and from one another. These workshops were founded on intentional kindness, rhetoric of respect, and the type of critical mentoring that graduate students were responding to. Undoubtedly, the canceling of these workshops caused some of the graduate students to doubt this type of mentorship.

I was upset by the decision to cancel these workshops and at my colleague's lack of understanding of the writing center, of the importance of co-learning and collaboration, and of the opportunity for graduate student professional development. However, I recognize that I did not effectively incorporate a rhetoric of respect or intentional kindness in planning these workshops. Much of Rousculp's (2014) *Rhetoric of Respect* explores how such rhetoric helps people analyze and think through the "complex interplay between strategic and tactical engagement, between institutional and deroutinizing purposes" (152). While the workshops were grounded in writing center pedagogy, to colleagues not aware of the work, they certainly were not part of the routine of common institutional practices, and I did not have explicit conversations with either the graduate students on tactical and strategic ways to work with the faculty member, or engage with my colleague to explain the pedagogy and purpose behind the workshops. As a director of the writing center, I should have known how to be a better and more critical mentor and to be more explicit in my own intent, which I believed was founded on kindness and respect. In my reflection on this situation, I am again reminded of Boquet's own admission of complicity in causing pain for others: "I do not exempt myself as an actor in these institutional scripts, either as someone who experienced or as someone who inflicted pain. . . . Perhaps pain is an inevitable part of the picture" (2016, 24). In this particular situation, I both experienced and inflicted pain, and it was a failed moment of mentorship. While these are obstacles to teaching for and fostering critical mentorship, they also highlight the importance and necessity of teaching for intentional kindness and rhetoric of respect, as this framework for mentorship can be a remedy for the academic harms all people—including myself—experience.

IMPLICATIONS OF INTENTIONAL KINDNESS AND A RHETORIC OF RESPECT FOR STAFF EDUCATION AND MENTORSHIP FOR GRADUATE WRITING TUTORS

While mentorship is important for all of us who work in academia, from first-year students to faculty members navigating tenure and promotion, I believe that mentorship is particularly crucial for the graduate students with whom we work. Not only do graduate students need mentorship for their own academic success, but they need to learn models of mentorship for the future. Incorporating intentional kindness and rhetoric of respect into our staff education can help writing center directors accomplish the following: professionalize graduate students with a focus on relationship building, create graduate spaces that advocate for inclusivity and equity in institutional structures that have historically been built on exclusion, and build supportive networks for graduate students for sustainable success.

Both concepts, intentional kindness and rhetoric of respect, focus on the importance of working with and learning from the people we encounter on a regular basis. Many scholars in writing studies have advocated for the serious need to explicitly teach graduate students about working conditions and have frank conversations with them on the difficulties of relationship building in the academy (Micciche 2007; Christoph et. al 2010; Leverenz 2010). Utilizing a rhetoric of respect when we critically mentor our graduate students can help prepare them to build better relations when they do become professionals and to treat with intentional kindness the students, faculty, and administrators with whom they work.

For example, I taught a Rhetoric of Respect graduate course last semester; in that course, there were several graduate writing center assistant directors. These graduate students discussed with me ways in which they were able to apply this work to their mentorship of new tutors, particularly those who were resistant to tutoring. Through listening to their fellow graduate students' serious concerns of time management and insecurities with tutoring, the more experienced graduate students were able to understand their concerns better and be more patient with these reluctant graduates as opposed to shutting down the conversation through warnings or threats. They reported to me that this text helped them rethink the way they saw their role and the way they mentor, especially since this text was framed as a way to think about mentorship in the local spaces in which we work. In their chapter "Three Models of Mentorship: Feminist Leadership and the Graduate WPA," Julie Nelson Christoph et al. (2010) specifically advocate for a feminist model of mentorship that "depends on decentralization and a leveling of hierarchy" (106). I believe teaching critical mentorship is built on principles of feminist leadership, particularly the way we think of relationships and hierarchies, and utilizing a rhetoric of respect to emphasize how we might decentralize and destabilize hierarchies is a necessary component. This approach allows for graduate students to reimagine their own relationships with faculty and administrators as they begin analyzing how they respond to the students and more junior graduates, and recognizing why certain policies and procedures are put into practice. As she narrates a particularly difficult experience with administration as a graduate student herself, teaching writing for the first time, Boquet (2016) writes, "I don't think faculty and administration were wholly indifferent. I think that they too were wildly underprepared" (20). Rhetoric of respect asks for people to analyze relationships and experiences in order to create better and new pathways; teaching for this type of analysis allows for graduate students to be more prepared when they enter their professional and academic careers as they learn how important establishing relations is in academia.

While kindness is often problematized, particularly when working in higher education, being kind does not mean being "doormats" (Nicolas 2016). In fact, I believe kindness, and teaching specifically for Boquet's theorizing of intentional kindness, entails very difficult and challenging work, particularly in working with graduate students to rethink the white and exclusionary spaces they work in and with, as Frankie Condon and Vershawn Young (2017) recently advocated. As Boquet argues, I too see intentional kindness as a core principle in social justice work, and one way is that we can critically mentor graduate students to become better advocates, and in turn become critical mentors. Feminist and critical theorist bell hooks advocates for teaching love as a way to combat racism and sexism in academia. In her work *Teaching to Transgress* (1994), she writes that "realizing that my students were uncertain about expressions of care and love in the classroom, I found it necessary to teach on the subject" (198). Teaching explicitly and intentionally on kindness to our graduate students for social justice work is a way for graduate students to rethink kindness, not as a trait for a "pushover" but as a reorientation of one's self in recognition of difference and how we can respond to conflict. Feminist activist scholars such as bell hooks and Sarah Ahmed (2017) discuss concepts of love and care as critical to social justice work as well as the difficult work involved in creating spaces of support for those marginalized by academia. Teaching graduate students for intentional kindness, particularly for social justice work, will be challenging and difficult; reorienting one's position often requires recognizing one's own complicity in continuing racist, sexist, or classist practices and reflecting on relationships and power dynamics on a daily basis.

One example of teaching intentional kindness to support social justice work for critical mentorship can be our approach in working with the multilingual writers we see in the writing center. While tutors often learn best strategies in working with multilingual writers, teaching for intentional kindness reminds tutors that these writers are humans, like them, who experience pain and emotional distress, especially as they write in the white spaces of academia, with faculty who have unrealistic expectations of a standardized academic discourse. Boquet (2016), similarly to Min-Zhan Lu's work on emotional distress (2003), explains that all people "are in pain on our campuses" and yet that our shared though wildly different experiences with pain "should render us more, not less, capable of responding to it everywhere" (Boquet 2016, 22). Teaching graduate students this explicit way of responding to pain, particularly the kind of pain a multilingual writer might experience with writing, means allowing for them to take time to share experiences of distress, and to create reciprocal learning environments in which people learn how they operate within academia, both as oppressed and oppressors (sometimes simultaneously). This pedagogy emphasizes a focus on the whole person—and not the individual's writing experience—to discuss larger implications of why this individual is struggling in the academy. Through these conversations, both consultant and writer can experience agency as they recognize they are not alone in their experiences with academia.

Teaching for intentional kindness and rhetoric of respect ultimately gives graduate students a sense of agency that allows for them to see both themselves and their peers as critical mentors. This mentorship helps create supportive environments for graduate students for sustainable success. Again, I echo Nowacek et al., chapter 12, concerning their focus on the importance of growing networks of camaraderie and mentorship for graduate students. As graduate students learn to treat their immediate colleagues with respect and kindness, and recognize the value of learning with and from differences, they may rediscover the amazing resources they have in each other. In understanding complex relationships, analyzing power dynamics, and advocating for more equitable spaces that push against exclusionary practices, graduate students can build tighter networks of support with each other and recognize that social change is possible.

REFERENCES

Ahmed, Sara. 2017. *Living a Feminist Life*. Durham, NC: Duke University Press.

Alexander, Jonathan, and Jacqueline Rhodes. 2014. "Flattening Effects: Composition's Multicultural Imperative and the Problem of Narrative Coherence." *College Composition and Communication* 65 (3): 430–54.

Anzaldúa, Gloria. 1987. Borderlands/La Frontera: The New Mestiza. San Francisco: Aunt Lute Books.

Boquet, Elizabeth. 2015. "It's All Coming Together, Right before My Eyes: On Poetry, Peace, and Creative Placemaking in Writing Centers." *Writing Center Journal* 34 (2): 17–30.

Boquet, Elizabeth. 2016. *Nowhere near the Line: Pain and Possibility in Teaching and Writing*. Logan: University Press of Colorado.

Boquet, Elizabeth, and Neal Lerner. 2008. "Reconsiderations: After 'The Idea of a Writing Center.'" *College English* 71 (2): 170–89.

Christoph, Julie Nelson, Rebecca S. Nowacek, Mary Lou Odom, and Bonnie Kathryn Smith. 2010. "Three Models of Mentorship: Feminist Leadership and the Graduate Student WPA." In *Performing Feminism and Administration in Rhetoric and Composition Studies*, edited by Krista Ratcliffe and Rebecca Rickly, 93–108. Cresskill, NY: Hampton Press.

Council of Graduate Schools. 2018. *Mental Wellness of Graduate Students*. Washington, DC: Council of Graduate Schools. https://cgsnet.org/pressing-issue-mental-wellness-graduate-students-0. Accessed February 13, 2021.

Denny, Harry. 2010. *Facing the Center: Toward an Identity Politics of One-to-One Mentoring*. Logan: Utah State University Press.

Eodice, Michele. 2019. "Participatory Hospitality in the Writing Center." In *The Rhetoric of Participation: Interrogating Commonplaces in and beyond the Classroom*, edited by Paige Banaji, Lisa Blankenship, Katie Deluca, and Lauren Obermark. Computers and

Composition Digital Press. https://ccdigitalpress.org/book/rhetoric-of-participation/eodice/. Access February 13, 2021.

Flaherty, Colleen. 2018. "Mental Health Crisis for Graduate Students." *Inside Higher Education.* March 6.

Grasso, Maureen, Melissa Barry, and Thomas Valentine. 2007. *A Data-Driven Approach to Improving Doctoral Completion.* Washington, DC: Council of Graduate Schools. https://cgsnet.org/ckfinder/userfiles/files/Paper_Series_UGA.pdf. Accessed February 13, 2021.

Grimm, Nancy. 1996. "The Regulatory Role of the Writing Center: Coming to Terms with a Loss of Innocence." *Writing Center Journal* 17 (1): 5–30.

hooks, bell. 1994. *Teaching to Transgress.* New York: Routledge.

Ianetta, Melissa, Catherine Quick, and Michael McCamley. 2007. "Taking Stock: Surveying the Relationship of the Writing Center and TA Training." *WPA: Writing Program Administration* 31 (1/2): 104–24.

Inoue, Asao. 2017. "Afterword: Narratives That Determine Writers and Social Justice Writing Center Work." *Praxis: A Writing Center Journal* 14 (1): 94–99.

Leverenz, Carrie. 2010. "What's Ethics Got to Do with It? Feminist Ethics and Administrative Work in Rhetoric and Composition." In *Performing Feminism and Administration in Rhetoric and Composition Studies,* edited by Krista Ratcliffe and Rebecca Rickly, 3–18. Cresskill, NY: Hampton Press.

Lu, Min-Zhan. 2003. "Reading and Writing Differences: The Problematic of Experience." In *Feminism and Composition: A Critical Sourcebook,* edited by Gesa E. Kirsch et al., 436–46. Boston: Bedford/St. Martin's.

Madden, Shannon, and Michele Eodice. 2016. "Access and Equity in Graduate Writing Support." *Praxis: A Writing Center Journal* 14 (1): 1–104.

Madden, Shannon, and Jerry Stinnet. 2016. "Empowering Graduate Student Writers and Rejecting Outsourced Mentorship." *Writing Center Journal Blog.* http://www.writingcenterjournal.org/new-blog//empowering-graduate-student-writers-and-rejecting-outsourced-mentorship. Accessed February 13, 2021.

Martinez, Aja. 2016. "Alejandra Writes a Book: A Critical Race Counterstory about Writing, Identity, and Being Chicanx in the Academy." *Praxis: A Writing Center Journal* 14 (1): 56–61.

Micciche, Laura. 2007. *Doing Emotion: Rhetoric, Writing, Teaching.* Portsmouth, NH: Boynton/Cook.

McKinney, Jackie Grutsch. 2013. *Peripheral Visions for Writing Centers.* Logan: Utah State University Press.

Nicolas, Melissa. 2004. "Where the Women Are: Writing Centers and Academic Hierarchy." *Writing Lab Newsletter* 29 (1): 11–13.

Nicolas, Melissa. 2005. "Writing Centers as Training Wheels: What Message Are We Sending Our Students?" *Praxis: A Writing Center Journal* 3 (1): 1–4.

Nicolas, Melissa. 2016. "5 Myths about Nice Academics." *Inside Higher Ed.* October 13.

O'Reilley, Mary. 1998. *Radical Presence: Teaching as Contemplative Practice.* Portsmouth, NH: Boynton/Cook.

Rousculp, Tiffany. 2014. *Rhetoric of Respect.* Studies in Writing and Rhetoric. Urbana, IL: National Council of Teachers of English.

Young, Vershawn, and Frankie Condon. 2017. *Performing Antiracist Pedagogy in Rhetoric, Writing, and Communication.* Fort Collins: WAC Clearinghouse and University Press of Colorado.

12
GRADUATE TUTOR PROFESSIONAL DEVELOPMENT—AND COLLABORATIVE LEADERSHIP—IN AN UNDERGRADUATE WRITING CENTER

Rebecca Nowacek, Matt Burchanoski, Danielle Clapham, Will Fitzsimmons, Alex Frissell, Lisa Lamson, and Anna Scanlon

Marquette University's Norman H. Ott Memorial Writing Center is staffed by a single faculty member, over forty undergraduate (or "undergrad") tutors, and a small team of four to seven graduate (or "grad") student tutors. These grad tutors arrive in the writing center from several disciplines and with varying degrees of writing center experience. Due to the rapid growth of our writing center, these graduate tutors have been asked to assume leadership roles in a center that is constantly changing—not only in terms of staffing (which turns over regularly in a center staffed primarily by undergrads)—but also because of expanding programmatic commitments across campus. Predictably, this context has posed challenges for professional development and for maintaining the culture of collaboration between grad tutors, undergrad tutors, and the faculty director that has long been at the heart of our work.

We are particularly inspired in this chapter by Anne Geller and her colleagues' 2007 work *The Everyday Writing Center*. They argue that writing centers can—and should—be a community of practice "based on something other than the familiar stratification between directors and tutors, tutors and writers," (7) and, in our writing center, graduate and undergraduate tutors. They point to the need for a culture of learning in which *all* members of a writing center staff are "in-the-moment-at-the-point-of-need knowledge producers" (9). But they also recognize that to build and sustain such a culture can be a challenge in the face of logistical constraints and bureaucratic pressures. In this chapter, we offer—through the interwoven narratives of the six grad tutor authors and the faculty director—an account of how we have worked together to cultivate a program of professional development that helps graduate students negotiate the power dynamics and build the interpersonal relationships necessary to sustain a culture of learning and collaboration. Although many of our choices are shaped (as we explain) by local institutional constraints, we believe that our account adds to the growing body of interrogations of everyday writing center practices. Specifically, we focus on how small choices can facilitate strong, professionally meaningful collaborative relationships between a faculty director, grad tutors, and undergrad tutors, a collaboration that resists the hierarchical relationships that often exist between these groups within higher education more broadly. To the degree that our graduate tutors have embraced a culture of mutual and collaborative learning with undergraduate tutors, we attribute that success to our onboarding process, our commitment to collaborative research involving a diverse cross-section of our staff, and a new leadership structure that functions less as a hierarchy and more as a network.

MAKING A VIRTUE OF NECESSITY: AN ACCOUNT OF OUR INSTITUTIONAL CONTEXT

Grad tutors in our writing center occupy a paradoxical space. For decades, the Ott Memorial Writing Center's organizational structure was a relatively simple hierarchy: a faculty director and one graduate student assistant director (AD) (see figure 12.1). In fall 2011 (when Rebecca began as director), the Ott was staffed by one faculty member, four grad tutors (one of whom served as AD), and eight undergrad tutors—a relatively small center with a ratio of one graduate tutor for every two undergraduate tutors. As we write this chapter in fall 2018, the Ott still operates with a single faculty director but now with six grad tutors and forty-six undergrad tutors. This growth in staff requires more clearly organized methods of mentoring new tutors; furthermore, the Ott has significantly expanded its mission, launching a course-embedded tutors program, a series of programs to support writers in area high schools, a writing accountability program for graduate writers, and an undergraduate research initiative. The ratio of one grad tutor to every seven undergrad tutors means that grad tutors are now decidedly in the minority—and that fact, combined with the need for knowledgeable leaders to guide our growing programmatic commitments, potentially sets up grad tutors to occupy a more rarified position in our center.

As we reflected on our changing institutional situation over the past several years, we recognized that the growth of our center and the larger

Graduate Tutor Professional Development—and Collaborative Leadership 167

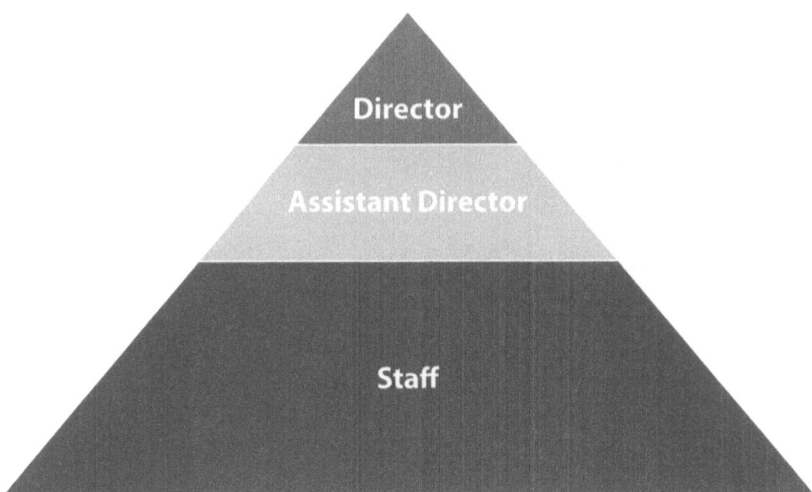

Figure 12.1. The original, more hierarchical leadership model

imbalance between graduates and undergraduates could calcify into a stratified leadership structure (figure 12.1), undermining the culture of collaboration we sought to maintain. However, we came to see this period of growth as an opportunity for us to significantly and intentionally restructure our center.

This chapter traces the ways we've attempted, over the past eight years, to make a virtue of our institutional necessities and how we've worked to structure professional development opportunities for grad students that prepare them to step into leadership positions while also encouraging active collaboration with and respect for undergrad tutors. The new leadership structure—represented in figure 12.2 and discussed at length later in this chapter—is more of a network. It relies far less on a top-down structure and much more on an integrated, collaborative administrative team that provides opportunities for the full staff (graduate and undergraduate student alike) to engage in leadership and professional development opportunities. As we've grown out of our clearer, smaller hierarchy of leadership toward a more distributed and inclusive network, we've also worked together to cultivate the type of "leaderful learning" (10) described in *The Everyday Writing Center*.

As the director, Rebecca initially resisted letting go of the existing organizational structure—in large part because when the staff was smaller, that structure often felt "flatter," more informal, and less hierarchical. She feared, for instance, that creating a second assistant director

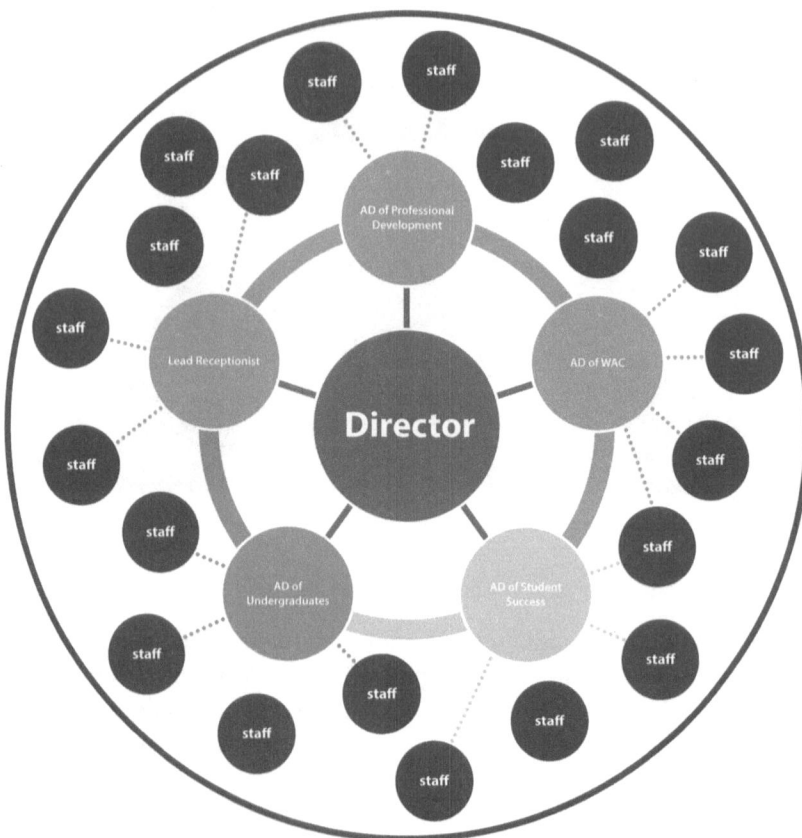

Figure 12.2. A subsequent, more distributed leadership model

and a "lead receptionist" position would stratify the staff in detrimental ways. Over time, though, she came to embrace the slowly emerging leadership network not merely as the only reasonable way to scale up our work across campus but also as an opportunity to offer challenging and rewarding professional development for grad and undergrad tutors. In the pages that follow, we offer accounts of how we have wrestled with the challenges of planning professional development for graduate tutors at two different stages: tailoring an introduction to writing center work for a wide range of grad tutors, and undertaking collaborative projects when our cohort of graduate tutors has more experience. We conclude by describing our current networked Leadership Team structure, and exploring how it invites grad tutors to collaborate both with undergrad tutors and the director, while also turning a critical eye to the limitations of this new system.

Community of Practice as a Community of Learning: Accounts of Onboarding from Will, Lisa, Danielle, and Matt

The institutional reality of funding for our graduate tutors has a direct bearing on the decisions we make about professional development. Marquette has no grad program in rhetoric and composition, and the writing center has no independent access to graduate assistant teaching (GTA) "lines." This situation leaves us with two avenues for obtaining graduate tutors. Some units on campus (most often English and occasionally history and other departments) choose to place one or more of their GTAs in the writing center; these grad tutors are salaried through the GTA line, work ten to fifteen hours each week of the semester, and sometimes balance their tutoring work with classroom teaching. In other cases, the writing center hires graduate tutors on an hourly basis; generally, these grad tutors have already established relationships with the Ott, either because they were an undergrad tutor or previously worked in the Ott on a GTA line. Some grad tutors stay for three or more years, others are on staff only a semester; most are on staff for two or three years. As a result, in any given year our cohort of grad tutors may consist of new and returning graduate tutors—and those new tutors may bring experience as tutors (at our writing center or elsewhere), bring experience as teachers, or have none of those previous experiences. Like Alex Wulff's work (chapter 14), we have found that hiring grad tutors from a variety of disciplines demands a program that "recognize[s] the diversity of [tutors'] experiences and allow[s] them to see the value of their own work."

Our response has been a fall "onboarding" program that assumes no previous tutoring knowledge, foregrounds practicalities, and introduces grad tutors to a small sample of writing center scholarship. We think of this first-semester onboarding as having two components: a crash course in learning through observation and a series of weekly "grad seminar" discussions. Whereas all undergraduate tutors are required to take a full-semester, four-credit class that involves fifteen hours of shadowing and deep engagement with writing studies scholarship, our grad tutors experience a highly condensed version of the undergrad curriculum. The observational component is meant to help graduate tutors build their knowledge and encourage reflective practice; it's also the first of many opportunities for graduate tutors to negotiate the power dynamics of a collaborative relationship with undergraduate tutors.

The learning through observation follows a pattern common in many writing centers. We block out the grad tutor's schedule for the first two weeks; instead of conducting appointments with writers, they bring their own writing into the center to get feedback. They watch experienced tutors and engage in reflective conversation about choices the tutor made; during this stage, it's not unusual for new grad tutors to observe and learn from experienced undergrad tutors. Eventually, the new grad tutor starts leading sessions with writers, with an experienced tutor observing and available for reflective conversation afterward. As the following accounts suggest, these observations play different roles for different grad tutors, offering opportunities to build confidence; reflect on the differences between tutoring and teaching; and challenge the hierarchical imbalance between graduate and undergraduate students that characterizes much of the rest of our university culture.

Some grad tutors begin their time in the Ott with a significant amount of tutoring experience. For instance, Will—a graduate tutor from the Philosophy Department—worked in the Ott as an undergrad and recalls that beginning as a grad tutor was fairly low stakes and streamlined. Not surprisingly given his participation in the four-credit class and year of experience at the Ott, Will didn't participate in the observational component of onboarding. Other tutors, though, found the observational onboarding crucial. Lisa, a graduate tutor from the History Department, recalls initially being terrified: "I had no previous experience at any of my former institutions at a writing center, and I wasn't an English major. I felt I was not qualified."

In Lisa's case, the observational onboarding process was central to decreasing her panic and increasing her confidence: "The grad student AD took me aside to ask about my concerns (there were many), and that day, away from the undergraduate tutors who seemed more qualified than I was, we had two conferences—one with his work, and another with mine—and wrote the conference reports together." Coming to the writing center with only the experience of teacher-student relationships, Lisa valued how her initial work with other grad tutors allowed her to learn about tutoring without having to reveal her anxiety to undergrad tutors who, in a different semester, might be enrolled in her history course. For Lisa, it was bringing her own writing to the writing center that allowed her to fully embrace her collaborative relationship with her undergraduate colleagues. At first, she worked primarily with other graduate tutors, but as she got to know some undergrad tutors during slow shifts, she began to schedule appointments exclusively with undergraduates. Discussing her dissertation with undergrad tutors created a context in which her disciplinary expertise was visible and yet she was actively and genuinely learning from the undergraduate tutors who helped brainstorm writing advice and modeled effective tutoring behaviors.

Danielle, a grad tutor from the English Department, also recalls feeling constrained, not only by her designation as a graduate tutor but also by her own experiences as an undergrad tutor in another university writing center. Although she initially felt she would be expected to function more as an expert than a peer, the fact that she was scheduled with undergraduate tutors and regularly turned to them with questions soon shifted her perception: "My early experiences in the center, particularly the first few weeks where undergrad tutors were walking me through every step of the tutoring process, Ott workshops, and our online system, led me to rethink my initial thoughts about authority and expertise." While Danielle still had experience as a tutor and a teacher, this was a new writing center, with different expectations and ways of doing things. Fortunately, for grad tutors such as Danielle who must navigate the space between instructor and tutor, the learning process of that initial onboarding experience invited her (and all the graduate tutors) to develop genuinely peer relationships with undergrad tutors.

Even for grad tutors who never felt anxious about ceding the authority that would seem to attend their graduate student status, the opportunity to observe experienced undergrad tutors in action was crucial to building genuine partnerships. Matt, a grad tutor from the English Department, recalls that his total lack of tutoring experience made it easier to seek help from his undergraduate colleagues: "I was able to observe several undergraduates lead conferences, work with them while prepping workshops, and just generally discuss practices and strategies at staff meetings and around the writing center. I felt like I was steadily finding my voice and identity in a unique and special environment rather than being thrown in as a presumed authority despite no experience." These challenges of negotiating authority and expertise are hardly unique to our writing center; in this collection, Megan Boeshart Burelle and Meagan Thompson as well as Anna Sicari (chapter 11, chapter 18) describe similar challenges. However, because our condensed observation "onboarding" process—made necessary by the limited time and diverse backgrounds of the grad tutors who come to work in our writing center—often places new grad tutors in the position of learning from experienced undergrad tutors, it has the advantage of laying the foundation upon which grad tutors build their habits of turning to undergraduate tutors as peers.

Strengthening Community: Anna, Lisa, and Alex Reflect on the Importance of Collaborative Inquiries

In addition to this intense two weeks of observation, the heart of our ongoing graduate tutor professional development is a weekly grad-tutor-only "seminar." Because our writing center is closed during the first week of classes, we take the ten hours GTAs would ordinarily work and redistribute them as a series of seven seventy-five-minute conversations. When we have new graduate tutors on staff, the meetings generally include three components: (1) a discussion of logistics (e.g., How do I create a client report in our center's database? What happens if a tutor calls out sick?); (2) a discussion of writing center scholarship (see the list of representative readings at the end of this chapter); and (3) a five-to-ten-minute period devoted to hearing an excerpt from a piece of writing in progress from one of the graduate tutors or the director. This three-part structure has several advantages: new tutors learn some of the logistical ropes, the grad tutors are introduced to a small body of scholarship that helps them contextualize and reflect on their everyday practices, and sharing our own writing makes us present to each other as writers ourselves. In addition, the weekly seminar offers a time for the director to recognize the particular academic strengths and ambitions of graduate tutors who are in the midst of advanced studies and helps cultivate an esprit de corps among the grad tutors.

Through these meetings, we seek a balance. On the one hand, our onboarding process helps graduate and undergraduate tutors to see each other as equals. On the other hand, graduate students are at the university for advanced study and to seek advanced opportunities—*and* the growth of our writing center calls out for us to draw on the skills of these more experienced individuals. Toward this end, during semesters when we have a cohort of more experienced grad tutors, we have adopted one of two approaches: either a research project intended for publication or a shared pedagogical project (often with immediate leadership implications). We readily confess that this was not always our conscious plan. For several years, the focus of the graduate seminar was serendipitous: We opted into shared inquiries because they spoke to the interests of the current cohort or responded to a sudden exigence.

But over time, we've come to recognize a pattern: the professional development provided in the grad seminar feels most valuable when it operates as site for what Jean Lave and Etienne Wenger call "legitimate peripheral participation" (LPP) in the community of practice that is our writing center. The term LPP refers to "the development of knowledgeably skilled identities in practice" in the context of a community of practice's "characteristic biographies/trajectories, relationships, and practices" (55). In other words, new members of the community gain experience and confidence by working together with expert members in ways that are mentored and meaningful contributions to the community. In the following passages, we provide two examples of how the director and graduate tutors have worked together on projects that provide genuine contributions to our writing center.

Sometimes our collaborative project is an inquiry that leads to publication. Without doubt, publications hold a uniquely powerful value in many realms of academic life; an active research agenda increases the regard upper administrators at our university have for our writing center. And publication experience potentially benefits individual grad tutors—not just by adding a line to their CV but in many cases by providing a closely mentored venture into the process of writing abstracts, submitting essays to editors, rebounding from revise and resubmits (or rejections), and seeing a project through to publication. What's more, though, these projects serve a powerful function in the everyday life of our writing center.

For instance, during the spring 2017 semester, what began as a modest staff meeting on keeping conference records grew into a semester-long mixed methods inquiry into the role conference records play in building a culture of reflection. Anna, a graduate tutor in the English department, recalls that "as we discussed reflective trends in client reports in our grad seminar, we realized that we had a lot to say about reflection in these reports. Rebecca asked if it should be an article and all of the graduate students eagerly took on the chance to explore the themes we'd started to notice in more detail." From Rebecca's perspective, the precedent for this collaborative research project with a cohort of grad tutors was set by an ongoing undergrad research initiative within our writing center; it is perhaps another instance of how we work to provide advanced learning opportunities for *all* the members of our staff, at the graduate *and* undergraduate levels. Lisa notes that this experience was particularly useful not only for learning about the writing center and reflective practices but because "it also gave insight into the processes involved in collaborative writing for publication." The findings of our research have cycled back into our everyday practices, through staff meetings and informal mentoring.

Other times, our collaborative project might more aptly be characterized as a venture in scholarly teaching. For instance, at the end of the fall 2017 semester, our tutors (especially our tutors from underrepresented populations) reported a significant uptick in appointments in which they grew very uncomfortable with the contents of drafts: for example, anti-Muslim arguments, assertions that all Black people in Chicago were violent, or a defense of a "good" slaveholder. We felt strongly the need to devote multiple staff meetings to giving tutors opportunities to reflect on these incidents and to helping each tutor reflect on their range of possible responses. Rebecca felt underprepared to plan and lead such staff meetings; it became, by necessity, a collaborative effort.

Grad seminars were devoted to reading works from Laura Greenfield and Karen Rowan's *Writing Centers and the New Racism* and elsewhere. We talked about what kind of writing center we'd like to be, what kind of university we'd like to be, what kind of humans we'd like to be. We argued with each other (and sometimes with ourselves) about the pros and cons of various in-conference strategies: for example, is it okay for a tutor to "tag out" and ask another tutor to take a triggering conference? And together we worked to adapt an approach to forum theater described by Rasha Diab et al. (2012). This collaborative project facilitated genuinely motivated collaborations between the director and graduate tutors. The legitimate peripheral participation was hardly peripheral, for graduate tutors were at the very center of planning and leading staff meetings (that often broke into two smaller groups to encourage more participation). Reflecting on the professional development involved in running forum theater staff meetings, Alex, a graduate student in English, notes,

> In addition to the collaborative process of developing forum theatre scripts, I found the forum theatre process also invoked a collaborative experience through group discomfort, laughter, and commiseration. As a grad tutor, the act of performing in a forum theater required me to engage with the head-space of problematic writers and confront my own biases and discomfort with confrontation and difficult conversations. In terms of professional development, this experience helped me develop skills for helping both myself and undergraduate tutors manage the emotions that may be evoked in "difficult" conferences. This helped me develop both as a tutor and leader and as a future educator.

Furthermore, because this particular collaboration around forum theater depends on a scripted remembrance of an actual situation, multiple undergrad tutors (who composed scripts from their own uncomfortable conferences) were central to this collaborative process as well. In this way, the grad tutors were asked to be, in the tradition of Anne Ellen Geller et al. (2007), leaderly learners—taking on new challenges and responsibilities while still operating within a culture of learning and collaboration.

LOOKING FORWARD: LEADERSHIP TEAM AND COLLABORATION

Our writing center—like so many writing centers—is an institutional unit in flux. Over the past eight years, we've grown in size and scope. We've changed reporting lines—from English, to arts and sciences, to the Provost's Office via our Center for Teaching and Learning. We've developed the onboarding strategies and collaborative inquiry projects described above, coming to see them as intentional choices rather than purely serendipitous responses to current conditions. And we have—as we noted at the start of this chapter—shifted away from a simpler to a more networked leadership structure. We now have a Leadership Team (which meets once a week) composed of seven ex officio members and three at-large members. The ex officio positions include four graduate tutor ADs (in charge of professional development, student success, and writing across the curriculum) as well as an undergraduate AD, an undergraduate lead receptionist, and an undergraduate public relations intern. The three at-large members rotate each semester and generally (but not always) are undergrads, selected to represent the diversity of experience and identities on our staff.

The new structure has several important advantages. We run many types of programming now, all of which require careful attention and thoughtful leadership; more ADs focusing on particular aspects of our work helps meet that need. The new networked Leadership Team builds an infrastructure that doesn't rely too much on any one person. It allows both grad and undergrad tutors to take on and grow into intellectual challenges and leadership responsibilities that not only serve the needs of our community but also prepare them for work beyond the Ott. It frequently positions undergraduate and graduate tutors to collaboratively organize and execute projects together; some recent examples include developing and leading workshops for high school students, planning and hosting a "Writer Fight Club" event on campus, planning and leading a series of staff meetings, revising our handbook, and developing and implementing a publicity campaign. And although we considered—when we shifted from one graduate AD to more—eliminating the three at-large positions, we instead doubled down on undergraduate representation. In addition to keeping the at-large members of our Leadership Team, we added an undergraduate AD position hoping it would clearly signal how much we value undergrad leadership and provide further opportunities for grad-undergrad collaboration.

But, as we conclude, we want also to be mindful of the various ways in which this structure remains imperfect. The institutional design of our university continues to influence our writing center's structure. For example, some, but not all, of our graduate tutors are part of our official Leadership Team. Generally, those who have more hours in the Ott—that is, those on a GTA line—are placed in AD positions. Thus, an unintended consequence of our revised leadership structure is a hierarchy within the grad tutor cohort, one in which salaried GTA-line graduate tutors hold official positions while other hourly graduate tutors do not. Will notes that because of his commitments to an accelerated MA program, he never sought an official leadership position. Because of that, he says, "I was viewed as above undergraduate students yet still below the other graduate tutors."

Furthermore, only a small fraction of our undergraduate tutors are a part of Leadership Team (6 of 42 tutors), but nearly all of our graduate tutors are automatically included ex officio. And even though our current Leadership Team excludes nearly 80 percent of our tutors, it remains large enough to complicate decision-making processes. In our attempt to maintain as inclusive a structure as possible, we have become less nimble in our ability to respond quickly to new situations and opportunities. Without doubt, our team decisions often benefit from a protracted and increasingly reflective discussion process, but such an approach does take time—and time sometimes feels like a luxury.

Nevertheless, we feel the advantages of this system of professional development and collaborative leadership outweigh the inevitable limitations. While our structure clearly responds to local affordances and constraints, we highlight, by way of conclusion, several strategic choices that other writing centers might consider closely in designing their own systems of professional development and leadership.

> **Hiring.** When interviewing new graduate tutors, we listen for a willingness to embrace collaboration with undergraduates and do so in multiple ways. We listen for the ways candidates talk about their own authority (perhaps in a classroom) and expertise (perhaps regarding previous tutoring work). We listen for how they talk about collaborating with writers. And we listen carefully to their answers when we ask directly about how they might bridge the gap between graduate students and undergraduate students that exists in most other parts of the university. Although we have no definitive code words or "right answers" that guide our hiring decisions, we do think that even including such questions signals these collaborative values to potential graduate tutors before they even join the staff.
>
> **Onboarding.** Given the multiple experiences documented in this chapter, we intentionally choose to schedule new graduate tutors with especially experienced undergraduate tutors, skilled at reflecting on their

tutoring practices. Doing so encourages graduate tutors to draw on the wisdom of their undergraduate colleagues from the start, and it clearly signals to the full staff that we believe that graduate tutors have much to learn from undergraduate tutors.

Structuring leadership. Our Leadership Team has broad representation from both undergraduate and graduate tutors. Whenever possible, we have large projects or events co-led by a pair of graduate and undergraduate tutors. At first, this was an unconscious choice forced by necessity. A new graduate tutor, for instance, might have had more time to see a project to completion, while a returning undergraduate tutor had extensive experience with the project in a previous year. Although these graduate-undergraduate pairings may have started by chance, because they relied on the genuine strengths of both tutors and enabled the pair members to accomplish more together than they could individually, we quickly learned that such pairings were crucial to handing down institutional knowledge from year to year and getting things done. Furthermore, while particular pairings emerged to solve specific programmatic challenges (how to make this event happen, or see that project through to completion), we came to recognize that a steady stream of such collaborative projects helped to promote a culture of collaboration that goes beyond individual pairings.

In sum, while we have turned some constraints to our advantage, we still work actively to structure our opportunities for legitimate peripheral participation in ways that we hope encourage—through small, everyday means—a culture of mutual and collaborative learning.

A SAMPLE OF READINGS FROM GRAD SEMINAR

From introductory semesters:

- Hall, R. Mark. 2017. *Around the Texts of Writing Center Work: An Inquiry-Based Approach to Tutor Education.* Logan: Utah State University Press.
- Harris, Muriel. 1995. "Talking in the Middle: Why Writers Need Writing Tutors." *College English* 57 (1): 27–42.
- Mackiewicz, Jo, and Isabelle Thompson. 2014. "Instruction, Cognitive Scaffolding, and Motivational Scaffolding in Writing Center Tutoring." *Composition Studies* 42 (1): 54–78.
- North, Stephen. 1984. "The Idea of a Writing Center." *College English* 46 (5): 433–46.

From more advanced semesters:

- Block, Rebecca. 2016. "Disruptive Design: An Empirical Study of Reading Aloud in the Writing Center." *The Writing Center Journal* 35 (2): 33–59.

- Bean, John. 2011. *Engaging Ideas: The Professor's Guide to Integrating Writing, Critical Thinking, and Active Learning in the Classroom.* San Francisco: John Wiley & Sons.
- Bitzer, Lloyd F. 1968. "The Rhetorical Situation." *Philosophy & Rhetoric* 1 (1): 1–14.
- Condon, William, and Carol Rutz. 2012. "A Taxonomy of Writing Across the Curriculum Programs: Evolving to Serve Broader Agendas." *College Composition and Communication* 64 (2): 357–82.
- Eodice, Michele, Anne Geller, and Neal Lerner. 2017. *The Meaningful Writing Project: Learning, Teaching and Writing in Higher Education.* Logan: Utah State University Press.
- Greenfield, Laura, and Karen Rowan, eds. 2011. *Writing Centers and the New Racism: A Call for Sustainable Dialogue and Change.* Logan: Utah State University Press.
- Melzer, Dan. 2014. *Assignments across the Curriculum: A National Study of College Writing.* Logan: Utah State University Press.

REFERENCES

Diab, Rasha, Beth Godbee, Thomas Ferrel, and Neil Simpkins. 2012. "A Multi-dimensional Pedagogy for Racial Justice in Writing Centers." *Praxis: A Writing Center Journal* 10 (1): 1–8.

Geller, Anne Ellen, Michele Eodice, Frankie Condon, Meg Carroll, and Elizabeth Boquet. 2007. *Everyday Writing Center: A Community of Practice.* Boulder: University Press of Colorado.

Greenfield, Laura, and Karen Rowan, eds. 2011. *Writing Centers and the New Racism: A Call for Sustainable Dialogue and Change.* Boulder: University Press of Colorado.

Lave, Jean, and Etienne Wenger. 1991. *Situated Learning: Legitimate Peripheral Participation.* Cambridge: Cambridge University Press.

13
(GRADUATE) FRIENDS WITH BENEFITS
Writing Relationships into the Center

Elise Dixon and Cassie J. Brownell

A few years ago, as Elise, a graduate consultant, and Cassie, her graduate student client, met for their weekly writing center (WC) appointment, they were gently teased by a WC administrator about standing appointments. He joked the WC was a place where "writers, and not necessarily their texts, are what get changed by instruction" (North 1984, 438), and the appointments seemed counterintuitive; after all, weren't standing appointments an academic crutch focused primarily on editing papers? We took the criticism in stride, arguing how beneficial our relationship was for us as a graduate student consultant working with a graduate student client. If the WC is supposed to be about peer-to-peer collaborative writing, where all participants develop as learners and writers, then ours is a relationship deeply rooted in writing center tradition and goals.

Indeed, perhaps standing appointments run counterintuitively to the "grand narrative" that "writing centers are comfortable, iconoclastic places where all students go to get one-to-one tutoring on their writing" (McKinney 2013, 3). Because this narrative stems from North's (1984) axiom "better writers, not better writing" (438), the assumption is that repetitive focus on the same text improves the *text* but not necessarily the *writer*, because such a focus could make a client reliant on the center to write in the first place. Standing appointments, then, offer *more than* one-to-one tutoring and seemingly go against the approach Jeff Brooks (1991) advocated. Still, as Kenneth Bruffee (1984) articulated, WCs provide "help that was not an extension of but an alternative to traditional classroom teaching" (637). Sustained working relationships between graduate consultants and graduate student clients create a support system outside the WC and provide help to both parties that is not an extension of, but an alternative to, an alienating graduate experience.

While sustained professional growth initiated our working relationship, our shared writing fostered opportunities for us to grow personally, together. Our standing appointments evolved into much more: Elise facilitated writing groups Cassie participated in; Cassie mentored Elise through academic moves; we both received a fellowship to work outside the WC; and Elise read nearly every draft of Cassie's dissertation. We became good friends whose relationship surpassed a typical client/consultant transaction to become one of mutual mentorship and support. In this chapter, we argue sustained working relationships—read here as feminist co-mentoring (Godbee and Novotny 2013)—are beneficial in WCs because they model the kinds of collegiality we anticipate as faculty, create better colleagues and writers, and create better writing.

WRITING CENTERS AND GRADUATE STUDENTS

As articulated by Elizabeth Boquet (1999), especially as WCs shifted from labs to collaborative centers in the 1970–80s, so too did the hierarchical teacher-student model change to peer-to-peer models of consulting. Bruffee (1984) argued this collaborative, peer-to-peer design was developed because undergraduate students not "fluent" in academic discourse were not seeking help provided before open enrollment created space for a diverse student population. Students did not want to visit yet more teachers in their free time, where they would surely be met with further discourse surrounding their unpreparedness for college. Instead, students wanted an alternative to the traditional classroom (Bruffee 1984). An alternative to the traditional classroom at this point in time for undergraduate students was a collaborative consulting session with a peer, the antithesis of the traditional teacher-student lecture model. In keeping with WC tradition and ethos, scholars might ask what help alternatives to the traditional classroom might look like for a graduate student today, as more WCs offer services for MA and PhD clients.

Before considering what an *alternative* to traditional graduate classrooms might look like, it is important to consider the characteristics of traditional graduate student education. Graduate classrooms certainly vary among disciplines and institutions. Many graduate classrooms exist in seminar form, with discussion highlighted more than lecture. Graduate students frequently work in labs, hold research fellowships, or teach undergraduates. They are traditionally expected to understand written academic genres, what Laura Brady and Nathalie Singh-Corcoran (2016) call "disciplinary conventions" (3) of their discipline with little-to-no instruction or supervision beyond feedback from advisors. Further, many professors do not see teaching disciplinary conventions as valuable, as articulated by a professor in Brady and Singh-Corcoran's study, who argued, "Graduate school is sink or swim—if you don't have these skills coming into it, you shouldn't be here. I'm not sure we should be spending our WC resources worrying about graduate students" (4). As discussed by Elizabeth Festa in chapter 17, traditional WC models of peer-to-peer sessions with an undergraduate tutor may also fall short of what graduate students need. The lack of consensus among faculty and some WC directors on how much (if any) writing instruction should be provided to graduate students only leaves them more in need of an alternative to the traditional graduate school model.

For these reasons, the process of enculturating into a graduate program and disciplinary field is deeply uncomfortable and fraught with tension. In her multidimensional study of the "writing games" undergraduate and graduate students must learn to play in the academy, Christine Pears Casanave (2002) notes that

> studies of doctoral students learning to participate authoritatively in their academic communities . . . all seem to point to the messy and unsettling nature of the very serious, identity-transforming academic literacy games in the enculturation process. Amidst this messiness, issues of authority . . . are at the heart of learning to write and of developing a professional identity in a graduate setting. In that setting, tensions are created between novices' pressure to identify and conform to convention on the one hand and the desire to assert other less academically conventional identities on the other. Tensions are also created in that the sources of authority-building knowledge and practice are so diverse and partial, encompassing the social, political, personal, and textual. (141)

Much of graduate studies is about navigating one's discipline. Gaining clarity on how to succeed depends on the advice and knowledge gleaned from advisors, lore, peers, seminar classes, and workshops; there are multiple ways to learn how to succeed—both writing and otherwise—but most are nebulous, illusive, and shrouded in myth. Thus, Bruffee's (1984) "traditional classroom" looks vastly different for graduate students.

It's no wonder a WC that resists a traditional classroom model for graduate students looks vastly different. Helping graduate students become "better writers" includes consultants seeing graduate clients more frequently (one-to-one and in a writing group), and developing a co-mentoring relationship and sometimes a friendship. This model worked well for us, whether similar to a traditional model or not. This chapter is a practice of "constellating stories in order to visualize a web of relations" that we share with the WC, the academy, and each other (Powell et al. 2014, act 1, scene 3). Our experience acts as a case study for what worked well for two graduate students, a consultant and client, who organically developed a routine to become professional and personal support for one another in an environment often reticent to transparently provide that support. The back-and-forth stories we detail can be read as personal encounters with what Beth Godbee and Julia Novotny (2013) describe as "feminist co-mentoring, or two-way (reciprocal and mutual) teaching, learning, and laboring together" (177). We illuminate *how* this model organically arose, provide arguments for *why* it worked, and offer suggestions for replicating this intentional approach to graduate-to-graduate consulting in other WCs.

PEERNESS AS GRADUATE STUDENTS—CASSIE

On advice from a peer two years ahead in my teacher education doctoral program, I made weekly appointments with various graduate consultants at the WC. In no time, these evolved into standing appointments with an advanced PhD student in rhetoric. These appointments scaffolded my writing by serving as a weekly deadline for me (ultimately, cultivating a daily writing habit) and by apprenticing me into genres of academic writing. Because my consultant was a seasoned graduate student, she provided insights about professional development on campus.

I maintained a weekly two-hour standing appointment at the WC, and meetings with consultants in my previous two years were focused on course papers or conference presentations; by year three, I shifted to programmatic milestones—such as comprehensive exams—and external funding and publications. Throughout, the voices of the past consultants I had worked with replayed themselves in my head as I wrote independently or provided peers with writing feedback. I continued to improve my writing skills and learned a great deal about myself as an academic writer.

I met Elise in the summer before my fourth year of study. I knew what I needed from consultants with whom I worked. I desired critical feedback on my work, preferring that the consultant I worked with "go for the jugular" rather than hold back for fear of hurting my feelings. I was aware of particular ticks I had as a writer (though, as I would later learn from Elise, I also had quite a few other habits of which I wasn't yet aware) and specific writing skills I still struggled with (organization, for instance). In our first meeting, I outlined for Elise the specific tasks I wished to accomplish and how they aligned with my long-term goals.

I wanted to engage one individual in my writing through standing appointments, as in the past three years, so I would have to do less work during sessions to provide context for my consultant about the research, the grant, or how I approached my work. Through standing appointments, I knew I could more readily dive in and out of writing projects. As a scholar of writing and rhetoric, Elise understood as a researcher and practitioner that writing was not a static, linear process. She understood writing as thinking (Hughes and Bridges-Rhoads 2013; Richardson 1997) and pressed me about the decisions I was making as a researcher and writer because she knew these processes were not separate. She provided targeted feedback to help me cultivate my skills as a researcher, writer, and thinker through specific feedback (Stanulis and Bell 2017). For instance, she did well to challenge me to consider my positioning as a white woman who frequently wrote empirical articles about children of Color.

PEERNESS AS GRADUATE STUDENTS—ELISE

What I remember most about my first meeting with Cassie is that, at the end of our first session, she announced we were going to be friends. I laughed but already felt similarly. Cassie had a clearly articulated plan for our session and immediately emailed the WC director to request a standing appointment at the conclusion. Her commitment to her own work, her already-existing comfort with the WC, and her faith in me, a second-year PhD student with less advanced training than Cassie, made me want to reciprocate her faith and commitment.

I also felt intimidated by Cassie. I was not sure what I offered her as a graduate student two years behind her in studies. Still, I had facilitated a year-long writing group with PhD education students senior to Cassie. This group met once weekly to discuss an alternating member's written work—I guided theory conversations and provided feedback, engaging in a cross-disciplinary approach not unlike what is described by Kristin Messuri in chapter 16. The writing group was appreciative of my help. As facilitator, I dissected the inner workings of academic disciplinary conventions, something at which my graduate work in rhetoric and writing made me adept. Although I felt like less than a peer to Cassie in terms of PhD experience, I knew I could offer my understanding of academic writing and extensive experience with WC consulting. Without realizing it, I was modeling what Godbee and Novotny (2013) describe as "writing as a practice of recording and extending what is said as a means of empowerment" (189); one of the greatest things I offered was a listening ear and the use of writing to empower Cassie.

During our first year, Cassie worked on her dissertation proposal that later became a grant proposal. We worked weekly for two-hour sessions over a month on the same document, pouring over examples of previous grant winners, the grant website, and tips provided to her. I became more emotionally invested in the project to the point at which it sometimes felt like my project as well, even though Cassie was writing it all. By submission time, I was sick of the project in the way I got sick of my own work after the recursive process of writing, revision, and editing. I was also very invested in Cassie as a client, as a graduate student, and as a friend.

In the final year as her consultant, I assumed Cassie would breeze through her dissertation. I had seen her piece together whole articles in a manner of weeks, both because of her skill with writing and with her willingness to send out material she knew was not necessarily perfect (a difficult mental hoop for many graduate students). I figured her dissertation would be the same. Instead, she struggled as I had seen other graduate students struggle: she wanted it to be perfect; she felt defined by it; she felt daunted by it; she distracted herself with job market materials to avoid it. Watching Cassie struggle helped me to realize my dissertating process would inevitably look similar, because no matter how prepared a person may be to write an article, the dissertation is a different beast.

CONCLUSIONS ON PEERNESS AS GRADUATE STUDENTS

While standing appointments might be frowned upon by some under the guise that such a service acts as a crutch for a writer, we found the opposite. Standing appointments allowed us to build the peer-to-peer relationship Bruffee (1984) and Stephen North (1984) both advocated. Due to our different disciplines, neither of us always felt like the expert or novice in a session (as discussed by Marcus Weakley and Mark Pedretti in chapter 9), allowing for what Godbee and Novotny (2013) refer to as "power with" as opposed to "power over" (180). The "power over" model of knowledge creation and mentorship is precisely the model Bruffee (1984) and North (1984) themselves hoped to avoid. Because of our consistent appointments, our relationship very quickly developed into one of co-mentorship and helped us to develop professionally and intellectually. As Godbee and Novotny (2013) argue, "it takes time to participate fully in this relational process, and so we need institutional structures—like writing centers—that provide this professional support" (190). Standing appointments allow for the time to develop a vulnerable, intimate co-mentorship relationship.

(FEMINIST) CO-MENTORING—CASSIE

Recently, I read an editorial from a journal in qualitative research that described the concept of "murmuration," a manifestation of collective behavior whereby the line of individuals blur as they begin moving as one. Although the authors noted murmuration as being associated with starlings (a kind of bird), they used the starlings' cohesion to describe how articles in their issue were "no longer discrete individuals but instead function[ed] as one organism, constantly in motion, continuing to change direction as additional shifts engage and interact with it" (Van Cleave, Bridges-Rhoads, and Hughes 2018, 2). I was taken by murmuration, feeling it spoke to my experience with Elise—as consultant and friend.

Jessica Van Cleave, Sarah Bridges-Rhoads, and Hilary Hughes (2018) write about how disagreement and the collision of ideas promotes a shift in response that, ultimately, impacts the whole. My memories with Elise are tied to instances when she did not let me off the hook in ways only the truest of friends perhaps can. Yes, like a "good" WC consultant she made me write (sometimes from scratch) or asked me pointed questions as she mapped my ideas on a nearby whiteboard. She also challenged the "I'm not good enough" refrain of imposter syndrome that often surfaced. Elise's engagement varied from words of encouragement to tough love. Yet, because she tied these actions to her own experience, she made herself vulnerable in similar ways to what she asked of me. Her willingness to share cemented our working relationship as one built on mutual trust, respect, and admiration (Godbee and Novotny 2013). Elise became not only a friend, but a critical one at that. In turn, she informed my writing and my personhood in ways less measurable and/ or accounted for than through typical means used by the WC to "track" a client's progress.

(FEMINIST) CO-MENTORING—ELISE

Because Cassie was two years ahead in her studies, she inadvertently modeled the practices of a successful graduate student. Cassie constantly submitted her work for publication, found opportunities to involve herself in department and discipline-wide service, and applied for multiple fellowships. Sometimes, as she worked on a fellowship application, she would look up from her work to tell me I should apply for the same fellowship. Other times, she described service she was doing and suggested I find something similar. I saw her strategically respond to revise-and-resubmit letters, practices I adopted myself. Cassie also always recruited graduate students for our writing groups who were ABD, dissertating, and on the job market. I learned from group members what a prospectus and dissertation defense looked like before I completed them, and I witnessed the hopelessness and frustration associated with the job market. Cassie was often the expert in the room with regard to her discipline and her specific research agenda and I was there to offer confirmation of that expertise, just as Godbee and Novotny (2013) noticed the client Andrea doing in her consultations with Charisse, "taking on the role of expert and gaining experience speaking from a position of *knowing well her work*" (191). By witnessing my client's expertise, I learned how to develop it myself.

Cassie mentored without being aware she was doing it. I acted as a sounding board and cheerleader to her writing; she led by example how to navigate a PhD. We mentored each other, sometimes unknowingly. This kind of co-mentoring "allows individuals to build group solidarity, and solidarity gained from the stance of *power with* enables shared empowerment—making the whole stronger than its parts—so that both co-mentors gain from the relationship, even when those gains are different in degree or kind" (Godbee and Novotny 2013, 180). Acting as co-mentors, we shifted back and forth between that of WC consultant/client, colleagues, and friends. We modeled the kind of working relationships we hoped for as faculty members, learning more from each WC session than just how to become better writers (though we did that too).

CONCLUSIONS ON FEMINIST CO-MENTORING

The description and embodiment of the consultant and client within Godbee and Novotny's (2013) article on feminist co-mentoring *felt* real to us. Across our shared stories here and in the following sections, we detail not only *that* our relationship shifted but *how* it shifted.

BECOMING (GRADUATE) FRIENDS WITH BENEFITS—CASSIE

In my field (teacher education), mentoring relationships between early career teachers and seasoned colleagues often take center stage. Scholarship in this area positions the relationship as "mentor/novice," but researchers are attuned to mentoring as not a one-sided relationship. Instead, and as others argue, the dialogue about mentoring must shift to account for the reciprocal learning that occurs, as in my relationship with Elise (Feiman-Nemser 2001; Stanulis and Weaver 1998; Stanulis et al. 2018).

Many topics discussed among mentors/mentees in K–12 education mirrored those Elise and I found ourselves discussing. For instance, sometimes despite the plan for our writing session, this "work" took "a backseat to the daily mechanics of school life" (Stanulis and Weaver 1998, 137). We sometimes departed from scheduled conversations to unpack happenings in our teaching or research. This detour facilitated a larger discussion about playing the grad school game—navigating department politics, writing for specific purposes, or strategizing problems of teaching practice. Referencing back to the concept of murmuration, the roles of mentor/mentee, reader/writer, consultant/consultee frequently became blurred as the boundaries of conversations shifted to account for the realities and responsibilities we encountered in our programs.

The work of our sessions facilitated peer-to-peer mentoring for us both. We were cheerleaders for one another, particularly when we felt uncomfortable sharing our successes with colleagues in our individual programs for fear of anger or jealousy from fellow graduate students. We held one another to high standards in work we produced and how we participated in life within and beyond the academy (Godbee and Novotny 2013). We became acutely attuned to one another's voices/bodies/needs. For instance, on days when I was frustrated with my writing, Elise would close our meeting with the advice to "get something to eat" or "take a nap." Similarly, I encouraged Elise to eat during our sessions and coached her through an afternoon of meal prep as it was a tool I had found useful. Other times, I picked up dinner when her partner was away, and I reluctantly worked on puzzles she was completing. This quality time enriched our working relationship as we learned to take pleasure in caring for one another as friends. What started as an intellectual professional relationship facilitated by the WC evolved to a personal one; we provided emotional and physical support as co-mentors and friends (Godbee and Novotny 2013).

BECOMING (GRADUATE) FRIENDS WITH BENEFITS—ELISE

For the remainder of our two years together before Cassie graduated, I noticed some shifts in the way our sessions unfolded. Some days, she would show up with nothing planned for me to go over with her; instead, she just needed someone to hold her accountable as she wrote. On these days, I felt connected to the cultural rhetorics methodological practice Andrea Mukavetz (2014) refers to as "thereness": an act of being present in order to build relationships with people and space—"being attentive to how relationships and space impact the opportunity for and construction of knowledge making" (180). I was simply there for/with Cassie, knowing my presence was a part of her relational knowledge-making practice.

Other days, we would get sidetracked as she offered me advice on which fellowships to apply for or conferences to propose to. As we became closer, sometimes our sessions would begin with personal stories, tears, or the sharing of snacks. Cassie recruited her friends for a writing group with me as a facilitator for two years, so we saw each other multiple times a week. We spent time together outside of the WC—going out for meals, getting drinks, or attending performances. Her friends from the writing group became my friends.

BECOMING (GRADUATE) FRIENDS WITH BENEFITS

Tutor guides suggest tutors should maintain a level of professional distance from a client, to develop boundaries and avoid overly familiar interactions. While this advice is certainly useful, it also doesn't really encompass the kind of relationship building in WCs, especially for graduate students. In some cases, like ours, friendship strengthened our consultant/client relationship and allowed us to model the kinds of professional, intellectual friendships we wish for as faculty members, but in a low-stakes environment such as the WC. The WC provided a perfect setting for us to develop as colleagues, co-mentors, and eventually very good friends.

IT'S NOT A CRUTCH: THE WRITING CENTER AS A FEMINIST CO-MENTORING SPACE

In their conclusion, Godbee and Novotny (2013) advocate for more institutional spaces to foster feminist co-mentoring practices among graduate students. They write,

> The writing center provides one example of an institutional space with the conditions to foster feminist co-mentoring: although relationships cannot be imposed or guaranteed, they can emerge when time and space is set aside for "just talking" about writing and other central intellectual activities. In this context, tutors are paid for their time and earn lines on their CVs, while writers who visit the center make tangible progress and receive significant feedback on their work—on a regular basis. (192)

When WC directors develop services for graduate students, *time* and *space* to allow graduate students to talk, sit in their work, and build relationships are a critical element to offering "help of a sort that is not an extension but an alternative to" the traditional graduate school model (Bruffee 1984:637). If Cassie could only set up her appointments week to week, she would invariably work with multiple tutors. She may have received help on her writing, but neither of us believe it would have been as beneficial because a key part of the knowledge-making process in graduate school is relational. Her writing might have improved, but she herself may not have become a better writer.

In addition to Cassie's improvement as a writer, Elise developed a greater sense of self as a graduate student. Cassie read over Elise's fellowship applications, encouraged her to apply for additional funding, and provided emotional support during the difficult times most graduate students experience. Cassie and her writing groups modeled for Elise the process of publishing, completing a dissertation, and progressing in the job market. Elise saw how much she was capable of accomplishing through outside service and publication, something she very likely would not have considered without Cassie's guidance. Elise also developed further as a writer, writing instructor, and writing consultant because of the multiple meta-discussions she facilitated with Cassie.

Unlike the Godbee and Novotny (2013) piece, which looks in on two women engaged in the WC, we presented arguments from a personal account. We discussed not just the act of feminist co-mentoring in the present but possibilities for scholars' futures. While Godbee and Novotny (2013) outlined the specific moves of feminist co-mentoring in a WC, through our shared storytelling, we articulated how feminist co-mentoring moves beyond the WC walls, and far past the time of graduate school. At the time of this writing, Cassie is a first-year faculty member at the University of Toronto, while Elise is preparing for the job market and concluding her dissertation. This chapter was written through multiple virtual meetings in which we, between writing sessions, discussed Cassie's role as a new faculty member alongside Elise's appointment as an interim assistant director of the WC and her need to turn attention to her own dissertation. Yet, as when we were co-located within the WC, our talks included personal matters—Cassie shared her experiences transitioning to a new country, and Elise described preparations for her first child in late 2018. What we learned about peerness, co-mentorship and friendship in the WCs carried into our professional lives, further convincing us that this model (standing appointments that facilitated a close relationship) is ideal for graduate student clients and consultants.

For WC directors with graduate student consultants and clients, we suggest a few potential takeaway points:

Allow for standing appointments for graduate students. Standing appointments helped us develop a professional rapport; Elise became very familiar with Cassie's work, which is especially useful for graduate students when clients and consultants are in different disciplines.

Allow for longer appointments. At our WC, students can make two-hour appointments. Graduate students use these appointments to workshop longer written works.

Consider providing graduate student writing groups and facilitators. Writing groups allowed for Elise to become even more familiar with Cassie's work. Likewise, Cassie, Elise, and the group members developed co-mentorship models as well. The writing group members remain friends and are still in contact, despite most graduating and becoming faculty members elsewhere.

We propose graduate consultants are particularly well positioned to develop meaningful, sustained relationships with peer clients because of their shared experiences in the wider university. Generally, the WC "status quo" suggests clients will "graduate" and work on their own. In our experience, our sustained relationship challenged this notion while modeling the kind of working relationships that are ideal for graduate and faculty writers—a co-mentorship that may last beyond the client/consultant relationship and guide both individuals in future collaborations and partnership. We argue sustained working relationships between graduate consultants and clients are not just an acceptable option in WCs, but the ideal. Such relationships, beyond helping the client become a better writer, also provide models for how to build reciprocal, professional relationships in the future as faculty members. In so doing, graduate students can rewrite the "rules" of the writing center for the benefit of client and consultant.

REFERENCES

Boquet, Elizabeth H. 1999. "'Our Little Secret': A History of Writing Centers, Pre-to Post–Open Admissions." *College Composition and Communication* 50 (3): 463–82.

Brady, Laura, and Nathalie Singh-Corcoran. 2016. "A Space for Change: Writing Center Partnerships to Support Graduate Writing." *WLN: A Journal of Writing Center Scholarship* 40 (5–6): 2–10.

Brooks, Jeff. 1991. "Minimalist Tutoring: Making the Student Do All the Work." *The Writing Lab Newsletter* 15 (6): 1–4.

Bruffee, Kenneth A. 1984. "Collaborative Learning and the 'Conversation of Mankind.'" *College English* 46 (7): 635–52.

Casanave, Christine Pears. 2002. *Writing Games: Multicultural Case Studies of Academic Literacy Practices in Higher Education.* New York: Routledge.

Feiman-Nemser, Sharon. 2001. "Helping Novices Learn to Teach: Lessons from an Exemplary Support Teacher." *Journal of Teacher Education* 52 (1): 17–30.

Godbee, Beth, and Julia C. Novotny. 2013. "Asserting the Right to Belong: Feminist Co-mentoring among Graduate Student Women." *Feminist Teacher* 23 (3): 177–95.

Hughes, Hilary E., and Sarah C. Bridges-Rhoads. 2013. "Beyond the Scope of This Paper: Troubling Writing across Paradigms in Education Dissertations." *International Review of Qualitative Research* 6 (1): 103–25.

McKinney, Jackie Grutsch. 2013. *Peripheral Visions for Writing Centers.* Boulder: University Press of Colorado.

Mukavetz, Andrea M. Riley. 2014. "Towards a Cultural Rhetorics Methodology: Making Research Matter with Multi-generational Women from the Little Traverse Bay Band." *Rhetoric, Professional Communication, and Globalization* 5 (1): 108–25.

North, Stephen M. 1984. "The Idea of a Writing Center." *College English* 46 (5): 433–46.

Powell, Malea, Daisy Levy, Andrea Riley-Mukavetz, Marilee Brooks-Gillies, Maria Novotny, and Jennifer Fisch-Ferguson. 2014. "Our Story Begins Here: Constellating Cultural Rhetorics." *Enculturation: A Journal of Rhetoric, Writing, and Culture* 25. http://enculturation.net/our-story-begins-here. Accessed February 13, 2021.

Richardson, Laurel. *Fields of Play: Constructing an Academic Life.* New Brunswick, NJ: Rutgers University Press, 1997.

Stanulis, Randi N., Lindsay J. Wexler, Stacey Pylman, Amy Guenther, Scott Farver, Amy Ward, Randi N. Stanulis, Lindsay J. Wexler, Stacey Pylman, Amy Guenther, Scott Faver, Amy Ward, Amy Croel-Perrien, and Kristen White. 2018. "Mentoring as More than 'Cheerleading': Looking at Educative Mentoring Practices through Mentors' Eyes." *Journal of Teacher Education* 70 (5): 567–80. https://doi.org/10.1177%2F0022487118773996.

Stanulis, Randi N., and Julie Bell. 2017. "Beginning Teachers Improve with Attentive and Targeted Mentoring." *Kappa Delta Pi Record* 53 (2): 59–65.

Stanulis, Randi Nevins, and Dera Weaver. 1998. "Teacher as Mentor, Teacher as Learner: Lessons from a Middle-school Language Arts Teacher." *Teacher Educator* 34 (2): 134–43.

Van Cleave, Jessica, Sarah Bridges-Rhoads, and Hilary E. Hughes. 2018. "Work/Think/Play in Doctoral Education." *Qualitative Inquiry* 24: 739–42. https://doi.org/10.1177/1077800418767215.

14

MAKING THE INVISIBLE VISIBLE
Valuing Labor in the Design of an Observation-Based Mentor Program for Graduate Student Writing Tutors

Alex Wulff

While this chapter focuses on the implementation and impact of an observation-based mentor program on the graduate student writing tutors at Saint Louis University's writing center, I want to start with a more general foray into what writing center scholarship makes observable. Even as writing center directors have traditionally identified centers as "marginalized" spaces (North 1984; Sunstein 1998; Denny 2010), writing centers are—at least from one perspective—deeply visible spaces. Directors work hard to ensure that all students know where their writing center is located. My writing center was even a stop on the orientation tour when I was a graduate student working as an assistant director. As Jackie Grutsch McKinney (2013) points out, the "grand narrative" of writing centers—that "writing centers are comfortable, iconoclastic places where all students go to get one-on-one tutoring in their writing" (6)—means that we spend a lot of time making sure all students know we are a service for them.

Yet, making a space—or service—visible does not necessarily make the labor performed in that space—in the act of service—visible. McKinney focuses on how the grand narrative impacts the labor of directors, indicating that this narrative undervalues the work of staff and faculty directors (2013, 52–53). I would like to extend McKinney's argument to include ways that positioning writing centers as comfortable and iconoclastic spaces can unintentionally make the labor of tutors within writing centers less visible and more prone to exploitation. Specifically, when directors position mentoring programs as an "informal" and unpaid expectation, they make the labor of their tutors even less visible—despite their best intentions.

While the term "invisible labor" has traditionally been applied to work that happens outside of employment (Daniels 1987), scholars

DOI: 10.7330/9781646420858.c014

such as those collected in *Invisible Labor: Hidden Work in the Contemporary World* (2016) have noted that current economic structures decrease the visibility of labor even inside places of employment. In the introduction to that collection, Marion Crain, Winifred R. Poster, and Miriam A. Cherry codify this expanded definition of "invisible labor as activities that occur within the context of paid employment that workers perform in response to requirements (either implicit or explicit) from employers and that are crucial for workers to generate income, to obtain or retain their jobs, and to further their careers, yet are often overlooked, ignored, and/or devalued by employers, consumers, workers, and ultimately the legal system itself" (qtd. in Daniels 1987, 6).

As someone who values what happens inside writing centers, I find this trend concerning—especially as I recommend a mentor program for graduate student tutors. I want to be careful as I frame takeaways for other centers and for graduate student practitioners. Even as I seek to demonstrate how creating an overt, intentional mentor program for tutors—specifically one focused on what Mark Hall (2017) has called a "culture of observation" (15)—became central to the training of, and sharing of practice between, graduate student tutors at Saint Louis University, invisible labor and its place in the field of writing center scholarship concern me. Without a significant financial investment, the program I am promoting looks more like exploitation than something I would want a writing center to undertake.

I think there is distinct value in this intensive, observation-based mentoring program. For one, I believe that this kind of mentoring program is one way to close the gap between undergraduate and graduate training models noted by Vicki Behrens and Alex Funt in chapter 15: "Investing in Graduate Tutor Training: A Sustained Approach." Like Behrens and Funt, I believe that the "return" on this kind of "investment" can be substantial. Most important, I contend that the assessment of this mentoring program increased the visibility of the space, the service, *and* the labor of graduate tutors.

Even still, it is easy to imagine a mentoring program that *relies* on the invisibility of graduate student labor, rather than pushing back against this invisibility. Cost cutting in higher education means that we work in environments looking for returns without investment. We cannot pass the cost on to our tutors. Mentoring takes time and effort, for which tutors must be compensated. I find mentoring models that rely on "volunteers," "downtime," and emails occurring after sessions without explicit models for paying for such time—as described in Matthew Klauza's (2010) article "Tutor Training Comes Full Circle:

From E-mail to Practicum and Back Again"—exploitative. That articles about these practices find themselves published in the mainstays of Writing Center scholarship—the *Writing Lab Newsletter* in the case of Klauza's article—makes it clear to me that the informal nature of writing center work, which scholarship has celebrated for so long (Bruffee 1984; Warnock and Warnock 1984; Boquet 2002), can just as easily be exploited by both practitioners and scholars.

A TWIST ON GOOD INTENTIONS

I am not suggesting that all writing center scholarship failing to mention how a mentoring program is funded is part of making the labor of tutors invisible. I acknowledge that the valuation and reimbursement look different across institutional situations. Reading Barbara Jensen's 1996 account of "The Benefits of a Tutor-Mentor Program" in a three-credit tutor-training course, my first instinct is not to be concerned that students receiving credit hours are being exploited. While I have seen writing centers solve budget cuts by offering more training classes to serve the same number of students (effectively turning paid staff positions into unpaid student labor), my concern here is with the sense that mentoring programs for hourly workers, or graduate students on assistantship, can be informal and unpaid. I think scholarship that explicitly involves the labor of tutors should find better ways to acknowledge how the labor of tutors is being valued. I also want to make clear that at Saint Louis University, this valuation meant paying for the time to create and design the program, time to train, time to prepare to observe, time to observe, and time to process the observation. As important, it also meant giving graduate tutors the flexibility to alter their schedules so that they had the freedom to do additional mentoring on a paid basis. Within our scheduling software, tutors could mark their time as "Mentoring" and be paid for that time. As we push for increasing professionalization and training opportunities for graduate students, we must be careful that those opportunities do not become opportunities to exploit those same individuals we are advocating for: A mentoring program is an implicit valuation of graduate student labor that must be made explicit.

I am not questioning the *intentions* of those writing about "informal" mentoring programs in writing center scholarship (Rouse, 1990; Buckley 1999; Zeppetello 2001, Fitzgerald et al. 2009; Klauza 2010). Yet, as Nancy Grimm explains in *Good Intentions: Writing Center Work for Postmodern Times* (1999), "writing centers are places where assimilation into the discursive systems of the university is facilitated" (xvi). A combination of Grimm's observation with Crain, Poster, and Cherry's collection on "invisible labor" might read like this—despite the "good intentions" of a director, the discursive system of the university, as currently constituted, is preparing students to take up roles in an economic system that increasingly demands "invisible labor." Further pacing Grimm, without raising significant awareness about how invisible labor permeates writing centers (and looking for ways to make it visible), directors will more than likely find themselves benefiting from this invisible labor, right along with the university structures they are part of. Writing center scholarship is largely unified about the need for training and mentoring (Gillespie and Lerner 2000; Murphy and Sherwood 2003; Ryan 2002), but it is very often unclear how training and mentorship are paid for. Worse still, it is—at times—quite clear that this work is not paid for.

LOOKING FOR VISIBILITY

The invisibility of graduate student labor within a writing center is heightened when the center is moved outside of an academic department and placed within a student success center. This was the situation I found when I began my job as director. One of the reasons I was hired was to integrate a graduate writing center—which had been entirely run by graduate students within the English Department—into University Writing Services, which had previously only served undergraduate students. While there were several graduate students who had come to feel as though the center was decidedly part of their institutional "home" on campus, this was not a wide-ranging sentiment.

Early on, it seemed clear to me that I needed to create a training program for graduate students that recognized the diversity of their experiences and allowed them to see the value of their own work. The answer my tutors and I came to (and we very much came to it together) was built on (1) mentorship, (2) observation, and (3) assessment. While R. Mark Hall's *Around the Texts of Writing Center Work: An Inquiry-Based Approach* (2017) had not yet been published, what my tutors and I were aiming for was what Hall names "a culture of observation." Like the story Megan Boeshart Burelle and Megan Thompson tell in chapter 18, "An Inquiry-Based Approach for Customizing Training for Graduate Student Tutors," I was setting out to design a new training program. While Burelle and Thompson based their approach directly on Hall's work, the appeal that Hall makes so effectively—building a training program around a local sense of what can be made visible in a tutoring session and seeking to use those observations as an ongoing source of dialogue in the center—speaks directly to what my tutors wanted to see built into the mentoring program.

Like Burelle and Thompson (and Hall), I asked for input about what my tutors felt was happening during their tutoring sessions. Like Hall, we built rubrics, and, like Hall, the process of building these rubrics made my tutors concerned about what it would mean to assess our practice. The process for building our rubrics was different from that proposed by Hall in that we first built observation tracking sheets and then holistic rubrics from their feedback. Where Hall's observation rubrics are analytic rubrics—each criterion is evaluated based on its presence or lack thereof—the rubrics that eventually formed our assessment documents were holistic rubrics. I wish I could say that the choice to create a holistic rubric was deeply intentional. It was not. Instead, it was a product of natural sticking points in a collective writing process: we had a difficult time organizing the information we wanted to collect. Because of this, we created provisional "observation tracking" sheets. Tutors liked these sheets, but they were not meant as a final stopping point in our process. The attempt to organize and evaluate the data collected on the observation tracking sheets pushed us in the direction of a holistic rubric.

"GOOD OBSERVING = GOOD TUTORING"

The value of observing sessions as an important source of training and mentoring was something I did not come to with much intentionality. Having been an assistant director at a very large but very tight-knit center at the University of Illinois at Chicago, I fully expected that tutors would have concerns about a new director. After calling an introductory meeting to get to know the staff, I realized I would need to find another way to meet with every tutor and get a sense of what was happening in the center. With over forty tutors working between three and twenty hours a week, over a seven-day period from 10 AM to 9 PM, in three locations, and on two different campuses, I realized it was going to take me a little while to even meet everyone.

It was at this point that I settled on observing as many tutors as I could in order to really understand what tutoring writing at Saint Louis University looked like. I could tell when I made this announcement that tutors were nervous. I wanted to be systematic and transparent about the observations, though systematic and transparent observations were not part of my previous experience. In fact, I came from a center where we talked a lot about the importance of passively observing tutors—especially tutors who were training to possibly become staff.

There was a sense that observations were something like mock tutoring sessions, never quite real enough to tell you things you really wanted to know about a tutor you were training.

In meetings with tutors after the observations, I found out that much of the methodology that I was seeing was being passed around informally. Tutors who had acted as informal resources for each other, or who had simply worked next to each other, had shared or absorbed strategies that were easily identifiable. When we talked and I asked about specific techniques, tutors would discuss whom they had learned a technique from. It was almost as if there were tutoring trees of influence coming from more experienced tutors. At one point, I tried to sit down and create a kind of map of practice trying to delineate influence upon practice among tutors.

I liked the idea of "tutor trees" and the informal mentorship that created these trees, but I was a little concerned about how haphazard those trees seemed to be. The center had grown so much, and expanded into several smaller satellite locations, that a training model that relied on who sat next to whom during any given shift was eventually going to break down. It was also overly reliant on experienced tutors taking it upon themselves to provide mentorship beyond the scope of their—often hourly—positions. Reflecting back on my decision to observe as many of the tutors as I could in the time that was left in my first semester, I realized that I could have gone a long time just talking to tutors, passively observing, reading session notes, or reading tutors, reflections, and would have had far less understanding of what was actually happening.

This realization, and interviewing graduate student tutors about what they would like to see in a training program, led me to believe that a mentoring program based on observation was the best way to address the separation from their departments that graduate students felt working in the center, the lack of an ongoing training platform, and the lack of a true community of practice outside of informal tutor trees. I felt supported in this decision by returning to Paula Gillespie and Neal Lerner's *The Allyn and Bacon Guide to Peer Tutoring* (2000). A text I had not used in tutor training for quite some time, its chapter "Observing in the Writing Center" literally equates good tutoring with observing: "GOOD OBSERVING = GOOD TUTORING" (58). If there was a relationship between good tutoring and good observing, it seemed as if trying to create a mentoring program that facilitated good observation would be a way to figure out what our center meant by "good tutoring."

The document we first negotiated was an outline of the program. One the most important lines in the document for me was "Mentors will be observed prior to the start of the program so that they have a clear sense of the philosophy Writing Services is hoping to impart." Potential graduate student mentors wanted me to observe them and train them to be observers of sessions. They wanted to ensure they had a model before they were asked to observe. This resulted from concerns that they would be thrust into the role of mentor simply based on seniority, with no experience observing writing consultations, or even experience observing in an educational setting. They wanted to make sure that they were trained on how to observe before they were asked to lead a mentoring relationship based around observation.

The graduate tutors also wanted the mentor program to be an opportunity to create consensus about things they wanted to change about the center. Hence, they wanted a line in the program proposal (which later just became the program outline, with all mentors and mentees receiving a copy) about mentors and mentees asking for trainings they would like to see offered. Tutors wanted to make sure that, if they saw the need for improvement, it was not entirely up to them to know how to make that improvement. They wanted to be able to say, "We saw X, and we have no idea what to do about it." I would then meet with the mentor pairing who were not sure of next steps and possibly create a training for all tutors.

Perhaps the line I was most excited to see make it into the proposal was "Mentors and mentees will create consultation goals to work on for the semester." Tutors wanted to be able to customize what they wanted to focus on for the semester, but they also wanted to make sure the observations were valuable. At a staff meeting, one of the more experienced tutors brought up that bad observing and bad mentoring could look a little like bad peer review; without clear feedback that address the stated concerns of the tutor, the process might feel more rote than valuable.

WHAT ARE WE LOOKING FOR?

We decided there would be three observations each semester with ten hours of additional training for graduate students at the start of each semester. But, we still needed to figure out what we were going to be looking for in these observations. Several staff meetings were dedicated to brainstorming what happens during tutoring sessions. We were looking for shared practices and practices we wanted to reproduce, but we needed to start with listing what we might be able to observe in a consultation. Some of what came up in those meetings were humorous responses to the question. Tutors acknowledged that sometimes they ran late and that their cell phones were a distraction.

Besides a list of tutoring outtakes, what emerged from our discussion was . . . messy. There is a lot that can happen in a consultation with a student. During our brainstorming sessions, phrases such as "inspire writers" were put onto the brainstorming document. We had discussions about what it means to inspire a writer, how you know a writer has been inspired to write something by a consultation, and what it would mean for someone observing a consultation to "see" inspiration. These were important conversations to have, and much of what we left off the list was important to think through. We talked a lot about the need for there to be space for notes on whatever it is that we ended up creating. Tutors wanted to be able to round out the picture of a consultation that would be created for only looking for what was observable. The notes that tutors took sometimes ran to full pages. I even had one tutor who always drew a rough sketch of the physical environment of the consultation.

Before we ended up with two sheets that tutors could be trained how to use, we still had some work to do. Using Google Docs, as well as large and small staff meetings, we were able to winnow our list of observable practices. The list we created was still difficult to organize. There were things we talked about that only made sense to observe if there was some type of counting involved such as of questions and positive comments. There were tutors who wanted questions to relate to the order in which they were most likely to happen during a consultation. We had extensive conversations about making sure we were properly valuing dialogue during consultations.

Finally, we had a list of what we thought our "best practices" looked like. Some of these things worked well on a checklist: getting a writer to write, finding patterns in a writer's writing, getting a writer to demonstrate learning. Other practices were more unwieldy, such as the number of positive comments. Rather than trying to figure out what would need to be eliminated from our list of observable practices, I created an observation sheet that incorporated all the elements that tutors wanted. They would simply be called observation tracking sheets, and they would be the basis for taking notes on the consultation in order to fill out the rubric.

Perhaps the most interesting and quickest change that occurred when we implemented the observation tracking sheets was that reading practices became a hot topic in the center. We spent a lot of time reading to students and reading in really different ways. Trainings were created on reading methods that would allow for tutors to avoid emphasizing errors if asked to read a student's papers aloud. We often stopped reading to address errors as they arose, rather than prioritizing those errors. In reflective documents tutors discussed how they prioritized errors, but that was not what they saw when they observed each other with an eye toward being strengths based and positive. As a result, tutors trained on reading texts without emphasizing error and then going back after having prioritized certain errors.

VALUING LABOR HOLISTICALLY

Hall (2017) makes an argument for observation needing to be more frequent in writing centers to avoid the perception that observation is a "high stakes" endeavor. Even after a semester of low-stakes observation, the idea of creating a rubric was still concerning to tutors. One way of registering the tutors' concerns about rubrics would be to follow Kirsten Komora's (2006) argument in her article "Mock Tutorials: A dramatic method for training tutors." Komora (2006) moves from a fear of traumatizing tutors through observations to eliminating observations and replacing them with "a role-playing session in which the senior tutor visits the Writing Center in the guise of a freshman with a poorly written paper and requests help from a tutor" (12). Setting aside the fact that spending time training tutors to be very good actors would have been a dramatic waste of tutor-training resources in a center where the graduate training program was limited to one day, the tutors were not making an argument akin to Komora's. They did not feel traumatized by the idea of being observed. What they were registering was that rubrics were tools for grading. They were worried about being scored.

The first draft of our rubric certainly did not help their concern with being scored. I had simply marked four categories with the numbers 1 through 4 on the top of the document and then filled them in with standard rubric scoring categories. I did not realize the impact those numbers were having until a staff meeting when I made it clear that the categories themselves were up for discussion. The outpouring of suggestions meant the meeting did not really end. It just flowed into my office. By the time we were done, we had new categories and even a logo for the mentoring program.

What we had decided upon was that since the goal of the rubric was not evaluative, the "meets" category—which became "on target" at the request of the tutors—would be the largest category. It was visually the largest category but also the category we wanted a large number of consultations to fall into. This aim created some difficulty for thinking about how we wanted to score "exceeds" and "outstanding." If the goal was simply to be on target, what would it mean to exceed and be outstanding? The solution we came up with was to have the rubric build from left to right in a fairly unique manner.

If a tutor was doing things that were "off target," even if they did things in the on-target category, the category would be scored as off target. If nothing was highlighted in "off target" and something was circled in "on target," then the category would be scored as "on target." If something was scored in "on target," and "exceeds," then the rubric would be scored as "exceeds." A mentor would need to highlight nothing in "off target," something in "on target," something in "exceeds," and something in "outstanding" for a category on the rubric to be scored as "outstanding."

I would not want to argue that our rubrics should be used in other centers. Quite the contrary, I believe that the development of the rubrics at the local level was responsible for much of their value. Over the course of the three years following the implementation of our mentoring program, visits went up from nearly 4,000 to more than 7,000. The in-year return rate for all students climbed from 29 percent to 50 percent. It became possible to measure the "value" of experienced tutors in relation to practice. Experienced graduate tutors were more likely to be positive with students, more likely to have students write during a consultation, and more likely to help students create a clear plan of action as they left a consultation. These were local findings, and our rubrics were not meant to be model assessment documents outside of our own institution, but the assessment work they allowed for supports the findings of Jo Mackiewicz and Isabelle Kramer Thompson (2014) in their book *Talk about Writing: The Tutoring Strategies of Experienced Writing Center Tutors*. I was able to make a case for defending part-time staff budget lines because of the clear difference experience made in so many of our categories. Two graduate students who were part of the mentor program design and revision are now working on writing center dissertations. Three graduate students now have administrative positions in writing centers.

The rubrics were the most difficult to construct, and they made the tutors more nervous than mentoring or observations with tracking sheets. At the same time, those rubrics became a central training document that became a point of pride for tutors. They also were instrumental in being able to show the value of the work being done in consultations, and they were also the documents we revised each year most thoroughly. We could, in a sense, come to easier consensus on what we were seeing or wanted to see in a tutoring session. Where consensus was more difficult to build was in the scoring of those things. It might not be necessary for a center to take this second step—as Hall does not—to see the benefits of a "culture of observation." At the same time, it was the holistic rubrics that created the most discussion and raised the visibility of the work being done in the center. Yet, that valuation would not be enough if the tutors had not been paid for each step of this process. If refusing to add to the invisibility of the labor occurring within centers means that we knowingly reduce the effectiveness of our centers, that is an outcome we should find ways to become comfortable with.

I believe that one of the reasons that labor within centers can so easily be rendered invisible—and why support for centers is such a consistent issue (Jolly 1984; Summerfield 2001; Schendel and Macauley 2012)—is that, unlike the desire to have students know they *can* be supported in a writing center, there is not widespread understanding of what happens *when* a student is supported in a writing center. That is, there is a general sense that this support should be available but not a specific valuation of the training and skill necessary to support student writing outside the classroom. Training programs are not inherently valued; they are oftentimes concessions that must be to be won or renewed through proposal (Stock 2012). In the meantime, it can seem to a director that some type of "informal" training or mentoring is the best option for a center to improve practices. Yet, the line between "informality" and exploitation is not as bright as it needs to be in writing center scholarship. "Informal" should not act as code for devalued and unpaid.

REFERENCES

Boquet, Elizabeth. 2002. *Noise from the Writing Center*. Logan: Utah State University Press.
Bruffee, Kenneth A. 1984. "Collaborative Learning and the 'Conversation of Mankind.'" *College English* 46 (7): 635–52. https://www.doi.org/10.2307/376924.
Buckley, Liz. 1999. "Distance Mentoring: The Mentoring Is in the Email." *Writing Lab Newsletter* 23 (10): 1–5.
Crain, Marion G., Winifred Poster, and Miriam A. Cherry. 2016. *Invisible Labor: Hidden Work in the Contemporary World*. Oakland: University of California Press.
Daniels, Arlene Kaplan. 1987. "Invisible Work." *Social Problems* 34 (5): 403.
Denny, Harry C. 2010. *Facing the Center: Toward an Identity Politics of One-to-One Mentoring*. Logan: Utah State University Press.
Fitzgerald, Lauren, Natasha Kohl, Liesl Schwabe, and Allison Smith. 2009. "Opening Doors to Diverse Populations—and Keeping Them Open." *Writing Lab Newsletter* 33 (6): 1–5.
Gillespie, Paula, and Neal Lerner. 2000. *The Allyn and Bacon Guide to Peer Tutoring*. Boston: Allyn and Bacon.
Grimm, Nancy. 1999. *Good Intentions: Writing Center Work for Postmodern Times*. Portsmouth, NH: Boynton/Cook.
Hall, R. Mark. 2017. *Around the Texts of Writing Center Work: An Inquiry-Based Approach to Tutor Education*. Utah: Utah State University Press.

Jensen, Barbara. 1996. "The Benefits of a Tutor-Mentor Program." *Writing Lab Newsletter* 21 (2): 11–12.

Jolly, Peggy. 1984. "The Bottom Line: Financial Responsibility." In *Writing Centers: Theory and Administration*, ed. Gary A. Olsen, 101–14. Urbana, IL: National Council of Teachers of English.

Klauza, Matthew D. 2010. "Tutor Training Comes Full Circle: From E-mail to Practicum and Back Again." *Writing Lab Newsletter* 35 (2): 1–5.

Komora, Kirsten. 2006. "Mock Tutorials: A Dramatic Method for Training Tutors." *The Writing Lab Newsletter* 30 (9): 12–15.

Mackiewicz, Jo, and Isabelle Kramer Thompson. 2014. *Talk about Writing : The Tutoring Strategies of Experienced Writing Center Tutors*. New York: Routledge.

McKinney, Jackie Grutsch. 2013. *Peripheral Visions for Writing Centers*. Logan: Utah State University Press.

Murphy, Christina, and Steve Sherwood. 2003. *The St. Martin's Sourcebook for Writing Tutors*. Boston: Bedford/St. Martins.

North, Stephen. 1984. "The Idea of a Writing Center." *College English* 46 (5): 433.

Rouse, Joy. 1990. "Tutor Recruitment and Training at Miami University." *Writing Lab Newsletter* 14 (8): 1–3.

Ryan, Leigh. 2002. *The Bedford Guide for Writing Tutors*. Boston: Bedford/St. Martins.

Schendel, Ellen, and William J. Macauley. 2012. *Building Writing Center Assessments That Matter*. Logan: Utah State University Press.

Summerfield, Judith. 2001. "Writing Centers: A Long View." In *The Allyn and Bacon Guide to Writing Center Theory and Practice*, ed. Robert W. Barnett and Jacob S. Blumner, 22–28. Boston: Allyn and Bacon.

Sunstein, Bonnie S. 1998. "Moveable Feasts, Liminal Spaces: Writing Centers and the State of In-Betweenness." *Writing Center Journal* 18 (2): 7–26.

Warnock, Tilly, and John Warnock. "Liberatory Writing Centers: Restoring Authority to Writers." In *Writing Centers: Theory and Administration*, edited by Gary A. Olson, 16–23. Urbana: NCTE, 1984.

Zeppetello, Joseph. 2001. "Great and Not-So-Great Expectations: Training Faculty and Student Tutors." *Writing Lab Newsletter* 25 (9): 11–14.

15
INVESTING IN GRADUATE TUTOR TRAINING
A Sustained Approach

Vicki Behrens and Alex Funt

In their call for proposals for this collection, Megan Swihart Jewell and Joseph Cheatle note that like faculty and professional tutors, graduate student writing tutors "often do not receive much, if any, formalized preparation." Constraints on time and resources prevent many institutions from investing much in graduate training. As many writers in this collection point out, graduate tutors are also often assumed to have some prior experience with teaching—perhaps even with teaching writing—so in some centers, training graduate students may be viewed as less of a priority than training undergraduates. Whatever the specific reasons may be, in general, graduate tutors tend to receive less formal training, mentoring, and support than do their undergraduate counterparts.

Scholarship on writing centers reflects this disparity. Writing center research has often addressed working with graduate student *writers*, including in a 2016 special edition of *WLN: A Journal of Writing Center Scholarship* that focused on graduate students (Barron and Cicciarelli 2016; Brady and Singh-Corcoran 2016; Chen 2010; Hixson et al. 2016; Lee and Golde 2013; Mannon 2016; Phillips 2013; Radke 2018; Reardon, Deans, and Maykel 2016). But myriad handbooks, guides, and articles regarding tutor training assume a primary audience of undergraduate peer tutors or writing center administrators who are supervising undergraduates (Fitzgerald and Ianetta 2016; Gillespie and Lerner 2000; McAndrew and Reigstad 2001; Rafoth 2000; Ryan and Zimmerelli 2016). While some scholars have addressed graduate tutor training and professional development (Bell 2019; Gillespie 2007; Gillespie, Heidebrecht, and Lamascus 2008; Nicolas 2008; Summers 2016), there have been few recent attempts to document training plans for graduate writing tutors.

We argue here that sustained, intensive training for graduate students can provide enough benefit to outweigh its costs, and we offer our program at the Writing Center at the University of North Carolina at Chapel Hill (UNC-CH) as an example. Our graduate writing tutors (we refer to them as coaches) receive more than 100 hours of training and mentoring over the course of an academic year. This extensive support encourages an atmosphere of experimentation and continuous refinement of skills among the coaching staff that mirrors the atmosphere we strive to create for student writers; it also allows our full-time professional staff to gain better insight into how each coach is progressing. And the Writing Center's reputation for providing excellent professional development helps us to recruit a strong coaching staff from departments across campus, with many coaches choosing to stay on at the Writing Center for multiple years.

In this chapter, we provide an overview of our graduate coach training program and explain how ongoing activities that focus on feedback and reflection, involvement in administration, and building community create an environment in which staff remain engaged while students receive consistently high-quality support. We hope that reading about our experiences may be useful to colleagues in a broad range of writing centers as they develop or expand their own graduate tutor-training programs.

BACKGROUND

Recognizing that institutional contexts vary and afford different opportunities and constraints, we begin by offering a brief description of our context. Our writing center began as an English Department service; the first coaches were English graduate students who were classified as teaching assistants. Our founding director was hired in the mid-1990s as the first full-time professional staff member; since then, she has moved the Center toward serving the entire university and has obtained funding to add full-time professional staff and graduate coach positions, extensive English language support services, and an undergraduate coaching program. During the 2017–18 academic year, the Writing Center coached approximately 3,000 distinct students in approximately 6,000 face-to-face and asynchronous online sessions, as well as offering programs and events such as workshops, write-ins, writing groups, and speaking groups that contributed approximately 10,000 additional hours of student participation.

The Writing Center's student coaching staff now consists of approximately twenty to thirty undergraduate and graduate coaches from majors and degree programs across the university. In recent years, there have generally been about fifteen graduate coaches during the fall and about ten during the spring; the number of undergraduates has fluctuated. Undergraduates take a course that focuses on academic writing and teaching one to one before they are eligible to apply to work at the Writing Center; graduate coaches do not. As Joseph Cheatle and Genie Giaimo point out in chapter 10, graduate students are often kept very busy by the demands of their departments and disciplines and simply "do not have time to complete long and extensive formal training." We have developed a different approach to give graduate coaches a firm foundation in the same pedagogy and practices undergraduates encounter during the course and, as Cheatle and Giaimo note, to "establish a shared common language among all consultants."

Graduate coach training begins with a roughly thirty-hour, week-long "boot camp" just before the start of classes; both new and returning coaches attend. New coaches spend the first few weeks of the semester completing a checklist of activities and readings and joining in sessions with returning coaches. After that, all grad coaches work fifteen consistently scheduled hours per week, one of which is a weekly staff meeting. Because graduate coaches are classified as teaching assistants, they are not paid hourly, as undergraduate coaches are; graduate coaches receive the same stipend, health insurance, and other benefits they would if they were teaching a course. While we have no funds to provide tuition support, teaching in the writing center helps many graduate students meet their home departments' conditions for receiving it. And many coaches continue to work in their home departments while coaching in the Writing Center; the fixed hours make Writing Center positions a popular source of additional income. Starting each year with a group of new graduate students who have competed for their positions and who are excited about making connections outside of their own disciplines influences the character of our graduate coach training program, as well as (we believe) the success of our center. The training practices and values we are about to describe are an important factor in our ability to recruit and retain these excellent graduate students.

FEEDBACK AND REFLECTION

After surveying 164 writing center professionals, Julia Bleakney (2019) found that "reflection is a touchstone of ongoing tutor education." Tutors, Bleakney argues, benefit greatly from "the opportunity to revise or 're-see' their practice" (n.p.). We agree, and feedback and reflection are the foundation of our training. During their fall training week, graduate coaches practice coaching each other at least once a day; a third coach observes each pair and facilitates a postsession discussion. Coaches also engage in reflection activities to learn about themselves as writers, such as creating a metaphor about what writing is like for them, discussing their writing histories, and reflecting on differences in their personal writing processes and disciplinary contexts.

Feedback and reflection continue during the coaches' first weeks on the job. Before working with students one to one, new coaches "co-coach" with experienced colleagues in a similar way to what Dagmar Scharold (2017) recently documented in the *Writing Center Journal*. Where possible, co-coaching sessions are followed by a quick discussion of the choices each coach made while working with the writer and alternative approaches to consider the next time. Megan Boeshart Burelle and Meagan Thompson, in chapter 18, emphasize the benefits of such conversations, pointing out that "dialogue often results in tutors sharing new strategies, resources, and techniques for their colleagues to try." Both new and veteran coaches receive feedback from their colleagues, creating an atmosphere in which observation, feedback, and experimentation are normalized and openly discussed. Co-coaching also helps coaches begin to form a supportive community. While we initially wondered how the student writers who were being coached would respond to co-coaching dynamics, we found that most appreciated having another person to consult.

Throughout the year, coaches continue to work with a list of training activities. These include observing other coaches, watching videos of past sessions, acquainting themselves with the handout and video resources that we use with students, and meeting with staff to try out strategies and resources. In conversation with our English language specialists, coaches also reflect on their history as language learners, complete a grammar resource scavenger hunt activity, and watch a video about writing and cultural differences.

In their discussion of training for new coaches, Cheatle and Giaimo remark in chapter 10 of this collection that "during onboarding, lines of communication ought to be established." Similarly, Burelle and Thompson in chapter 18 recommend "setting up channels of communication between the director and tutors, and between the tutors themselves, so there are chances for tutors to ask about and work through the complicated roles they are asked to inhabit." For Burelle and Thompson, these channels of communication "provide tutors with the ability to collaborate and teach each other, as well as name what they need to know." We agree that open communication is extremely important. Many of our training activities require coaches to share their thoughts and progress on Slack, a team communication app that allows us to organize discussions on various topics, as well as message each other, post announcements, and arrange for shift swaps. All coaches and full-time staff have access to most "channels," which are spaces for designated discussion topics. But private direct messaging and channels restricted to certain subsets of the staff (say, coaches who are working on a project together) are also options.

After their initial training, coaches are together as a large group only during our weekly staff meeting; Slack allows them to maintain their connections and share ideas and experiences. We provide prompts for training-related reflections, but coaches are also welcome to ask for input from their colleagues on any topic. Each week, a coach is responsible for asking the group a question; while discussion topics range widely, examples from this past year included student writing that made coaches uncomfortable, favorite resources, strategies for turning around difficult sessions, and coaches' most dreaded parts of the writing process. Weekly discussions help coaches take a step back from their intense day-to-day work with students and learn from their colleagues' perspectives. While we monitor the discussion channels, we have never had any difficulties with inappropriate conversations; the training coaches receive regarding how to preserve student confidentiality and interact respectfully seems to transfer smoothly to their online interactions.

During the third or fourth week of the semester, each coach has a scheduled, hour-long meeting with our writing coach specialist or another full-time professional staff member to check in about how things are going. The coaches reflect on their strengths and weaknesses, any particularly interesting sessions they have had so far, questions they have about training assignments, and anything else they want to discuss. The meetings typically end with goal setting. These conversations help coaches process their experiences; they also help full-time staff build working relationships with coaches and better understand what types of additional support coaches might need. Similar meetings are scheduled throughout the year, with typically one or two more meetings in the fall and one or two more meetings in the spring. Subsequent meetings are also an opportunity for staff to share feedback.

R. Mark Hall (2017) has pointed out how video recording sessions have the potential to give tutors more control over the observation process (41). Our coaches routinely record their sessions with students using an iPad; they are currently required to capture one video each month. Videos facilitate reflection and conversation by allowing coaches to accurately remember what happened during a session and share key moments with colleagues. Each coach uses a survey form to comment on their own videos and record timestamps of especially effective strategies or moments that warrant further discussion. During a designated staff meeting, coaches watch and reflect on clips that they have selected in small groups and share takeaways with the larger group. One-on-one meetings with staff offer additional opportunities for coaches to review portions of their videos and receive feedback. While coaches are often initially nervous about recording their sessions, we were pleasantly surprised when a survey revealed that a majority of them valued this process because it gave them a self-aware and objective perspective on their coaching, reassured them of what they were doing well, helped them see their progress, and allowed them to observe and improve upon communication dynamics with students. More than half of the staff (eight out of thirteen coaches surveyed) even expressed a preference for video over live observation (Funt and Esposito 2019).

In addition to reflecting on their face-to-face sessions, coaches also receive feedback from one another on their online responses to students, via an activity called "Online Superstars." Coaches are sorted into groups and offer feedback round-robin style to their colleagues using Slack. The central idea is that each coach reads responses written by several others and offers comments on their strengths, shares ideas for improvement, and asks questions about the reactions that the student writers receiving the responses might have had. This process also naturally invites coaches to reflect on the ways in which their own online responses might be improved. The coaches share their takeaways from the exercise in writing on Slack, as well as during a designated staff meeting, and many report borrowing particular strategies that they observed their colleagues using. We recently implemented a similar activity for video recording—"Video Superstars"—in which coaches watch colleagues' video-recorded sessions and offer feedback through Slack on whatever coaching issues the recorded coach asks for (e.g., body language or the implementation of a particular strategy).

INVOLVEMENT IN ADMINISTRATION

Bleakney (2019) reports that in her interviews with writing center directors, many raised the issue of involving tutors in their centers beyond the work of direct tutoring. Examples of such involvement included helping with day-to-day operations, signing up to run staff meetings, sharing their areas of expertise, and creating written materials. Bleakney's survey participants reported that these activities help tutors develop as leaders and increase buy-in and investment. At UNC-CH, graduate writing coaches contribute in critical ways to the operation of the Writing Center. They play a significant part in our outreach, helping to represent us on campus by staffing tables at large campus events, serving on panels, and visiting classrooms to give an overview of our services. And they sometimes organize, as well as participate in, writing-related events such as our biannual "Write Night," which serves more than 100 students each semester and requires considerable coordination and planning.

We take full advantage of graduate coaches' special skills and campus connections. Coaches who have training in working with data help to create reports. A detail-oriented coach might be asked to help inventory our technology; one who is software-savvy might help us explore relevant writing and learning apps (this is how we began using Slack). Coaches who have some hardware expertise do much of the routine maintenance on our computers and serve as liaisons to the university's IT staff. Library science graduate students have helped us work on file architecture and accessibility. One past coach started a collaboration with a local library in which high school students formed a creative writing group. In general, whenever we find ourselves asking, "Hey, does anybody know anything about X?" or "Can anyone do Y?" that question goes out to our coaches, not just our full-time staff.

Graduate coaches also play instructional and mentoring roles within the Writing Center, sharing both their coaching knowledge and their broader expertise with each other. Each returning coach has the opportunity to lead or co-lead a training week session, and all coaches lead or co-lead staff meetings; topics have included working with scientific writers, multimodal composition, mental health, and a variety of other subjects that have been at the intersection of coaches' personal interests and the Writing Center's needs. As Alex Wulff explains in chapter 14 in this collection, tutors are sometimes worried about whether they are prepared to serve as mentors simply because they have tutoring experience, particularly since they may have no formal training in observing others. We attempt to allay such concerns by gathering veteran graduate coaches for a discussion of effective mentoring practices during a portion of the fall training week when new coaches are being introduced to our space and day-to-day operations.

One of our graduate coaches' most enduring contributions to the Writing Center has been the creation of resources. Many of the handouts in our collection of over 100 online resources were written (and later revised) by graduate coaches. In some cases, coaches write about their own disciplines or areas of expertise; in others, they research a topic such as writing anxiety or procrastination and share what they learn. While full-time staff work closely with coaches and make the final editorial decisions regarding the materials on the site, the handouts are very much a product of graduate students' efforts and a source of pride for their authors.

Involving coaches in the center's administration has lent a more collaborative and less "top down" feel to our training and professional development. There is a sense of freshness, energy, and variety to our trainings because they are not all coming from the full-time staff and because the approaches, styles, and interests of our coaches vary from year to year. Involving the coaches in program administration has also established a culture of teaching, learning, and growth that mirrors the work that we do with students. As Burelle and Thompson note in chapter 18, "view tutoring as a form of valuable professional development rather than just a job or assistantship."

The opportunity to contribute to the Writing Center in a variety of ways, and in considerable depth, has also been of benefit to our coaching staff in the longer term. One graduate coach decided to leave her master's program in English for the world of IT after volunteering to try to help create a computerized file management system for the Writing Center; she is now a director in University of North Carolina at Chapel Hill's Teaching and Learning division. Another, a historian who acquired tech skills and administrative experience as one of three graduate co-directors during a year when the director was on leave, directs a teaching and learning lab at Harvard. And a third, who took on an administrative role as a graduate mentor, is now a full-time academic coaching and data specialist at the UNC-CH Learning Center, using both his coaching expertise and his knowledge of statistics. Directors dedicate the final staff meeting of each year to a discussion of how skills and traits developed at the Writing Center can be used and marketed both within and beyond academia.

We believe that while both undergraduate and graduate tutors benefit from considering how to apply their writing center experience in the wider world, graduate coaches in particular deserve our help in developing skills that will serve them in a variety of professions. As David Ball, William Gleason, and Nancy Peterson point out, while tenure-track jobs have traditionally been the goal of graduate education in many fields, "the reality is that an increasing number of doctoral students, sometimes because of personal interest and often because of the reality of a constricted academic job market, have already begun to look at their careers more broadly" (2015, 109). Writing Center work, and similar forms of training, helps graduate students "develop relevant job experience and . . . learn to see university and academic culture from a broad perspective—qualities essential for a successful alt-ac job search" (112). We are hopeful that our training may benefit coaches long after they have left our center.

COMMUNITY

Involving coaches in the Writing Center's administration also helps to create the strong sense of community, one of our most important goals. We begin with the shared experience of training week, one day of which is devoted to a "challenge course" visit in which coaches and staff play team-building games, reflect on group dynamics, brave ziplines, and generally get to know each other better. While devoting a full day to a challenge course might appear to be inefficient, we have found that it builds community in a way that is invaluable. We are grateful to have the resources to provide such an experience for our coaches, and we find that the event communicates right from the start that we are all on the same team and can depend on one another.

As we described earlier, Slack is an important forum for facilitating training and reflection on coaching—but with our staff spread over a range of hours and working in multiple locations, it also plays a useful role in keeping us all in touch. We encourage participation by immediately introducing coaches to Slack: we post all announcements there, use the direct messaging feature to communicate with individual coaches, and ask them to manage their shift swaps there. Coaches can even show off pictures of their children and pets. Since we began tracking stats in May of 2016, approximately 80,000 messages and 1,500 files have been exchanged on Slack among full-time staff as well as between coaches. Slack has significantly expanded our communication, especially across locations, and enabled quick questions and exchanges that are not always possible in person.

Beyond Slack, our graduate coaches support each other both informally and through shared activities. One such activity is a friendly competition we call "Try 'Em." In 2011, a coach had the idea of using "chore charts" as inspiration for encouraging everyone to try different coaching strategies during sessions. Each spring, we make a chart that is displayed in the front of the Writing Center with things to try on one axis and coach names on the other axis. Strategies might include switching seats with a student, working at a table rather than in a cubicle, using an online tool such as mind-mapping software, or helping a student cut up a draft and rearrange the sentences. All coaches are invited to give input as to what strategies are featured. When a coach completes a "Try 'Em," they put a sticker next to their name, and when the row is full, they receive a small prize. This activity makes coaches publicly accountable to their peers, and it encourages experimentation at a point in the year when stagnation is a risk, especially for veteran coaches.

Our sense of community is enhanced when we each play a role in maintaining our shared space. We have a long-standing system in which coaches volunteer to take on different responsibilities to benefit the group. Each coach can make up a name for their special role—so, for example, the "Time Lord" is in charge of keeping all of the clocks in sync, the "Marquis of Markerboards" makes sure the whiteboards are clean and the markers are working, and the "Defender of the Library" fights the chaos on our bookshelves. The "Birthday Fairy" (the current holder of the office refers to himself as "Father Time") plays a particularly important role in making sure each person receives a card that the rest of us have signed. Coaches also help to take out the recycling, clean dusty desks, run updates on computers, wipe flash drives, wrangle the copier and coffee maker, assess our stock of supplies, and other office tasks. Staff never ask coaches to do anything that we do not also routinely do ourselves, but we do frequently request their help—which both keeps our center running smoothly and lets all workers know they have an important part to play.

Finally, we sustain community by creating opportunities to have fun together both at and outside of work. Our last staff meeting each year is "Waffle Day": everyone brings in waffle irons, batter, ingredients, and toppings, and we spend an hour cooking and eating together. We have taken groups to visit two local animal sanctuaries, the Carolina Tiger Rescue and the Duke Lemur Center. We recently held a movie night in which coaches and their friends and partners gathered in the Writing Center and pulled our furniture into a comfortable configuration so they could eat popcorn and watch *Arrival* together. Last semester, the staff visited a farm to pet baby goats, carve pumpkins, and eat ice cream. Leaders among the coaches typically plan these events. While these adventures are not training, per se, much like our day at the challenge course before the start of the fall semester, they help to create an atmosphere that facilitates learning.

CONCLUSION

While the training, support, and community building the UNC-CH Writing Center provides for graduate coaches consumes a considerable amount of time and energy for both coaches and staff, we have seen that this is a worthwhile investment. Our high-quality services and resources benefit student writers and our campus as a whole. Our graduate coach "alumni" have gone on to found and lead writing centers and use all that they have learned about students, teaching, and writing in academic positions; many report that they believe their writing center experience was what made them stand out on the job market. And the satisfaction of working in depth with, and forming ongoing relationships with, these exceptional graduate students helps us retain our full-time staff.

Our professional staff have stayed in touch with many former coaches. In a survey modeled after the work of Harvey Kael, Paula Gillespie, and Bradley Hughes's Peer Writing Tutor Alumni Research Project (Kael, Gillespie, and Hughes 2010), we contacted graduate coach alumni who graduated from 1995 to 2015. Fifty-two out of sixty (86.67%) coaches who responded rated the importance of their writing center training and experiences to their development as graduate students as "highly important." Only two described their training as "unimportant." One former coach summarized the prevailing sentiment by saying, "It is simply a shame that all graduate students, particularly those in writing-heavy disciplines, can't have this same in-depth level of training." If our experience is any guide, a greater emphasis on graduate writing tutor training would be an excellent investment for individual writing centers, their institutions, and the writing center profession. We encourage other practitioners to consider how they might promote feedback and reflection, involvement in administration, and community for the mutual benefit of their graduate tutors and their writing centers, in the ways that best align with their institutional contexts and missions.

REFERENCES

Ball, David, William Gleason, and Nancy Peterson. 2015. "From All Sides: Rethinking Professionalization in a Changing Job Market." *Pedagogy* 15 (1): 103–18.

Barron, Paul, and Louis Cicciarelli. 2016. "Tutors' Column: 'Stories and Maps: Narrative Tutoring Strategies for Working with Dissertation Writers.'" *WLN: A Journal of Writing Center Scholarship* 40 (5–6): 26–30.

Bell, Katrina. 2019. "Our Professional Descendants: Preparing Graduate Writing Consultants." In *How We Teach Writing Tutors: A WLN Digital Edited Collection*, edited by Karen Johnson, Ted Roggenbuck, and Crystal Conzo, n.p. WLN: A Journal of Writing Center Scholarship. https://wlnjournal.org/digitaleditedcollection1/Bell.html.

Bleakney, Julia. 2019. "Ongoing Writing Tutor Education: Models and Practices." In *How We Teach Writing Tutors: A WLN Digital Edited Collection*, edited by Karen Johnson, Ted

Roggenbuck, and Crystal Conzo, n.p. https://wlnjournal.org/digitaleditedcollection1/Bleakney.html.

Brady, Laura, and Nathalie Singh-Corcoran. 2016. "A Space for Change: Writing Center Partnerships to Support Graduate Writing." *WLN: A Journal of Writing Center Scholarship* 40 (5–6): 2–10.

Chen, Cheryl Wei-yu. 2010. "Graduate Students' Self-Reported Perspectives Regarding Peer Feedback and Feedback from Writing Consultants." *Asia Pacific Education Review* 11 (2): 151–58.

Fitzgerald, Lauren, and Melissa Ianetta. 2016. *The Oxford Guide for Writing Tutors: Practice and Research*. New York: Oxford University Press.

Funt, Alex, and Sarah Miller Esposito. 2019. "Video Recording in the Writing Center." *WLN: A Journal of Writing Center Scholarship* 43 (5–6): 2–10.

Gillespie, Paula. 2007. "Graduate Writing Consultants for PhD Programs Part 1: Using What We Know: Networking and Planning." *Writing Lab Newsletter* 32 (2): 1–6.

Gillespie, Paula, Paul Heidebrecht, and Lorelle Lamascus. 2008. "From Design to Delivery: The Graduate Writing Consultant Course (Part 2)." *The Writing Lab Newsletter* 32 (8): 8–11.

Gillespie, Paula, and Neal Lerner. 2000. *The Allyn and Bacon Guide to Peer Tutoring*. Boston: Allyn & Bacon.

Hall, R. Mark. 2017. *Around the Texts of Writing Center Work: An Inquiry-Based Approach to Tutor Education*. Logan: Utah State University Press.

Hixson, Cory, Walter Lee, Deirdre Hunter, Marie Paretti, Holly Matusovich, and Rachel McCord. 2016. "Understanding the Structural and Attitudinal Elements That Sustain a Graduate Student Writing Group in an Engineering Department." *WLN: A Journal of Writing Center Scholarship* 40 (5–6): 18–26.

Kael, Harvey, Paula Gillespie, and Bradley Hughes. 2010. "What They Take with Them: Findings from the Peer Writing Tutor Alumni Research Project." *Writing Center Journal* 30 (2): 12–46.

Lee, Sohui, and Chris Golde. 2013. "Completing the Dissertation and Beyond: Writing Centers and Dissertation Boot Camps." *Writing Lab Newsletter* 37 (7–8): 1–5.

Mannon, Bethany Ober. 2016. "What Do Graduate Students Want from the Writing Center? Tutoring Practices to Support Dissertations and Thesis Writers." *Praxis: A Writing Center Journal* 13 (2): 59–64.

McAndrew, Donald A., and Thomas J. Reigstad. 2001. *Tutoring Writing: A Practical Guide for Conferences*. Portsmouth, NH: Boynton/Cook Publishers.

Nicolas, Melissa, ed. 2008. *(E)merging Identities: Graduate Students in the Writing Center*. Southlake, TX: Fountainhead Press.

Phillips, Tallin. 2013. "Tutor Training and Services for Multilingual Graduate Writers: A Reconsideration." *Praxis: A Writing Center Journal* 10 (2): 1–7.

Radke, Chuck. 2018. "A Space for Grad Students: Peer-to-Peer Collaboration in a Writing Studio Startup." *WLN: A Journal of Writing Center Scholarship* 42 (7–8): 10–17.

Rafoth, Bennett A., ed. 2000. *A Tutor's Guide: Helping Writers One to One*. Portsmouth, NH: Boynton/Cook Publishers.

Reardon, Kristina, Tom Deans, and Cheryl Maykel. 2016. "Finding a Room of Their Own: Programming Time and Space for Graduate Student Writing." *WLN: A Journal of Writing Center Scholarship* 40 (5–6): 10–18.

Ryan, Leigh, and Lisa Zimmerelli. 2016. *The Bedford Guide for Writing Tutors*. 6th ed. Boston: Bedford / St. Martin's.

Scharold, Dagmar. 2017. "'Challenge Accepted': Cooperative Tutoring as an Alternative to One-to-One Tutoring." *Writing Center Journal* 36 (2): 31–55.

Summers, Sarah. 2016. "Building Expertise: The Toolkit in UCLA's Graduate Writing Center." *Writing Center Journal* 35 (2): 117–45.

16

DISCIPLINARY AMBASSADORS IN THE GRADUATE WRITING CENTER

A Professional Development Framework for Graduate Consultants from Diverse Fields

Kristin Messuri

Writing centers have been described as "interdisciplinary and cultural contact zones," multifaceted spaces where different disciplines, discursive practices, and cultures interact (Monty 2016, 12). Graduate writing centers (GWCs), defined here as centers primarily staffed by graduate-level consultants who serve graduate-level writers, are particularly complex contact zones. Graduate students have acquired extensive discipline-specific content knowledge but are still developing their professional identities. Both graduate consultants (GCs) and the graduate writers they serve must produce complex, high-stakes writing projects while acculturating to academic communities whose unwritten rules are often unintuitive and contradictory. The non-discipline-specific GWC, in particular, is one of only a few institutional spaces designed to facilitate interactions between graduate students from different disciplines. These complicated interpersonal dynamics are influenced by disciplinarity, among other factors, as discussed by Elise Dixon and Cassie Brownell as well as Marcus Weakley and Mark Pedretti in chapters 13 and 9, respectively.

Because GCs are asked to interact with advanced disciplinary texts and the experts-in-training who produce them, GCs represent a challenging case in the debate surrounding the effectiveness of specialist consultants, who have disciplinary knowledge relevant to the consultation, versus generalist consultants, who lack such knowledge. Scholars have recognized the centrality of discipline-specific knowledge to graduate writers' work. Talinn Phillips (2013), for example, identifies it as the bedrock of a holistic approach to engaging with graduate writers' texts, specifically in the context of consultations with multilingual writers. Discussions of field-specific graduate writing initiatives, such as

DOI: 10.7330/9781646420858.c016

GWCs and embedded fellows programs, have shown how shared disciplinary knowledge has helped GCs successfully support graduate writers (Gillespie 2007; Gillespie, Heidebrecht, and Lamascus 2008; Simpson et al. 2015; Snively 2008). These results corroborate research performed in undergraduate contexts, in which knowledge of the discipline or genre allowed consultants to facilitate more robust, effective consultations (Dinitz and Harrington 2014; Gordon 2014; Walker 1998).

However, generalist consultations may also provide graduate writers with valuable feedback, especially regarding clarity and language usage, from a nonspecialist perspective (Mannon 2016). In practice, GCs negotiate both generalist and specialist roles during consultations with graduate writers (Snively 2008; Summers 2016). Since "the notion of disciplinary expertise is . . . fluid and relational," GCs and graduate writers alternately inhabit positions of expertise and inexperience in their interactions (Summers 2016, 128). Taken as a whole, this body of scholarship demonstrates the need for GCs to navigate often-idiosyncratic disciplinary-specific writing genres and complex subject matter while drawing on common consultation strategies to meet graduate writers' needs.

This chapter will present a theoretical framework for professional development that engages GCs' experiences of writing in their home disciplines and invites them to act as disciplinary ambassadors—that is, experts in their disciplines who understand how disciplinary knowledge shapes their identities as writers and who are familiar with writing practices and conventions in other disciplines. The framework is based on the consultant training and professional development curriculum of the Texas Tech University (TTU) GWC. The GWC's consultants featured in this chapter are both GCs and professional consultants with master's or doctoral degrees in their fields. While this chapter focuses on GCs, the learning opportunities and intellectual exchanges afforded by this framework are also applicable to professional and faculty consultants, who may have more established professional identities but could still benefit from examining how their disciplinary backgrounds inform their consulting practices.

This framework is significantly different from other GC professional development models. Despite the complexity of graduate writers' work, researchers have documented a lack of specialized training for consultants working with other graduate students (Phillips 2013; Summers 2016). Several scholars provide valuable insight into consultations on specific genres, such as Elizabeth Festa's account, chapter 17, of a training initiative for GCs working with graduate writers developing proposals for a prestigious fellowship program. Consultations for thesis and dissertation writers have also received attention (Mannon 2016). In addition to addressing specific genres, scholars have described preparing GCs or fellows embedded in specific departments or schools, initiatives that implicitly depend on shared disciplinary knowledge (Gillespie, Heidebrecht, and Lamascus 2008; Simpson et al. 2015). Although these strategies are effective for targeted genres or programs, they cannot be generalized as a professional development framework in the context of a non-discipline-specific GWC. I follow Catherine Savini (2011) in training consultants and, by extension, writers to "actively investigate unfamiliar disciplines" during consultations (4). However, the framework proposed here extends beyond the individual GC's disciplinary knowledge and the context of the writing consultation. Rather, this framework invites the entire GWC staff to engage in an ongoing, collaborative, multidisciplinary dialogue to develop a more holistic body of shared knowledge.

DISCIPLINARY AMBASSADORS: A FRAMEWORK

In a non-discipline-specific GWC, graduate writers' need for discipline-specific writing support almost certainly eclipses the staff's knowledge of writing in the disciplines (WID). Therefore, this professional development framework leverages GCs' experiences of writing in their home disciplines and invites them to act as disciplinary ambassadors. I use the term "ambassador" here because the writing consultant is bringing disciplinary writing knowledge to the larger GWC staff, thereby contributing to the group's knowledge of writing in different fields. The GWC becomes what Jean Lave and Etienne Wenger (1991) have termed a "community of practice," where individuals interact in "an activity system about which participants share understandings concerning what they are doing and what that means in their lives and communities" (98). Like Anne Geller et al. (2007) and Cheatle and Giaimo (in chapter 10), I find this term to be an apt description for writing centers. I believe writing center practitioners can use the proposed framework to build such communities, as the knowledge that disciplinary ambassadors develop is socially constructed and relational. Furthermore, disciplinary ambassadors carry their experiences in the GWC to their home departments and disciplines. In this sense, they become "writing center ambassadors" in those communities of practice.

In their writing center work, GCs represent their disciplines insofar as they are drawing on their experiences and knowledge of writing conventions and articulating them in a way scholars from other fields can understand. Although we must recognize the limitations of having an individual or small group "stand in" for an entire field, disciplinary ambassadors give a voice to each represented discipline in the GWC. Implicit in this framework is the case for recruiting and hiring GCs from across the university, which may be dependent on local circumstances, particularly funding sources. However, GCs in every discipline are deeply immersed in highly specialized fields, dynamics that writing center practitioners can replicate even in a staff from a single academic department. For example, a GWC staffed by GCs from an English department may still have disciplinary ambassadors from rhetoric and composition, linguistics, and literature, subfields whose research and writing conventions vary widely. There may be benefits to employing the disciplinary ambassador framework in discipline-specific writing centers, where GCs are likely to engage with the professional community they will fully join after graduation.

Graduate writers from all disciplines, including GCs, often have a strong grasp of the content they mean to convey but may not be able to assess and respond to the complex rhetorical situations posed by unfamiliar discourse communities. Most academic programs—including those in English, writing studies, and rhetoric and composition—provide very limited to no writing support or training at the graduate level (Aitchison and Lee 2006; Aitchison and Paré 2016; Micciche and Carr 2011). Instead, graduate writers may feel that they are expected to learn to write highly complex scholarly texts by "osmosis" with little or no writing-related training (Micciche and Carr 2011, 479; Shapiro 2015, 2). Therefore, GCs may not have explicit knowledge of writing conventions and practices in their disciplines. Moreover, GCs may not conceptualize writing (especially "academic" writing) in the same ways as writers in other disciplines and, further, may be unaware of their assumptions. As Charles Bazerman (2015) notes, writers who are "deeply embedded in a set of writing practices associated with their profession or career," as graduate-level writers often are, may unreflexively assume "that what they learn in that specific context are general rules and models for effective writing" (37). Discussions of WID provide the entire staff with opportunities to examine their assumptions about writing. One goal of GC professional development should be to help them concretize and articulate their understandings of, and experiences with, writing in their home disciplines. Christopher LeCluyse and Sue Mendelsohn (2008) encourage writing center administrators to ask of GCs, "What are their interests and academic specialties? What assumptions about their professional personae and writing do they bring to the job?" (104). This line of questioning is expanded in the disciplinary ambassador framework, which relies on reflective practice and interaction among GCs and, through consultations, graduate writers from different disciplines.

Graduate students' development of discipline-specific writing knowledge is inextricable from their development of professional identities. Mary Jane Curry (2016) has defined writing as "disciplinary becoming," that is, "a means of developing and displaying an identity as a scholar, researcher, or other professional" (80). By definition, graduate students occupy a liminal space: they are not faculty members, but they engage in high-level research and teaching. Graduate consultants take these multifaceted identities into the GWC, where "graduate students . . . can and often do occupy the roles of client, tutor, and administrator, conceivably even within the same day" (Nicolas 2008, 3–4). Consultations allow GCs and graduate writers opportunities to practice professional identities as they engage with discipline-specific writing (Summers 2016). I believe professional development initiatives provide similar opportunities. As disciplinary ambassadors, GCs are asked to adopt positions of authority by discussing writing conventions in their home disciplines with writing center colleagues. In such interactions, GCs both articulate their knowledge of disciplinary writing and are encouraged to question the assumptions underlying those practices. For example, STEM writers may be surprised to learn that first-person pronouns are often employed by writers in the humanities, and humanities writers may be stymied by the Introduction, Methods, Results, and Discussion (IMRaD) structure common to many science disciplines. Graduate consultants do not always recognize the context- and discipline-specific nature of their knowledge until such interchanges occur.

The final element of the disciplinary ambassador framework is the writing center practitioner, who acts as the disciplinary ambassador for writing center studies, tasked with introducing GCs to our discipline's values, conceptualizations of writing, and pedagogy. Writing center practitioners may come from a variety of disciplinary backgrounds, which would help them implement the disciplinary ambassador framework. In the context of GC professional development, the practitioner, like the GCs, draws on disciplinary knowledge to introduce GCs to the field of writing center studies. In theorizing writing center studies as a discipline with its own history and discourse community (Monty 2016) and incorporating threshold concepts from the broader field of writing studies (Adler-Kassner and Wardle 2016), the writing center practitioner acts as a disciplinary ambassador, making these issues concrete and relevant for GCs from all disciplines. This knowledge allows GCs to draw on writing studies principles during consultations, either implicitly or explicitly.

Weakley and Pedretti (chapter 9) found that articulating such principles to graduate writers may help GCs mitigate disparities in discipline, degree levels, and seniority. In the GWC under study, GCs have been enthusiastic about joining this community of practice and are quick to identify writing conventions, areas of research, and values that overlap with their own. These interdisciplinary exchanges have the potential to enrich both GCs' education and the field of writing center studies.

Although the disciplinary ambassador framework is beneficial, there are some challenges to enacting it. As noted above, institutional structures and local circumstances may limit the ability to recruit and hire graduate students from a variety of disciplines. Limits on graduate student workloads may also prevent those with research or teaching assignments in their home departments from also working in the writing center. Or, such conditions may mean that GCs can only work very limited hours, minimizing their ability to consult with graduate writers and engage in professional development. In other cases, academic culture may dissuade graduate students from seeking appointments with writing consultants; graduate students, faculty, and administrators may not see the value in writing center work or may feel that students in some disciplines are less qualified to pursue such work. The disciplinary ambassador framework may address some of these assumptions, as it demonstrates the value of discipline-specific writing support. Moreover, the treatment of writing as peripheral in many disciplines or institutional contexts—another assumption that disciplinary ambassadors challenge—may also increase GCs' need for professional development. Graduate consultants from all disciplines benefit from discussions of writing, but those who have not received writing pedagogy training may have difficulty identifying or explaining writing issues in a way that graduate writers can easily understand.

Like any writing center initiative, this approach to GC professional development must be adapted to fit local circumstances. In the section below, I describe how the TTU GWC enacts this framework in order to offer one example of how it can be put into practice. Writing center practitioners may wish to use this model as a starting point when building GC professional development that fits the needs of their staff, writers, and institutional contexts.

"DISCIPLINARY AMBASSADOR" PROFESSIONAL DEVELOPMENT ARTIFACTS

In this section, I describe how the disciplinary ambassador framework is put into practice in the TTU GWC. This center has employed consultants from disciplines as diverse as atmospheric sciences, English literature, natural resources management, and theater and dance, among many others. To better respond to the needs of a disciplinarily diverse staff, the TTU GWC has formalized and expanded its professional development practices. Positioning GCs as disciplinary ambassadors now forms the theoretical framework for this GWC's professional development curriculum.

To enact this curriculum, the TTU GWC employs a multipronged approach involving the training strategies Summers (2006) identifies as being common to other GWCs: asking new consultants to observe more experienced consultants and vice versa, requiring new consultants to read training materials aimed at university writing center tutors (e.g., *The Bedford Guide for Writing Tutors*), and holding in-service meetings. I understand these activities as part of a larger constellation of professional development practices and opportunities available to GCs specifically because of their positions as disciplinary ambassadors. In the TTU GWC, weekly in-service meetings—or colloquia, as we call them—act as the primary site of professional development. In colloquium, the TTU GWC staff gathers to compare experiences from consultations, learn from guest speakers, and discuss assigned readings. Between colloquia, GCs are often asked to engage in reflective writing, which they then post in an online forum so that they can read and comment on one another's responses. Colloquia, the attendant readings, and writings are intended to promote a collaborative learning environment in which each GC can take on the role of disciplinary ambassador by engaging in a dialogue about their writing experiences. As disciplinary ambassadors from writing center studies, GWC administrators also participate in all activities and writing prompts, providing them with another avenue for professional development as they encounter new information about WID and explore their own experiences with writing. This participatory framework also promotes a democratic structure, as it does not privilege any one discipline's epistemologies or writing practices.

In the sections below, I include selected artifacts from the TTU GWC's ever-evolving professional development curriculum. Although these descriptions are merely examples of possible professional development activities, they demonstrate how a GWC might provide opportunities for GCs to act as experts interacting with other experts. Note that while the materials below emphasize cross-disciplinary interactions, GCs are also asked to read writing center scholarship. I believe the disciplinary ambassador framework allows GCs to take more nuanced approaches to discussions of consultation techniques, writers' autonomy and authority, social justice, and other topics common to writing center research.

Disciplinary Self-Assessment

Although most GCs have years of experience reading and writing in their disciplines, they may not recognize the degree to which their disciplinary backgrounds inform their approaches to writing consultations. Early in the academic year, GCs are asked to complete a "disciplinary self-assessment," a reflective writing activity in which they examine and concretize their understanding of writing in their discipline. This writing prompt frames later discussions about WID and encourages GCs to openly consider and discuss their individual experiences as writers in different disciplines.

Writing prompt: Describe your experiences as a writer in your home discipline. This writing activity is meant to be reflective and therefore subjective. You need not research writing in your discipline; instead, you may simply discuss your understandings and experiences.

You can approach this writing prompt as you see fit, but you may wish to consider the following questions:
- How does your field conceptualize writing? (How do members of your field talk about writing? How do they understand the relationship between writing and research, the writing process, etc.? What are their assumptions, values, and beliefs with regard to writing?)
- Which writing genres are most common to your field?
- How would you describe the tone and voice typical of writing in your field?
- How does your field use evidence, and which forms of evidence are appropriate?
- How do authors in your field establish credibility as scholars?
- How does your identity as a writer in your discipline influence your consultations?

Asking GCs to identify and describe their experiences with, and understanding of, writing helps them to make their implicit knowledge about writing in their home discipline more explicit. In doing so, they come to better understand their knowledge, background, and assumptions about academic writing. The assignment also exposes GCs to conventions of writing in multiple disciplines. They may or may not be able to draw on this specific knowledge in a consultation, but they will become more cognizant of how widely approaches to academic writing may vary, even when scholars from different disciplines write within the same genre.

Disciplinary Ambassador Reflection

Once GCs have gained experience both engaging in conversations about disciplinary writing and consulting with graduate writers, it is useful for them to reflect on how their understanding of writing and of writing center work has developed. This prompt acts as a counterpart to the disciplinary self-assessment, as it asks GCs to inhabit the roles of both disciplinary ambassador and "writing center ambassador"—a writer with discipline-specific expertise in writing center studies whose knowledge of that field informs their practices as both GCs and scholars in their home disciplines.

Writing prompt: This reflective writing activity builds on your prior writing about disciplinary knowledge and literacy, especially the Disciplinary Self-Assessment. Return to your first self-assessment and reevaluate your thinking and conceptualization of writing in your discipline.

Consider the following questions:
- How has your understanding of writing in your field changed or remained the same as a result of your work in the GWC?
- How have you developed as a writer as a result of this work?
- How have you drawn on your expertise as a writer in your discipline during consultations with graduate writers?
- How might you draw on your GWC experience to be a "writing center ambassador" to others in your discipline, the university, and the broader community?

Emphasizing GCs' growth as disciplinary ambassadors allows them to reframe their GWC work as writing center ambassadors. Taking on a new (secondary) disciplinary affiliation encourages them to synthesize their experiences and place them in the context of larger communities both within and beyond the university.

Developing a Disciplinary Ambassadors Curriculum

In the TTU GWC, specific assignments, readings, outreach opportunities, and other professional development activities are constantly being adapted to fit our ever-changing needs. The disciplinary ambassador framework is dynamic enough to be adapted to a number of circumstances. In the TTU GWC, we consider the following goals when planning professional development curricula:

- Help GCs make their implicit knowledge about writing, especially in their home discipline, more explicit
- Facilitate GCs' understanding of how their identities as writers from specific disciplines inform their work in the writing center, particularly in interactions with graduate writers
- Learn collaboratively about the conventions of writing in multiple disciplines

Writing center practitioners may wish to consider these concepts as starting points when planning their own disciplinary ambassador activities or curricula. Regardless of how writing center practitioners choose to enact this framework, they should consider documenting GCs' contributions to the group's knowledge so that they persist after their time in the GWC ends. Committing this information to institutional memory is especially important, as GCs in many disciplines can only spend a semester or two in the GWC before moving back to their home departments. Over time, this framework presents the opportunity for practitioners to develop a rich understanding of WID and a more tangible collection of related resources for their communities of practice.

EMPOWERING GCS AND GRADUATE WRITERS, ENRICHING GWCS

The disciplinary ambassador framework allows GCs to better respond to the sociorhetorical complexities of graduate writers and their texts. In doing so, GCs themselves are asked to examine and articulate knowledge about writing in their home disciplines and to reflect on their own writing experiences and practices. When GCs interact with writers in other disciplines—both their fellow GCs and other graduate student writers—they can better understand their personal and disciplinary epistemologies regarding writing. Since asking questions about WID is so central to GCs' professional development, they become more adept at asking graduate writers about their writing projects and disciplinary writing conventions. Ultimately, this approach has the potential to help GCs empower graduate writers to make important decisions about how to intervene and participate in academic discourse.

Moreover, consultations provide both GCs and graduate writers with what Claire Aitchison and Anthony Paré (2012) have termed "regular authentic opportunities to learn about the kinds of writing they need to master" by participating in a writing-focused community—in this case, in the GWC (23). Consultations provide an opportunity for graduate writers to embody the position of disciplinary expert as they explain their research verbally and through writing. They practice professionalism in an environment with lower stakes and often more support than an academic conference, a job interview, or even a seminar. This culture of cross-disciplinary exchanges benefits graduate writers, who have their own discipline-specific writing practices and professional identities. In consultations, the cross-disciplinary interaction between GCs and graduate writers is especially powerful because writing is the primary means of communication in all academic disciplines. This environment, as Elise Dixon and Cassie Brownell note in chapter 13, also allows GCs and graduate writers to develop the types of professional relationships they may wish to build as faculty. The social dynamics of the consultation are, in many ways, as significant as discussions of the text.

Most GCs will not pursue careers in writing center administration, but they will carry the skills they honed in the GWC beyond its walls. This cross-disciplinary approach to professional development encourages GCs to be more self-aware communicators and, in turn, equips them to engage with others who have different backgrounds, values, and knowledge. GCs who go on to academic jobs will be better prepared to help their students develop strong written communication skills. Those who seek work in other sectors can apply their communication and collaboration skills to those professional contexts. In other words, GCs can transfer these communication skills and practices to act as "writing center ambassadors" in future communities of practice.

The disciplinary ambassador framework has the potential to enrich not only GCs, but also the larger GWC, especially as it establishes a multidisciplinary community of graduate writers (including GCs). In the TTU GWC, positioning GCs as experts has empowered them to take greater ownership of their own professional development and other aspects of writing center work. Evidence of this shift includes the development of several consultant-led initiatives that have grown from their increased abilities to assess their own needs as well as those of their fellow graduate writers. For example, GCs proposed, organized, and now run drop-in writing groups, thereby growing the network of GCs and graduate writers from many fields who identify themselves as part of our writing community. In addition to these innovations, the development of a multidisciplinary staff helps build campus partnerships, facilitates the recruitment of future GCs from represented departments, and increases the visibility of the GWC within the institution. Ultimately, engaging GCs in professional development using the disciplinary ambassador framework has the potential to promote a more robust culture of writing on campus.

REFERENCES

Adler-Kassner, Linda, and Elizabeth Wardle, eds. 2016. *Naming What We Know: Threshold Concepts of Writing Studies.* Logan: Utah State University Press.

Aitchison, Claire, and Alison Lee. 2006. "Research Writing: Problems and Pedagogies." *Teaching in Higher Education* 11 (3): 265–78. https://doi.org/10.1080/13562510600680574.

Aitchison, Claire, and Anthony Paré. 2016. "Writing as Craft and Practice in the Doctoral Curriculum." In *Reshaping Doctoral Education: International Approaches and Pedagogies,* edited by Alison Lee and Susan Danby, 12–25. London: Routledge.

Bazerman, Charles. 2015. "Writing Speaks to Situations through Recognizable Forms." In *Naming What We Know: Threshold Concepts of Writing Studies,* edited by Linda Adler-Kassner and Elizabeth Wardle, 35–37. Logan: Utah State University Press.

Curry, Mary Jane. 2016. "More than Language: Graduate Student Writing as 'Disciplinary Becoming.'" In *Supporting Graduate Student Writers: Research, Curriculum, and Program Design,* edited by Steve Simpson, Nigel A. Caplan, Michelle Cox, and Talinn Phillips, 78–96. Ann Arbor: University of Michigan Press.

Dinitz, Sue, and Susanmarie Harrington. 2014. "The Role of Disciplinary Expertise in Shaping Writing Tutorials." *Writing Center Journal* 33 (2): 73–98.

Geller, Anne Ellen, Michele Eodice, Frankie Condon, Meg Carroll, and Elizabeth Boquet. 2007. *The Everyday Writing Center: A Community of Practice.* Boulder: University Press of Colorado.

Gillespie, Paula. 2007. "Graduate Writing Consultants for PhD Programs Part 1: Using What We Know: Networking and Planning." *Writing Lab Newsletter* 32 (2): 1–6.

Gillespie, Paula, Paul Heidebrecht, and Lorelle Lamascus. 2008. "From Design to Delivery: The Graduate Writing Consultant Course (Part 2)." *Writing Lab Newsletter* 32 (8): 8–11.

Gordon, Layne M. P. 2014. "Beyond Generalist vs. Specialist: Making Connections between Genre Theory and Writing Center Pedagogy." *Praxis: A Writing Center Journal* 11 (2): 1–5. http://www.praxisuwc.com/gordon-112.

Lave, Jean, and Etienne Wenger. *Situated Learning: Legitimate Peripheral Participation.* Cambridge: Cambridge University Press, 1991.

LeCluyse, Christopher, and Sue Mendelsohn. 2008. "Training as Invention: *Topoi* for Graduate Writing Consultants." In *(E)merging Identities: Graduate Students in the Writing Center,* edited by Melissa Nicolas, 103–18. Southlake, TX: Fountainhead Press.

Mannon, Bethany Ober. 2016. "What Do Graduate Students Want from the Writing Center? Tutoring Practices to Support Dissertation and Thesis Writers." *Praxis: A Writing Center Journal* 13 (2): 59–64. http://www.praxisuwc.com/mannon-132.

Micciche, Laure R., and Allison D. Carr. 2011. "Toward Graduate-Level Writing Instruction." *College Composition and Communication* 62 (3): 477–501.

Monty, Randall W. 2016. *The Writing Center as Cultural and Interdisciplinary Contact Zone.* London: Palgrave Macmillan.

Nicolas, Melissa. 2008. "Introduction (E)merging Identities: Authority, Identity, and the Place(s) In-Between." In *(E)merging Identities: Graduate Students in the Writing Center,* edited by Melissa Nicolas, 1–8. Southlake, TX: Fountainhead Press.

Phillips, Talinn. 2013. "Tutor Training and Services for Multilingual Graduate Writers: A Reconsideration." *Praxis: A Writing Center Journal* 10 (2): 1–7. http://www.praxisuwc.com/phillips-102.

Savini, Catherine. 2011. "An Alternative Approach to Bridging Disciplinary Divides." *Writing Lab Newsletter* 35 (7–8): 1–5.

Shapiro, Elliott. 2015. "Towards an Integrated Graduate Student (Training Program)." *Across the Disciplines* 12 (3): 1–13. https://wac.colostate.edu/docs/atd/graduate/shapiro2015.pdf.

Simpson, Steve, Rebecca Clemens, Drea Rae Killingsworth, and Julie Dyke Ford. 2015. "Creating a Culture of Communication: A Graduate-Level STEM Communication Fellows Program at a Science and Engineering University." *Across the Disciplines* 12 (3): 1–15. https://wac.colostate.edu/docs/atd/graduate/simpsonetal2015.pdf.

Snively, Helen. 2008. "A Writing Center in a Graduate School of Education: Teachers as Tutors, and Still in the Middle." In *(E)merging Identities: Graduate Students in the Writing Center*, edited by Melissa Nicolas, 89–101. Southlake, TX: Fountainhead Press.

Summers, Sarah. 2016. "Building Expertise: The Toolkit in UCLA's Graduate Writing Center." *Writing Center Journal* 35 (2): 117–41.

Walker, Kristin. 1998. "The Debate over Generalist Tutors: Genre Theory's Contribution." *Writing Center Journal* 18 (2): 27–32.

17
GENRE KNOWLEDGE AND (CROSS)DISCIPLINARY AWARENESS
Preparing Graduate Consultants to Support Proposals

Elizabeth Festa

As many scholars have observed, academic proposals are uniquely challenging to write. This task proves especially true for graduate students, who must compete for grants and fellowships long before they have oriented themselves to the critical landscape of their discipline, become familiar with its methods and methodologies, or discerned its politics. Because proposals are a crucial means of securing financial support for research, they have serious consequences for the research process (Curry 2016). They are a "prestige genre" (Tardy 2011, 145) in which applicants must persuade experienced reviewers of the originality and impact of their work to gain the imprimatur of a research award. Such a "powerful assertion of individual identity" (Poe, Lerner, and Craig 2010, 82) is a social and emotional gamble for novice researchers, who are often unaware of how their work may be perceived by disciplinary arbiters.

The question of how best to support graduate students in proposal writing intersects with broader concerns about the nature and extent of communication instruction that graduate students need across their course of study. As Mary Jane Curry (2016) asserts, it is challenging for students to become "comfortable making epistemological claims about the state of knowledge or research methodologies in their discipline" (88) and to discern the subtleties of disciplinary genres (88). In the writing center community, specifically, concerns over how best to support graduate writing have been articulated within ongoing debates on the merits and limitations of the "generalist tutor" who provides non-directive support across disciplinary divides and levels of study. As research suggests, the prevailing model of the generalist tutor is often inadequate for graduate writers who may need consultants with greater content expertise, familiarity with research genres, and awareness of

DOI: 10.7330/9781646420858.c017

the sociorhetorical complexity of disciplinary writing (Leverenz 2001; Phillips 2016; Savini 2011).

A number of institutions have attempted to redress this gap in support through the development of graduate writing groups (Aitchison 2014; Garcia, Eum, and Watt 2013; Starke-Meyerring 2014); dissertation camps and writing retreats (Knowles and Grant 2016; Lee and Golde 2013); and graduate-exclusive writing centers, some campuswide and others within particular schools of study (Phillips 2016; Snively 2008; Summers 2016). Such endeavors create pockets of intellectual community among graduate students within and across disciplines. With respect to proposal writing in particular, some of the most innovative initiatives have been situated within departments. For instance, Steve Simpson et al. (2015) describe how a student in a graduate "communication fellows" program collaborated with faculty in her department to develop curriculum for a proposal-writing course. Mya Poe, Neal Lerner, and Jennifer Craig (2010) describe grant-writing modules and mock review panels within a single graduate course. Each of these initiatives benefited from nearness to disciplinary authority and more authentic contexts for understanding the substantial rhetorical dimensions of proposal writing.

Although such projects represent an ideal in that proposal support is closely tailored to a specific audience, this model may not be scalable for large projects across disciplines, sustainable over time, or realistic within the context of campus or departmental cultures. This lack of scalability proved true for us at our writing center at Rice University. Five years ago, our Graduate and Postdoctoral Studies Office (GPS) requested our support in conceptualizing a centralized, peer support plan for graduate fellowships. In particular, they had located an immediate need among those students applying for the National Science Foundation Graduate Fellowship Program (GRFP).

The GRFP supports science, technology, engineering, and mathematics (STEM) and social science students who show very high potential as researchers and as leaders who will contribute to the "broader impacts" goal of the National Science Foundation (NSF), among them increasing the participation of underrepresented groups in the sciences; improving public outreach and engagement with science; and enhancing national security, the economy, and other domains (National Science Foundation 2018). Each year, our university has roughly sixty graduate students who are very competitive for this award. Among graduate applicants to the GRFP, only first- and second-year doctoral students are eligible to apply, and applicants may only submit one time. Therefore, students are often inexperienced research writers when they apply and have no opportunity to benefit from reviewer feedback. Typically, applicants revise their proposals many times, and while most advisors provide feedback, they seldom have the time for intensive mentoring.

We recognized that supporting this project would present a number of challenges. Because the *outcome* of this extremely competitive fellowship competition was as important to our institution as the applicants' development as writers, consultants would need to assist students in realistically imagining the reader-reviewer and strategizing about how best to package complicated research, a role that brings them closer to that of a faculty member. While our center has even proportions of undergraduate and graduate consultants, we decided to draw only upon our graduate cohort and to provide training that confers greater expertise than the modular instruction we use to train undergraduate consultants who support writing-in-the-disciplines projects.

In the sections that follow, I discuss the crucial partnership we forged with our GPS office during this project and some of the difficult compromises to our center's philosophy and pedagogical practices that this collaboration required us to make. As I explain, however, these changes not only helped us to develop a flexible and effective program but also deepened our cross-campus collaborations, increased our credibility, and empowered us to expand our graduate student communication initiatives. I then describe the training plan we co-developed to build graduate consultant expertise. We ultimately chose a diverse cohort of consultants that included senior graduate writing consultants from our center as well as graduate students selected by our GPS who had no prior writing center experience. To bridge gaps in knowledge and experience, we decided to take a genre analysis approach in which we focused on the formal, processual, and sociorhetorical dimensions of this fellowship (Tardy 2009). We focused on developing consultant confidence in facilitating conversations with students outside their discipline and increasing consultant awareness of the context in which fellowships, as a genre, are read and evaluated.

To prepare consultants for this new mentorship role, we foregrounded the challenges of fellowship writing for novice writers. As part of this process, we prompted consultants to reflect on their own evolving disciplinary identities (Curry 2016). As Kristin Messuri explains in chapter 16 on "disciplinary ambassadors" in the writing center, graduate consultants are often unaware of their own assumptions and limitations until these differences emerge through exchange. In cross-disciplinary conversations during training and after the fellowship cycle ended, consultants reflected on how they developed through this project and situated this experience within their growth over their graduate career. Through their participation in this project, graduate students gained insight into the challenges of entering a discourse community and valuable experience practicing their future roles as faculty members.

RETHINKING THE WRITING CENTER NARRATIVE WITH GRADUATE PROPOSALS IN MIND

In their article advocating for a "systems based" approach to supporting graduate writing, Simpson et al. (2015) argue that the "'problem' of graduate writing instruction" is one that must be recognized as a "problem affecting the entire institution" (103). Viable solutions, as these authors suggest, depend on networks that link departments, writing centers, and other organizations on campus (Simpson et al. 2015). While we concur, collaborations seldom proceed without philosophical differences coming into play. In our case, these differences required us to compromise on writing center beliefs that we had come to take for granted.

For instance, our GPS office assumed all the logistical and financial obligations of supporting this project. However, they made this investment with an eye to raising our institution's number of winners. While we shared their desire, we were surprised to discover how wedded we were to certain aspects of the writing center "grand narrative" (Grutsch McKinney 2013, 67), such as privileging the development of the writer over perfecting a particular piece of writing. We confronted a more significant hurdle in determining which graduate students would be most effective as fellowship consultants. Our GPS office preferred appointing past winners of the GRFP, whether or not they had writer center training. While we were receptive to hiring students without writing center training, we believed, nonetheless, that writing center consultants from the GRFP-ineligible humanities disciplines could also be trained to provide this support.

While these were not easy compromises, revising our policies ultimately led us to produce a stronger model for graduate student support. Like many centers, we limit the length, number, setting, and nature of consultations to promote the writer's independence. Standard consultations in our center are synchronous, forty minutes in length, limited to two sessions per week and fourteen per term, and take place in our space. We were persuaded to deviate from our standard practice, however, by research that suggests the benefits of continuity and flexibility in supporting graduate writers. As Helen Snively (2008) speculates, graduate students may benefit from having consultants support the development of their project over time, "holding the process" (97), much like a faculty mentor. More recently, in chapter 13, Dixon and Brownell describe the benefits of co-mentorship between consultants and graduate student clients in which frequent meetings within and beyond the center offer indispensable moral support. In a similar way, we assigned applicants to a single consultant across the fellowship cycle and allowed consultations to take place both synchronously and asynchronously for any number of sessions, at any location, and through any form of mediation (in-person, Skype, email). This new approach created space for authentic working relationships to emerge.

We further compromised on our selection of consultants. We agreed to give priority to past winners of the GRFP—including those with no writing center experience—if they possessed a strong interest in learning how the conventions of proposals manifest *across* disciplines. In addition, we included in our cohort graduate consultants from our center who had previously won the GRFP and senior humanities graduate students from our center who were ineligible for the fellowship. We limited the experience to those who were in their third year of study or beyond so that consultants would have greater experience with the writing process than their mentees. In the most recent iteration of this project, we hired six consultants to support thirty-five students.

TRAINING GRADUATE CONSULTANTS TO SUPPORT THE NSF GRFP
Foregrounding the Acquisition of Genre-Knowledge

To promote the success of our diverse cohort, our GPS office funded consultant time spent on related professional development activities. These vary from year to year but have included an orientation workshop on the GRFP; a presentation on how fellowships are evaluated, led by one of our university faculty members who has been a reviewer for the GRFP; a workshop given at our institution by a steering committee member of the National Alliance for Broader Impacts (NABI) on developing authentic and credible broader impacts initiatives for the GRFP; and a training module on best practices in proposal writing offered through the American Association for the Advancement of Science (AAAS) website. These activities enable us to establish a framework for consultants that conceptualizes the proposal within a broader sociorhetorical context and reinforces best practices as set forth at the departmental, institutional, and national grant-making levels.

The centerpiece of our training, however, is a two-hour workshop at our center. We begin at the ground level each fall, assuming no prior knowledge of proposal writing—even among those consultants who have supported previous cycles. This type of yearly "onboarding," as Rebecca Nowacek et al. write in chapter 12, this collection, is effective for working with diverse consultant cohorts. We begin by underscoring the challenges of working with first- and second-year graduate students on fellowships. In these early years of graduate school, they are not likely to have internalized the conventions of this genre or developed self-awareness of their own writing practice. We draw upon Christine Tardy's 2009 framework, which describes how graduate students gain expertise as they "integrate" the domains of *subject-matter knowledge, rhetorical knowledge, formal knowledge,* and *processual knowledge* (21–22; emphasis added). As she points out, novice researchers are unlikely to discern the ways that these epistemic categories might influence one another (21). As just one example, we share Tardy's (2009) recollection of a graduate student who located the formal conventions of the proposal on the Internet but had not internalized how those formal features performed specific rhetorical functions (118–21). We remind consultants that the "movement towards expertise" (Curry 2016; Tardy 2009) is a gradual and uneven process that far exceeds the span of a fellowship cycle.

With this information in mind, we advise consultants to understand their role as intermediaries between students and advisors. To enable them to serve in this capacity, we draw upon authentic models to illustrate how the exigencies of form, process, and rhetoric intersect within particular disciplinary communities. Our GPS solicits winning fellowship applications each year, and we annotate key conventions and structural moves as these are expressed in the language of different disciplines. We occasionally add the national reviewers' commentary (such as critiques or praise of various components of the proposal) if students are willing to share these. We weave samples from our consultant GRFP winners into our discussion and invite them to further explain their writing process as a part of the workshop. Through this process we concretize proposal conventions, develop consultant skill in using these models, and learn the varied ways in which writers across the disciplines compose a research story.

Promoting Consultant Expertise in Teaching the Genre

In chapter 9, on "sites of incommensurability" during consultations, Marcus Weakley and Mark Pedretti observe that disciplinary or field-based disparities between consultant and student are most likely to influence power dynamics within a session. To address the potential of such disparities, we organize our training around giving consultants what Sarah Summers (2016) has referred to as "tools . . . that create feelings of expertise and that balance feelings of inexperience" (133). Such a "toolkit," as Summers (2016) clarifies, may include approaches from a more generalist repertoire, such as referring students back to a content expert, as well as tactics that require substantial experience, such as sharing knowledge about how to produce a particular genre.

In a similar way, we encourage consultants to draw upon generalist approaches, such as putting the proposal aside and asking students to explain their research and pinpointing areas where they do not follow the argument. But we also focus on developing expertise in working with scientific proposals. We rely heavily on scientific writing books by Angelika Hoffman (2010) and Christine Feak and John Swales (2011); trade books on proposal writing such as those by Joshua Schimel (2012), Sandra Oster and Paul Cordo (2015) and Lawrence Locke, Waneen Spirduso, and Stephen Silverman (2014); scholarship on the rhetorical dimensions of academic discourse such as by Kenneth Hyland (2005); and articles on proposal instruction such as by Lynne Flowerdew (2016) to model principles and best practices. We frame our discussion around identifying common missteps that novice writers make that undermine their research story and strategies for addressing problematic areas. A few examples illustrate this approach:

1. Adapting consultant genre knowledge to the student's discipline

    Throughout training we emphasize that learning how to intervene in the knowledge of a field is among the greatest challenges that graduate writers must confront (Curry 2016; Poe, Lerner, and Craig 2010). We spend a generous amount of time discussing the rhetorical importance of the first two paragraphs of the research statement in which writers contextualize the research problem or question and situate their efforts in this landscape. We note that these paragraphs are *crucial* to the reception of the proposal; while they are read by field experts, consultants must also be able to follow the logic of this section.

    We hone in on two related missteps students make in crafting these paragraphs: the failure to identify the *knowledge* they are providing through their work and their ability to contextualize that knowledge with the appropriate scope. For instance, less-experienced STEM students may simply offer the device or computational model they are developing as the culminating contribution of the project. Such a move makes it challenging for them to situate themselves in the critical landscape because they have not linked the material outputs of their research to a knowledge gap. Not dissimilarly, social scientists may advance an idea simply because it has never been researched before but neglect to connect it to other scholars' interests. We encourage consultants to use visual strategies to help students organize their literature review and to locate and frame this opening. Students in the social sciences may benefit from visualizing their research, using conceptual maps that locate points of departure and overlap, and positioning their inquiry in relation to key interlocutors. Students in STEM, in contrast, may prefer a much more linear approach. One of our graduate consultants from chemistry (and also a recipient of the GRFP) shared that she simply draws an apex-down isosceles triangle on the page, writes "your research question" at the bottom of it, and works backward with the student to consider this question in relation to the history of questions and findings that preceded it.

2. Fostering productive conversations with advisors

In their article on campuswide initiatives to support graduate writing, Simpson et al. (2015) call for efforts that enhance rather than attenuate "the feedback students receive from advisors and peers" (106). Many applicants are hesitant to show their advisors work in progress. With this in mind, we focus on giving consultants a specific vocabulary for asking questions that students can take back to their labs. For example, STEM students may struggle to create key aims that build upon one another without completely depending upon one another. Here, we provide consultants with questions they can pose to improve this section, such as "Which aim are you most certain will be successful?"; "Which aim is your 'pie-in-the-sky' aim?"; "How does aim 3 develop what you expect to find in aim 2?"; and "What will you do if your hypothesis for aim 1 is wrong?"

Common errors in methods, which usually follow the aims, include not explaining the rationale for a method, adding too many details to the protocol, and not considering potential pitfalls. As one of our faculty members acknowledged, reviewers are much more easily convinced that students can *do* an experiment than that they understand the rationale for an experiment. Here, we invite consultants to ask students questions such as "Which aspects of your methods are novel?"; "Which are standard protocols?"; "What will this approach allow you to find?"; and "What potential roadblocks do you imagine as you complete this portion of the experiment?" We do not expect consultants to be able to gauge the accuracy of student responses. Rather, we use these questions to signal familiarity with the genre, lower students' psychological barriers to seeking support, and channel feedback toward those areas where it might be most beneficial.

3. Mapping the "research story" onto the proposal

In training, we identify common ground between consultants and proposal writers by introducing the classic Introduction, Methods,

Results, and Discussion (IMRaD) storytelling structure that we find in STEM and quantitative social science disciplinary writing. As we point out, these content categories are found in *all* scholarly writing, including the humanities and qualitative social sciences; differences reside primarily in organization and style. We then draw upon Joshua Schimel's (2012) description of how IMRaD maps onto the fast-paced and efficient structure of proposal storytelling (28). The proposal assumes an impatient reader who is looking for a concise and persuasive research story. We assist consultants in becoming master interpreters of our models; while students also have access to models, they do not always recognize the strategies that proposal writers employ.

We further encourage consultants to map research storytelling onto the personal statement. Personal statements often lack an overarching point and fail to contextualize the societal issues that the student wishes to pursue. We advise consultants to take an inductive approach in which they work with students on locating how their experiences suggest the interlocking and increasingly ambitious *aims* that inform their research and societal goals. We further ask them to draw upon the principles of the literature review and methods sections to strengthen student accounts of the broader impacts they hope to achieve. We reference a talk given at our institution by a steering committee member for the NABI who noted that applicants rarely recognize that these societal issues are also subjects of scholarly inquiry. Although consultants may lack familiarity with these societal issues, they are experienced library researchers who can increase students' credibility by helping them to contextualize the "what, why, and how" of their impacts through the literature.

DEVELOPING "DISCIPLINARY MATURITY" THROUGH CROSS-DISCIPLINARY ENCOUNTERS

We knew that a primary benefit of our consulting program was enhancing consultant knowledge of the proposal genre. We did not anticipate, however, how multidisciplinary consultations and training sessions would hone consultants' ownership of their own disciplinary writing conventions. As Claire Aitchison (2014) has written of the benefits of multidisciplinary writing groups, they make students "acutely aware of their own disciplinary and methodological requirements through the process of negotiating . . . different perspectives" (60). Similarly, Elena Garcia, Seung hee Eum, and Lorna Watt (2013) describe the pleasures of "practicing expertise" in their multidisciplinary writing group as they received feedback from "differently-disciplined experts-in-training" and, as they noted, "found a need to negotiate our thinking . . . and stand up for the epistemologies of our disciplines when they were challenged by contradicting ways of thinking" (273). We found a similar dynamic at play during training.

As one example, a consultant from bioengineering confessed that she was perplexed on how to give feedback to students from disciplines that do not construct hypotheses. She remarked, "How can you research something you can't test?" An anthropologist and a sociologist explained how they developed research questions contextualized through extensive literature review work and tested the validity of these questions in pilot studies. A biochemist interjected to describe her GRFP proposal, which centered on a chemical screen that was essentially exploratory and did not include a hypothesis, though she had an idea of some substances they might find. The anthropologist confirmed, "My research is similar to that chemical screen." Through this comparison, the biochemist and the anthropologist located common ground and explained a difficult concept. At the same time, each had staked a claim for the particularities of her own discipline and, in so doing, strengthened their disciplinary identities.

A closely related benefit of this project was the opportunity it gave consultants to practice the intellectual and emotional work of mentorship. Such work requires internalizing academic genres while maintaining a sensitivity to the self-doubt that often emerges amidst the pressures of high-stakes writing. Even those consultants whose academic path has been relatively unfettered recall the frustration of justifying early-stage projects. For instance, one consultant remembered "pushing back" against suggestions her consultant had given her when she was preparing her own GRFP during the previous cycle. Only later did she recognize that her proposal stopped short of the tensions, conflicts, and broader interests—the "so what and the *why*?"—that together are the mark of more developed projects. She could not yet imagine how she might frame her project less as something she was studying "because it is new" but rather "because it was interesting in some specific way." Learning to connect to "the questions that other scholars find interesting," she concluded, was the essence of "disciplinary maturity." In witnessing novice writers becoming researchers, reexamining their own paths toward expertise, and sharing the heirlooms of their hard-won knowledge, graduate consultants gained valuable self-insight through demystifying the writing process for their peers.

As we discovered through this project, reenvisioning our role in supporting graduate writers from a broader and more collaborative perspective resulted in approaches that better approximated the realities of graduate student needs and patterns of development. Our involvement also increased our credibility and opened the door to new communication efforts campuswide. Indeed, since our initial meeting five years ago, our consulting program has expanded to include fellowships funded by the National Institutes of Health, National Aeronautics and Space Administration, and the Fulbright Program. Moreover, the relationships we established led to our inclusion in an NSF grant that aims to scaffold communication skills among doctoral students in the natural sciences from their first year of study.

Most significant, though, we discovered the benefits of training graduate consultants to develop expertise in a high-stakes genre and raising their awareness of the process by which graduate students become members of a disciplinary community. As they distilled the knowledge they had gained about writing within their own disciplines and applied it in a cross-disciplinary context to guide more junior students, graduate consultants had the opportunity to see the conventions, assumptions, expectations, and boundaries of academic discourse from a bird's-eye-view. In occupying this broader perspective, they grew beyond the role of student peer-mentors and experienced their future roles as professional research writers and advisors.

ACKNOWLEDGMENTS

With thanks to Joff Silberg, Mary Purugganan, Kiri Kilpatrick, Anneli Joplin, Kim Gonzalez, and Jennifer Wilson for their insights and contributions to this project and this chapter.

REFERENCES

Aitchison, Claire. 2014. "Learning from Multiple Voices: Feedback and Authority in Doctoral Writing Groups." In *Writing Groups for Doctoral Education and Beyond: Innovations in Practice and Theory*, edited by Claire Aitchison and Cally Guerin, 51–64. London: Routledge.

Curry, Mary Jane. 2016. "More than Language: Graduate Student Writing as Disciplinary Becoming." In *Supporting Graduate Writers: Research, Curriculum, and Program Design*, edited by Steve Simpson, Nigel A. Caplan, Michelle Cox, and Tailinn Phillips, 78–97. Ann Arbor: University of Michigan Press.

Feak, Christine B., and John M. Swales. 2011. *Creating Contexts: Writing Introductions across Genres*. Ann Arbor: University of Michigan Press.

Flowerdew, Lynne. 2016. "A Genre-Inspired and Lexico-grammatical Approach for Helping Postgraduate Students Craft Research Grant Proposals." *English for Specific Purposes* 42 (April): 1–12.

Garcia, Elena Marie-Adkins, Seung hee Eum, and Lorna Watt. 2013. "Experiencing the Benefits of Difference with Multidisciplinary Graduate Writing Groups." In *Working with Faculty Writers*, edited by Anne Ellen Geller and Michele Eodice, 260–78. Boulder: University Press of Colorado.

Grutsch McKinney, Jackie. 2013. *Peripheral Visions for Writing Centers*. Logan: Utah State University Press.

Hofmann, Angelika H. 2010. *Scientific Writing and Communication: Papers, Proposals, and Presentations*. Oxford: Oxford University Press, 2010.

Hyland, Kenneth. 2005. *Metadiscourse: Exploring Interaction in Writing*. London: Continuum Press.

Knowles, Sally S., and Barbara Grant. 2014. "Walking the Labyrinth: The Holding Embrace of Academic Writing Retreats." In *Writing Groups for Doctoral Education and Beyond: Innovations in Practice and Theory*, edited by Claire Aitchison and Cally Guerin, 110–27. London: Routledge.

Lee, Sohui, and Chris Golde. 2013. "Completing the Dissertation and Beyond: Writing Centers and Dissertation Boot Camps." *Writing Lab Newsletter* 37 (7–8): 1–5.

Leverenz, Carrie Shively. 2001. "Graduate Students in the Writing Center." In *The Politics of Writing Centers*, edited by Jane Nelson and Kathy Evertz, 50–61. Portsmouth, NH: Boynton Cook Publishers.

Locke, Lawrence F., Waneen Wyrick Spirduso, and Stephen J. Silverman. 2014. *Proposals That Work: A Guide for Planning Dissertations and Grant Proposals*. Los Angeles: Sage.

National Science Foundation. 2018. "National Science Foundation Graduate Fellowship Program, NSF, 18–573." Last modified July 27, 2018. https://www.nsf.gov/pubs/2018/nsf18573/nsf18573.htm.

Oster, Sandra, and Paul Cordo. 2015. *Successful Grant Proposals In Science, Technology, and Medicine: A Guide to Writing the Narrative*. Cambridge: Cambridge University Press.

Phillips, Tailinn. 2016. "Writing Center Support for Graduate Students: An Integrated Model." In *Supporting Graduate Writers: Research, Curriculum, and Program Design*, edited by Steve Simpson, Nigel A. Caplan, Michelle Cox, and Tailinn Phillips, 159–69. Ann Arbor: University of Michigan Press.

Poe, Mya, Neal Lerner, and Jennifer Craig. 2010. *Learning to Communicate in Science and Engineering: Case Studies from MIT*. London: MIT Press.

Savini, Catherine. 2011. "An Alternative Approach to Bridging Disciplinary Divides." *Writing Lab Newsletter* 35 (7–8): 1–5.

Schimel, Joshua. 2012. *Writing Science: How to Write Papers That Get Cited and Proposals That Get Funded*. Oxford: Oxford University Press.

Simpson, Steve, Rebecca Clemens, Drea Rae Killingsworth, and Julie Dyke Ford. 2015. "Creating a Culture of Communication: A Graduate-Level STEM Communication Fellows Program at a Science and Engineering University." *Across the Disciplines* 12: n.p. https://wac.colostate.edu/atd/graduate_wac/simpsonetal2015.cfm.

Snively, Helen. 2008. "A Writing Center in a Graduate School of Education: Teachers as Tutors, and Still in the Middle." In *(E)merging Identities: Graduate Students in the Writing Centers*, edited by Melissa Nicholas, 89–102. Southlake, TX: Fountainhead Press.

Starke-Meyerring, Doreen. 2014. "Writing Groups as Critical Spaces for Engaging Normalized Institutional Cultures of Writing in Doctoral Education." In *Writing Groups for Doctoral Education and Beyond: Innovations in Practice and Theory*, edited by Claire Aitchison and C. Guerin, 65–81. London: Routledge.

Summers, Sarah. 2016. "Building Expertise: The Toolkit in UCLA's Graduate Writing Center." *Writing Center Journal* 35 (2): 117–45.

Tardy, Christine M. 2011. "ESP and Multi-method Approaches to Genre Analysis." In *New Directions for Specific Purposes Research*, edited by Diane Dewhurst Belcher, Anne M. Johns, and Brian Paltridge, 145–73. Ann Arbor: University of Michigan, Press.

Tardy, Christine M. 2009. *Building Genre Knowledge*. West Lafayette, IN: Parlor Press.

18
AN INQUIRY-BASED APPROACH FOR CUSTOMIZING TRAINING FOR GRADUATE STUDENT TUTORS

Megan Boeshart Burelle and Meagan Thompson

Picture it: A Writing Center (WC) in a new space, with a new director, and with almost all new graduate tutors. We were both new to our roles at Old Dominion University (ODU). Megan, a PhD student, was a new WC director and lecturer faculty member, and Meagan was a new master's student. We both relied on past experiences and the institutional memory of the WC within texts and materials to help us navigate that first day of orientation—and while we continued to rely on the past, we also began to question how these texts, materials, and the experiences of other tutors came to be and how they might continue to change. We quickly realized that part of the struggle was that this was a year of massive change and turnover, one not unfamiliar to the institutional memory of our WC. Our WC has had multiple directors, moved multiple times, and is entirely staffed by graduate student consultants who change from year to year—a struggle we believe is not unfamiliar to other WCs. This set of circumstances prompted us to ask how we could provide consistency and create a more solid institutional memory within our WC to prepare tutors for their work while still being open to change. We decided to use an inquiry-based approach to help us determine how to train graduate tutors in our WC. This inquiry-based approach was not something that only the director, Megan, took up, but also many of the graduate tutors, including Meagan. While all the tutors and their remarks throughout the year helped define the direction of the inquiry, Megan and Meagan collaborated closely to work toward crafting new tutor training and professional development for graduate consultants. R. Mark Hall argues that "tutor education, then, encourages an inquiry stance, which involves ongoing questioning, asking why and whether, wondering, researching, generating alternatives, testing, reviewing, and revising options" (2017, 128). We agreed and set about doing just that.

DOI: 10.7330/9781646420858.c018

The inquiry stance helped us set goals and come up with a clear vision for how we imagined tutor training for the future of our WC. An inquiry approach allows WC tutors and administrators to look at their particular context and determine how to best revise and reimagine tutor education. We think it is necessary for WCs to continually question the decisions made in regard to tutor training in order to revise and improve tutor training; we especially encourage administrators to question the assumptions we have about what kind of training graduate tutors need.

Our inquiry approach encouraged us to consider the constraints or limitations of our particular context and to see that our training continually needs to adapt to any new changes our WC may experience. Christopher LeCluyse and Sue Mendelsohn draw on Lloyd Bitzer's definition of the rhetorical situation to point out how we must be aware of our constraints so we can best identify and meet institutional and departmental expectations within the WC (LeCluyse and Mendelsohn 2008). By examining our center's constraints, in addition to our tutors' needs, we developed questions that will serve as a heuristic to invent, evaluate, and revise training specifically for graduate student consultants. The heuristic we developed asks WC administrators to consider their WC philosophy, the pedagogies enacted regularly, the history within past training materials, and past experiences.

The inquiry at our WC led us to these goals for future tutor training: (1) helping graduate tutors negotiate their roles as tutors within the WC, (2) fostering student agency during tutoring sessions, (3) prioritizing educational accessibility and addressing the needs of various student populations, (4) providing adequate technology training to reach ODU's online student population, and (5) encouraging collaboration between tutors to develop new strategies for working with students. We realize that these goals may not be exactly the same for other WCs, that some other goals may be prioritized, or that these goals for us may in fact shift in the future, but these became a foundational point for us to begin to formulate more questions about how to design our tutor training.

By creating a heuristic for developing graduate tutor training, we hope to emphasize the importance of using an inquiry-based approach, rather than provide a one-size-fits-all "how to guide." We see this approach as one that all WCs could use, and the questions we pose are applicable for all centers. Of importance, though, answers may change based on individual institutions. Therefore, we focus on the questions, rather than our answers, to reinforce the idea that institutional context will determine how centers implement new training strategies. Often, we are focused on having a set of "universal" best practices, but we encourage readers, instead, to focus on asking the right questions that lead to practices best fitting each institution's needs. Hall writes,

> Novice tutors, in my experience, are eager to know the "right way" to tutor, a formula for engaging in a writing consultation. But no such formula exists. As helpful as a list of shared practices may be, it is no panacea. Sometimes particular valued practices aren't appropriate. Sometimes they don't work. What is more valuable for novice tutors are multiple opportunities over time to develop critical habits of mind that encourage them to reflect on practices in the moment, then, when tutoring isn't working, to innovate new, more effective strategies, based on a sound theory of teaching and learning grounded in research. (2017, 45)

So, too, are administrators eager to know the "right way" to train tutors, but no such formula exists. Instead, administrators must be open to continual reflection and evaluation of their practices. What we hope to offer in this chapter is a set of heuristic questions that can be used as a guiding tool so that informed decisions can be made about how to train and support graduate student tutors while carefully considering local and institutional contexts. We divide the heuristic into four sections: institutional and WC context, texts and technologies, agency and power dynamic, and tutor collaboration as learning method. Each section is organized by the types of questions we think are necessary to consider when making decisions about graduate tutor training. For each section, we offer a list of questions we felt were necessary to consider, as well as provide explanations of how these questions worked in connection to WC scholarship and our own WC context. We hope that providing a sense of how we used these questions to guide our own thinking as an example might provide a clearer idea of how to put this kind of inquiry into practice.

INSTITUTIONAL/WC CONTEXT AND LOGISTICS OF CREATING SUSTAINED GRADUATE TUTOR TRAINING

We began with a set of questions focused on our particular institutional and local WC context, knowing that many of the limitations and constraints we might encounter would be necessary to address in order to create graduate tutor training that could continue to change and still be sustainable. We think these questions are necessary for each individual WC to consider as they design and/or revise graduate tutor training.

- What is the WC's mission, and how has this determined how tutors have been trained in the past? How should it determine how tutors are trained now and in the future?

- What services has the WC offered in the past? What are the expectations of the WC services from the institution? The department the WC is housed within? Faculty across campus? Students being served by the WC? Our graduate tutors?
- In what ways do WC philosophies, pedagogies, and scholarship bump up against institutional expectations or limitations?
- How is labor in our WC distributed (tutoring hours, position types, job expectations of the tutors)?
- When is it possible to incorporate training based on institution schedules, tutor schedules, and compensation available for tutors? Is it possible to provide orientation? Front-loading training? Weekly staff meetings? Asynchronous ongoing training? Other options?
- What does our institution/department/etc. expect tutors to have learned or expect our tutors to have received in terms of professional development when they leave the position as graduate student tutors?
- What student populations and demographics does our particular WC serve? How should the student populations served influence tutor training?
- What WC data has our WC collected that may help determine what tutors or student needs are from the WC?
- How do we plan training and craft training materials that we know will need to continue to evolve and change?

Reflection is often discussed in WC scholarship, both by tutors and administrators. Reflection was a critical first step for us because "through critical reflection, theories and decisions remain open to inspection, evaluation, and revision" (Hall 2017, 106). As we navigated and negotiated the process of revising our tutor training, we reflected on our institution, and our WC's current practices and mission, as well as the student populations we served and how those populations were served by our WC currently and in the past. Our stance of inquiry led us in many directions, including exploring the WC's history and faculty perceptions of our services. The examination of our WC's history helped us realize that our WC was in a moment of significant change, as was our institution. For example, our online student and international student populations have grown significantly, and our graduate student population has made it clear that they need more writing support from our university. We don't think the major changes our WC or institution are undergoing are unique. Rather, we imagine that while the specific changes might be different, many WCs and institutions are experiencing some sort of change. As Joseph Cheatle and Genie Giaimo write in chapter 10, WCs are sites of high employee turnover, and those employees may be part time or, because of a lack of time or funding, underprepared for WC work. As such, the inquiry-based approach we are advocating is a possible way for WCs to confront those challenges. For our center, it allowed us to better respond to change and we think it would allow others to better respond to ongoing change.

By asking ourselves the questions in the heuristic above, we began to create a clearer idea of what we might imagine tutor training looked like, as well as how to shape our goals for what we wanted tutor training to accomplish. Two points became particularly salient during our reflections and following conversations. First, we wanted to address the needs of the student populations frequently using our center. Second, we wanted to ensure our graduate tutors had sufficient professional development to provide excellent tutoring services for those student populations. We used data collected throughout the year in various ways (i.e., tutorial session notes, student satisfaction surveys, weekly meeting notes from discussions among tutors, written weekly tutor reflections, and intraoffice communication via a Google Doc) to help determine what the student and tutor needs were. This data helped us shape the training so it better addressed what students and tutors said they needed. Much of the data we used to come to these conclusions were collected without the intention of using it for this purpose. Rather, these were texts that were already part of our WC's daily/weekly workflow. As Kim Jackson (1996) reminds us, though, we should be the primary audience of our own records and use them to educate ourselves on our practices.

The initial line of inquiry about our local context also helped us to recognize the constraints placed on us through various parts of the institution. In recognizing these constraints and keeping them in mind, we could better formulate a realistic and feasible plan. For example, almost all of our tutors spend only one year in the WC during the first year of their master's degree program (and there are various emphases within our department). All of our tutors are graduate students in the English Department and hold the position through an assistantship line, with one of them being a doctoral student, each year. Many of the master's-level tutors will go on, in their second year, to teach first-year composition. For this reason, our staff turnover rate is high, even for most WCs. The expertise of all our graduate tutors varies (in really great ways, we think!), but our staff often lacks expertise outside of English. Our tutors are expected to carry things they learned from the WC into their work as writing instructors. We think that all of these constraints should inform the way our training is designed and imagine that WCs with other institutional constraints may need to respond to their context's constraints differently. The local context inquiry provides WC administrators and tutors with a starting point to build further inquiry off of—to see the places where our theories and practices collide with the logistics of our very real constraints and situations.

One particular challenge we faced was the variance in our yearly number of tutors and the way that our tutors are compensated at our institution. Since all of our tutors are on assistantships, tutors are named within graduate programs (based on budgets and enrollment, of course) and not by the WC director. Our graduate tutors are required to put twenty hours a week into their assistantship responsibilities. In an effort to make our graduate students' labor "visible," as Wulff suggests in chapter 14, we also took into account that the stipend (like so many graduate assistantships) is quite low and still leaves our graduate tutors in precarious financial circumstances. We felt that professional development should be both formal and compensated. In order to provide adequate training, but not put an extra burden on graduate tutors to provide labor they are not compensated for, we created a training module for all of our tutors to work through during the first week of classes. We chose activities that could be done alone and others that required tutors to work with other tutors who shared shifts with them. Tutors came the first week of classes for their regular schedule but spent most of those hours actively working through the module and activities, since few students visit the WC during the first week. This timing allowed us to provide training, including collaborative training that involved the tutors discussing and working through training and workplace scenarios together, without requiring everyone to be present at the same time.

We also use a weekly staff meeting as part of ongoing training that counts as one hour of the required twenty so that tutors are compensated for attending staff meetings. We also used the initial week of training to solicit feedback from tutors on what they felt they still needed to know more about to be effective tutors and crafted built-in training into the weekly meetings. For example, we have our tutors complete an LGBTQIA+ Safe Space training provided for students and faculty on our campus during a couple weeks of staff meetings so tutors will be Safe Space certified. Previous tutors felt the training was helpful, and new tutors expressed that they wanted training on how to discuss LGBTQIA+ issues with writers. While the logistics of when we could build in time to provide this type of ongoing training were important, so too were the texts and technologies we decided to utilize within the WC.

TEXTS AND TECHNOLOGIES

- What theories, scholarship, and/or texts are guiding training, professional development, and workflow design choices in our WC? How do these texts and technologies align with our WC goals and mission? With our particular context?
- How do we make choices about technology (hardware, software, and document formats) that are based on institutional resources and systems but that are still accessible to everyone? What kind of technology is it possible/feasible for the WC to have (budget, hardware, etc.)?
- What technology is required for online appointments? Scheduling? How do we ensure that tutors are proficiently using our technology that is necessary to serve students? What kind of training is necessary to ensure tutors feel comfortable at using technology for tutoring?

After reflecting upon our local and institutional expectations and needs, we looked to WC scholarship and theory to develop a canon of core texts and materials that could serve as institutional memory and guide us in planning professional development opportunities. Like Lisa Cahill et al., "we discovered that grounding our practices in principles derived from carefully selected scholarship was a successful approach, both for meeting our goals and for professionally developing our peer writing tutors" (2017, 10). Much of that scholarship, such as Hall's *Around the Texts of Writing Center Work: An Inquiry-Based Approach to Tutor Education* and Melissa Nicolas's edited collection *(E)Merging Identities: Graduate Students in the Writing Center*, guided the development of the heuristics presented in this chapter.

The primary challenge our WC faces when determining what texts and technologies we can utilize and provide for our tutors (and students) is our lack of an operational budget. We wanted to provide a set of core texts for tutors to use during training and tutoring but needed to keep in mind the accessibility of these documents for both the WC and tutors. All tutors are given a copy of *The Bedford Guide for Writing Tutors* (Ryan and Zimmerelli 2010) to read and work through during the initial orientation. We also host a set of in-house resources in Google Drive folders, a suite that all faculty and students at our university have access to. The folders include a manual with policies, procedures, best practices for sessions, technology guides, and campus resources. Diane Boehm (2009) suggests that all WCs have such a collection of go-to texts, in addition to available handouts of common problems seen during sessions. Over the years, our WC has created and collected "help documents" on various writing topics, from citation styles to comma usage, which tutors and students have access to both in hard copy and electronically.

We have limited access to the hardware and software we might need to effectively hold tutoring sessions, especially online tutoring for our growing population of distance and nontraditional students. We chose a service that worked both as a scheduler and a host for online appointments and that could work on an online browser without additional downloads. While we chose the vendor WCOnline, we encourage everyone to evaluate their own needs and limitations to choose an appropriate platform. Previously, our online tutoring system required so many steps that our students did not utilize the service, despite the large number of entirely online students at our institution. This platform meets our student population's needs, but it also requires extensive training for our tutors so they are equipped to handle scheduling appointments and holding online appointments. For this reason, we devoted a significant amount of time during orientation to learning the various technologies. Tutors are guided through a hands-on practice session with the online schedule and appointments. Then they have ample time to practice independently or with each other during the first week of classes. In addition to this practice and available how-to guides, we encourage tutors to troubleshoot potential technology issues that commonly arise in our online sessions. It brings our inquiry-based approach to WC work down to the nitty-gritty. Just as tutors must develop, incorporate, and assess strategies for working with students, they must do the same when working with computers. While this may seem like a "small" part of the tutoring session, having access to, and proficient use of, the available technologies allow the tutor to focus on the writing rather than the logistics of running a session. When tutors and students have access to all of the texts and technologies they need in order to succeed, the WC functions as it should and the goals of the center and institution are more likely to be met.

AGENCY AND POWER DYNAMICS AS GRAD TUTORS

- What are the power dynamics of being a graduate student tutor? How does a grad student negotiate those power dynamics?
- What previous experiences and academic backgrounds do tutors bring with them to the WC? How does this affect how they see their role in the WC as a tutor?
- How do tutors negotiate the role of not being a peer (at least to the undergrads) but also not in an instructor role either (especially when most scholarship is focused on peer tutors)?
- How do we create a professional development environment where tutors can work through the tension of the roles they inhabit?

Graduate students operate within a liminal and often precarious role in the university, having more experience and knowledge than undergraduates but lacking the expertise and security of faculty. LeCluyse and Mendelsohn describe this tension as being in a "professional limbo," where graduate students must "take on the persona and responsibilities of a confident professional at the same time that they have neither the institutional power nor the experience to fully do so" (2008, 103). Within the WC, graduate student tutors must constantly face and navigate this tension, which is a challenging task. Brooke Rollins, Trixie G. Smith, and Evelyn Westbrook explain that graduate student tutors must rely on, and feel confident in, their writing expertise while still leaving the authority of the work in the clients' hands, "striking the appropriate note of judiciousness and flexibility" (2008, 121). This push and pull between who has expertise and authority within a session is often one of the biggest challenges our tutors face when they begin working at the WC.

Our tutors tend to exist on two planes, depending on their previous experiences in tutoring or teaching. New graduate students without any tutoring or teaching experience often express anxiety at not having enough expertise or authority because they do not know any pedagogical strategies or best practices. One tutor compared it to having imposter syndrome; she felt like she was chosen for a position based on assumed knowledge she had, but because she was still a student herself she felt unsure if she had enough expertise. On the other hand, those tutors who have previously been instructors, either in secondary or postsecondary settings, typically struggle to relinquish the "teacher" role to assume the position of collaborator. One author of this chapter, Meagan, struggled with this as a former high school teacher. She often felt the need to impart a certain quantity and quality of knowledge upon the student.

Finding a balance between these two poles is a difficult task because it often involves a lot of individual work on the part of each tutor. As administrators, we can offer strategies, best practices, and resources for tutors to individually explore how they might negotiate authority and agency within consultations, while emphasizing Anna Sicari's suggestion in chapter 11 to value kindness, empathy, and respect. To model these values, we spend a considerable portion of our weekly staff meetings devoted to problem solving and peer collaboration, so tutors can talk about and learn from the experiences and advice of their colleagues. We recommend setting up channels of communication between the director and tutors and between the tutors themselves, so there are chances for tutors to ask about and work through the complicated roles they are asked to inhabit. Channels of communication also provide tutors with the ability to collaborate and teach each other, as well as name what they need to know.

ALLOWING TUTORS TO COLLABORATE, TEACH EACH OTHER, AND NAME WHAT THEY NEED TO KNOW

- How can activities be included in orientations and ongoing training that allow tutors to teach other tutors? To collaborate with other tutors?
- How do we set up an environment that encourages tutors to develop new strategies for tutoring and push themselves outside their comfort zone?
- How can we set up consistent feedback loops to learn what tutors need help with? Still need more support on?
- How can we use tutor expertise to build in professional development activities that allow them to take a leading role in providing support to other tutors?

An environment of co-learning within the WC encourages graduate student tutors to engage more directly in their work as a writing tutor, allowing them to view tutoring as a form of valuable professional development rather than just a job or assistantship. Believing that tutors should take an active role within the WC and in the education of their fellow tutors, we established several opportunities for tutors to work and learn from each other. We rely on the few returning tutors we have to assist and lead training activities. During orientation, veteran tutors were called upon to lead training activities, such as role-playing potential consultation scenarios. We also held a returning and former tutors panel in order for new tutors to comfortably ask questions about any aspect of being a graduate student tutor. This panel immediately established an environment where tutors could come to each other for information and problem-solving strategies.

We carry the collaborative culture of orientation into the remainder of the year during weekly meetings and intraoffice communication channels. During meetings, tutors pose questions, challenges, and successes they had during the previous week. Rather than the director being the sole responder, other tutors offer their own experiences and suggestions. This dialogue often results in tutors sharing new strategies, resources, and techniques for their colleagues to try. In this way, tutors are involved in their own, and each other's, learning processes. These meetings also serve as an opportunity for the director to hear feedback on what additional support tutors need, whether that be resources for working with a special population or a request for new technology. If tutors are hesitant to share challenges or requests in front of the group, they also keep a reflective journal where they can pose questions directly to the director. This is a feedback channel between individual tutors and the director that serves both as a communicative tool and reflective practice.

To avoid reflective practices becoming an activity restricted to a limited audience (self and director), we responded to Hall's (2017) call for dialogic reflection, so reflective writing becomes a conversation rather than a private journal. To facilitate dialogic reflection and critical engagement with their own practices and current WC scholarship, we incorporated asynchronous training opportunities for tutors to engage with theory and then discuss it with each other on an intraoffice communication channel. These reflective writings, to be completed during "flexible" hours, become a starting point for discussions during weekly meetings. Fostering a collaborative culture places value on reflection and dialogue, key components to an inquiry-based approach.

EMBRACING THE OPPORTUNITY FOR CHANGE

Implementing an inquiry-based approach to tutor training using the heuristic questions we've shared in this chapter has improved our WC training for both the tutors and the administrator. An inquiry-based approach allowed us to have a flexible, responsive training that made room for tutor needs to be addressed in the moment. It also encouraged the recognition that the training may need to evolve and be revised in the future because the answers to the heuristic questions may change. By starting with questions, we were able to personalize our training to our student and tutor needs, with both our strengths and limitations in mind. Answering our heuristic questions allowed us to get a better sense of how our system was functioning. Without this knowledge, we would not have been able to address the challenges our WC faces, whether it was our nonexistent operational budget, high rate of employee turnover, or the diverse student population we reach at our WC. In other words, we all need to recognize the ways in which our particular WCs, institutions, departments, tutors, and even the student populations we serve affect what training we can put into place.

Perhaps the most important point we hope readers take away from our chapter is that they see the need for ongoing inquiry into their tutor-training practices, considering especially their tutor population and how having graduate student tutors brings new challenges and varied concerns for how to implement training in our WCs. We want to encourage WC administrators and tutors to embrace adaptation and change in our pedagogies and practices; by doing so, we may continue to meet our tutors and students where they are as well as help them become better tutors and writers using a sustainable inquiry-based model.

We hope that readers consider the heuristic questions we've provided as a beginning point for sorting through all the considerations that are necessary to create tutor training that is both embedded in WC scholarship and pedagogy but also considers local and institutional contexts, especially the student and tutor population. While we cannot provide everyone with a "how-to guide" for the best training, we do think these questions help provide a how-to guide for beginning the necessary inquiry process into making graduate tutor-training decisions.

REFERENCES

Boehm, Diane. "The Work and Art of Writing Center Tutor Training." *Zeitschrift Schreiben.* https://zeitschrift-schreiben.ch/globalassets/zeitschrift-schreiben.eu/2009/boehm_tutor_training.pdf. Accessed September 21, 2018.

Cahill, Lisa, et al. 2017. "Developing Core Principles for Tutor Education." *Writing Lab Newsletter* 42:1–2, 10–17. https://wlnjournal.org/archives/v42/42.1-2.pdf.

Hall, Mark R. 2017. *Around the Texts of Writing Center Work: An Inquiry-Based Approach to Tutor Education.* Logan: Utah State University Press.

Jackson, Kim. 1996. "We Can Be Our Own Audience: Using Our Records to Educate Ourselves." *Writing Lab Newsletter* 21:2, 1–3, 10. https://wlnjournal.org/archives/v21/21-2.pdf.

LeCluyse, Christopher, and Sue Mendelsohn. 2008. "Training as Invention: *Topoi* for Graduate Writing Consultants." In *(E)Merging Identities: Graduate Students in the Writing Center,* edited by Melissa Nicolas, 103–18. Southlake, TX: Fountainhead Press.

Nicolas, Melissa. *(E)Merging Identities: Graduate Students in the Writing Center.* Southlake, TX: Fountainhead Press.

Rollins, Brooke, Trixie G. Smith, and Evelyn Westbrook. 2008. "Collusion and Collaboration: Concealing Authority in the Writing Center." In *(E)Merging Identities: Graduate Students in the Writing Center,* edited by Melissa Nicolas, 103–18. Southlake, TX: Fountainhead Press.

Ryan, Leigh, and Lisa Zimmerelli. 2010. *The Bedford Guide for Writing Tutors.* 5th ed. New York: Bedford / St. Martin's.

INDEX

Academic Writing Center (AWC), 58, 59, 68; background of, 60–63; standards of, 60, 61
accountability, 139, 147–48, 149, 166–74, 187
Actor Prepares (Stanislavski), 69
administration, 214; involvement in, 209–12
administrators, 7, 46, 47, 139; considerations for, 81–84; PCs and, 45; takeaways for, 28–29; training/development and, 51–53; WC, 4, 87, 140, 204, 242, 246, 252
agency, 127, 163, 243; tutors and, 248–50
Ahmed, Sarah, 162
Aitchison, Claire, 225, 237
Aldrich, Howard E., 83
Alexander, Jonathan, 156
Allison, Fallon N., 8, 9, 47
Allyn and Bacon Guide to Peer Tutoring, The (Gillespie and Lerner), 197
American Association for the Advancement of Science (AAAS), 233
anxiety, writing, 18, 121, 152, 211
APA, 50, 102, 105, 106, 107
applications, 37, 38, 39, 40–41, 42
appointments, 5, 49, 60, 75, 190
approaches: directive, 62, 68; evidence-based, 126; non-directive, 61, 62
Around the Texts of Writing Center Work: An Inquiry-Based Approach to Tutor Education (Hall), 195, 247
Association of Writers and Writing Programs conference, 108
authority, 11, 77, 92, 95, 107, 126, 223; asymmetries in, 127; classroom, 89; collaboration and, 87; consultant, 9–10; differential, 127; disciplinary, 79; institutional, 103; instructional, 47, 102–4; lack of, 132–33; peer support and, 68; student-teacher, 6, 79; tutor, 91, 132–33
AWC. *See* Academic Writing Center

Baker, Ted, 83
Ball, David, 211
Bartholomae, David, 89
Bazerman, Charles, 219

Bedford Guide for Writing Tutors, The (Ryan and Zimmerelli), 6, 19, 21, 47, 72, 222, 247
Behrens, Vicki, 12, 142, 193
being directive, 91
being me, 84
Beltman, Susan, 145
"Benefits of a Tutor-Mentor Program, The" (Jensen), 194
Bennion, Elizabeth, 146
Bitzer, Lloyd, 242
Blackboard, 22, 35, 37, 39, 40
Bleakney, Julia, 206, 209, 210
Boehm, Diane, 247
Boquet, Elizabeth, 3, 34, 40, 41, 152, 160, 180; on faculty/administration preparedness, 161; intentional kindness and, 153, 155, 161–62; on universities/people, 157–58
Brady, Laura, 180–81
brainstorming, 121, 171, 199
Brent, Rebecca, 120
Bridges-Rhoads, Sarah, 185
Bright, Alison, 33, 35
Brooks, Jeff, 61, 114–15
Brownell, Cassie, 11, 216, 226, 233
Bruce, Shanti, 6, 20
Bruffee, Kenneth, 31, 40, 41, 86–87, 180, 181, 184
Bryant, Scott, 146, 147
Building a Character (Stanislavski), 69
Burchanoski, Matt, 13
Burelle, Megan Boeshart, 5, 6, 7, 12, 141, 171, 195, 196, 207, 211, 241
Burke, Kenneth, 18
Burns, Deborah, 115, 127

Cahill, Lisa, 247
Caldwell, Cam, 141
Canvas, 35, 117, 118
Carino, Peter, 62, 114, 127
Case Western Reserve University Writing Resource Center, 6
Caza, Brianna Braker, 71, 72, 73, 74, 76, 79, 84
Center for Teaching and Learning, 175
change: opportunity for, 251–52; responding to, 245, 252

Cheatle, Joseph, xi, xii, 159, 204, 206, 207, 218, 244; mentoring and, 13; training and, 12, 17
Cherry, Miriam A., 193, 195
Chilbert, Elizabeth, 92, 94, 95
Christoph, Julie Nelson, 161
Clapham, Danielle, 13
clarification, 67, 131, 133, 134; duty, 141, 142
clients, 100, 189; consultants and, 188, 190
closing the loop, 37, 38, 39–40, 41
"Cloud, Castle, Lake" (Nabokov), 64, 65
co-mentoring, 11, 233; feminist, 182, 185–86, 188–90
coaches: graduate, 210, 211; peer, 12; undergraduate, 206
collaboration, 6, 12, 13, 41, 48, 74–75, 77, 142, 152, 169, 170, 173–77, 180, 190, 210, 211, 218, 226, 232, 238, 246; authority and, 87; cross-, 144, 231; culture of, 166, 167, 174, 250, 251; discussion and, 36; importance of, 172–74; leadership and, 175–77; mentorship and, 156; online, 36; peer, 179, 249; strengthening, 120, 121, 167; tutors and, 250–51; understanding of, 159; WC, 113–15
"Collaborative Learning and the 'Conversation of Mankind'" (Bruffee), 31
comments: qualitative verbatim, 87; suggestive, 87
communication, 50, 97, 98, 141, 212, 229, 230, 239, 249; dynamic, 89, 209; intraoffice, 250, 251; open, 207–8; shortcomings in, 64; STEM students and, 120; writing and, 136
community, 13; building, 54, 139, 140, 141, 144, 149, 172–74, 214; disciplinary, 239; discourse, 8–9, 35, 126, 219, 232; higher education, 17; lack of, 34; learning, 18, 25–29; professional, 18, 26, 27, 28, 219; sense of, 42, 148, 212, 213; tutor, 22; WC, 17, 26, 42, 109, 229; writing, 226
composition, 77, 135, 169; program, 86; teaching, 92, 101; theory, 104
Condon, Frankie, 162
Conference on College Composition and Communication, 108
conferences, 108, 173, 188, 226; video, 53; WC, 88
consultants, xii, 7, 39, 48, 54, 135–36, 139, 158, 236–37; agency and, 163; approaches of, 38, 235; awareness of, 231; clients and, 187, 188, 190; expertise of, 234–36; faculty, 8–10, 55, 105, 111, 140, 217; graduate, 135, 140, 142, 143, 144, 148, 149, 179, 189, 190, 220; part-time, 51; peer, 5, 6, 31, 32, 33, 34, 35, 37, 42, 47, 107, 110, 113, 119, 144; power dynamics and, 134; responses from, 133, 135; role of, 9–10, 12; students and, 50; training, 6, 8, 9, 36, 41, 49, 52, 105, 137, 145, 233–37; undergraduate, 8, 140, 142, 143, 144, 231; WC, 3–4, 34, 185; writing, 32, 37, 102, 103, 119, 121, 221. *See also* professional consultants
consultations, 7, 10, 74–75, 92, 149, 199, 200, 217–18, 220, 226, 232, 234–35; asynchronous, 104, 109; disciplinary, 224; effective, 217; graduate, 126, 182; multidisciplinary, 237; online, 108, 109; peer-to-peer, 125; synchronous, 108; undergraduate, 143; writing, 223, 243
conversations, 47, 98, 208, 209; cross-disciplinary, 231–32; in-person, 28; productive, 236; unending, 28
Cooper Union, 112–13, 114
coordinators, 24, 42, 82; program, 149
Corbett, Steven J., 19
Cordo, Paul, 235
costs: assumptions about, 53–55; direct/indirect, 52; turnover, 52
Craig, Jennifer, 230
Crain, Marion, 193, 195
Creating a Role (Stanislavski), 65, 69
"Creative Staffing for the Community College Writing Center in an Era of Outsourced Education" (Reglin), 33
Crime and Punishment (Dostoyevsky), 64, 65
"Critique of Pure Tutoring, A" (Burns), 127
"Cultivating Professional Writing Tutor Identities at a Two-Year College" (Bright), 33
culture, 46, 48; academic, 212, 221; collaborative, 166, 167, 174, 250, 251; learning, 166, 174; observation, 193, 202; organizational, 141, 174; WC, 139, 140, 141, 144; workplace, 12, 142, 143
Curry, Mary Jane, 220, 229

Dambruch, Steffani, 79–81, 82, 103, 113, 120
demographics, 45, 46, 92, 244
development: argument, 106; costs of, 53, 55; holistic, 81–84; intellectual, 146; opportunities for, 28, 52, 56; patterns of, 238; professional, xii, 7, 10, 12–13, 17, 18, 20–21, 22, 23, 27, 45, 47, 54–55, 73, 83, 92, 99, 104, 107, 136, 143, 148, 149, 159, 165–166, 167, 168, 169, 172, 175, 176, 182, 204, 211, 217, 219, 220,

221–25, 226, 233, 247, 248, 250; staff engagement/retention and, 55–56; students and, 52–53; sustainable, 28; synchronous, 51; thesis, 102; time for, 51–53; training and, 46, 50, 51–52, 53, 56
Diab, Rasha, 174
Dinitz, Sue, 115, 128, 132
directors, 153, 165, 192; assistant, 166, 176
disabilities, 50; students with, 18, 20, 23, 27, 28
disciplinary ambassadors, 218–19, 221–25, 231; curriculum for, 224–25; framework for, 218, 219–20, 221, 225
disciplinary conventions, 12, 115, 127, 180–81, 183
disciplinary maturity, 237–39
discourse, 35, 48, 89, 126, 132, 155, 219; academic, 92, 239; analysis, 87; deferential, 79; disciplinary construction of, 135; WC, 109, 113
discussion boards, 22, 27, 28, 37, 38, 51, 117
discussions, 21, 38; collaboration and, 36; community, 35; goal-setting, 135; monitoring, 208; synchronous/asynchronous, 37
disparity, 132, 134; power, 129, 136, 137
dissertations, xii, 116, 184, 186, 189
Dixon, Elise, 11, 216, 226, 233
Dostoyevsky, Fyodor, 65
dynamics: communication, 89, 209; group, 212; interpersonal, 14; power, 11, 126, 129, 130, 133, 134, 155, 163, 166, 169, 235, 248–50; social, 226

economic realities, 81–84, 193
editing, 20, 59, 96, 97
"Editing Line-by-Line" (Linville), 20
education, 18, 32, 35, 38, 45, 140, 198; higher, 54, 193; staff, xii, 160–63; training and, 34; tutor, 114, 242; tutoring and, 18
Electrical and Computer Engineering (ECE) Department (NJIT), 117
(E)Merging Identities: Graduate Students in the Writing Center (Nicolas), 247
engagement, 9, 37, 169; development and, 55–56; mutual, 139; strategic/tactical, 159, 160; training/development and, 55–56
English language learners, 18, 20, 28
Eodice, Michele, 158
epistemology, 225, 229, 237–38
ESL Writers: A Guide for Writing Center Tutors (Bruce and Rafoth), 6, 20

Eum, Seung hee, 237
Everyday Writing Center, The (Geller et al.), 80, 139, 165, 167
expectations, 97–98, 136, 239; curricular, 104; institutional, 104; managing, 135
experiences, 6, 32, 52, 68, 78, 208, 214, 249; analyzing, 161; collective, 19; diversity of, 175; educational, 20, 33, 49; graduate student, 152; learning, 49; mentorship, 148; professional, 18, 27, 72; teaching, 61, 112, 249; tutor, 21, 72, 171; writing, 159
expertise, 98, 126, 127–28, 235; disciplinary, 128, 217, 224
expert outsider, 10, 113–15, 115–17

faculty, xii, 22–23, 80, 87–88, 99, 161, 165, 233; adjunct, 21, 117; full-time, 21; rhetoric/composition, 86; tutor model, 87; writing, 86
Faculty SEED Grant, 121
Fahle Peck, Kimberly, 9, 32, 81–84, 103, 113, 120
Feak, Christine, 235
feedback, 19, 25, 37, 80, 93, 102, 103, 107, 170, 180, 183, 196, 198, 205, 209, 217, 231, 237, 238; asynchronous, 51, 104, 105; channel, 236; direct/indirect, 23; directive, 106; effective, 50; online, 105; peer, 12; providing, 97, 101; reflection and, 206–7; sharing, 208, 250–51; soliciting, 246; student, 81; training and, 18, 24; tutoring, 78; writing, 182
feeling me, 73, 84
Felder, Richard M., 120
fellowships, 185, 229, 234
Festa, Elizabeth, 11, 181, 217
First Year Writing Program, 112, 121
Fitzgerald, Lauren, 87, 92
Fitzsimmons, Will, 13
"Flattening Effects: Composition's Multicultural Imperative and the Problem of Narrative Coherence" (Alexander and Rhodes), 156
Flower, Linda, 89
Flowerdew, Lynne, 235
Ford, Clinita, 149
Fralix, Brandon, 17
Frissell, Alex, 13
Fulbright Program, 239
Funt, Alex, 12, 142, 193

Garcia, Elena, 237
Gardner, Clint, 41
GCs. See graduate consultants

Geller, Anne Ellen, 137, 165, 174, 218
genres, 14, 117, 118, 180, 238; disciplinary, 217, 229; research, 229–30
Giaimo, Genie, 159, 206, 207, 218, 244; mentoring and, 13; training and, 12
Gillespie, Paula, 90, 197, 214
Gladstein, Jill, 17
Gleason, William, 211
goals, 81, 84, 97, 149; development, 50, 84; long-term, 76; pedagogical, 134, 137; personal/professional, 83
Godbee, Beth, 183, 186, 188, 189; co-mentoring and, 182; peerness and, 184
Gomez, Amanda, 103, 113, 120; story of, 76–78
good intentions, twist on, 194–95
Good Intentions: Writing Center Work for Postmodern Times (Grimm), 194–95
GPS. *See* Graduate and Postdoctoral Studies Office
graduate consultants (GCs), 3, 6, 8, 10–14, 216, 217, 218, 220, 222, 223, 224, 231, 233–37, 238, 239; development of, 92, 218, 225; education of, 221; empowering, 225–27; recruiting/hiring, 219; reflection/interaction among, 220
Graduate and Postdoctoral Studies Office (GPS), 11, 230, 231, 232, 233, 234
graduate students, xii, 107, 135, 145, 156, 197, 204–5, 214, 216, 249; academic hierarchy and, 158; appointments for, 190; of color, 150; consultants and, 233; invisibility of, 195; isolation for, 152; limits on, 221; networks of, 160, 163; peerness and, 182–83, 183–84; support for, 232; training for, 195, 198; WCs and, 180–82; working with, 119; writing experiences of, 159
graduate teaching assistants (GTAs), 169, 172, 176
graduate writing centers (GWCs), 216, 217, 218, 220, 221–22; enriching, 225–27; GCs and, 219; grammar, 97, 106, 107; grants, 184, 229, 233; professional development at, 222, 224–25
Graybill, Jolie, 142
Greenfield, Laura, 174
GRFP. *See* National Science Foundation Graduate Fellowship Program
Grimm, Nancy, 194–95
growth, 110; lack of, 52; personal, 146; professional, 179–80
GTAs. *See* graduate teaching assistants
GWCs. *See* graduate writing centers

Hall, Mark, 195, 196, 202, 208, 247, 251; culture of observation and, 193; on tutors, 243
Hanlon-Baker, Patti, 79
Harasim, Linda, 35–36, 37
Harrington, Susanmarie, 115, 128, 132
Harris, Muriel, 6, 79, 89, 115
hazing, academic, 154, 158
Healy, Dave, 91, 94, 95
Hedengren, Mary, 77
Hewett, Ben, 105
Higher Order Concerns, 36, 38–39
Hoffman, Angelika, 235
Honors College (NJIT), 113
hooks, bell, 162
Hubbuch, Susan M., 115, 116, 127–28
Hughes, Bradley, 113, 116, 214; expert outsider and, 115; on tutor education, 114
Hughes, Hilary, 185
Huwe, Jennifer, 146
Hyland, Kenneth, 235

Ianetta, Melissa, 87, 92, 157
ICC. *See* Illinois Central College
Idea Generating, described, 36
Idea Organizing, described, 36
"Idea of a Writing Center, The" (North), 104
identity, 58, 71, 79, 84, 172–73, 220, 226; addressing, 10; careerist, 9; consultant, 9–10; conventional, 181; cultural, 92; disciplinary, 238; disparate, 74, 75–76, 175; individual, 229; integrated, 76; markers, 148; merging, 78; multiple, 73; peer tutor, xi; personal, 71; professional, 32, 72, 73, 80, 81, 83, 84, 217; relinquishing, 81; spatial, 92; struggles, 73, 74, 76; workplace, 79; writer-tutor, 76, 77
Illinois Central College (ICC), 31, 32
imposter syndrome, 76, 185, 249
IMRaD. *See* Introduction, Methods, Results, and Discussions
Inoue, Asao, 158
Inside Higher Ed, 152
institutional contexts, 106–8, 135; accounting for, 166–74
instruction, 4, 103; classroom, 90, 105; learning and, 34–35; writing, 81, 132, 133, 232
instructors: adjunct, 32, 34, 74, 79, 80, 82; tutors and, 90, 91, 92, 94; writing, 76, 245. *See also* teachers
Intellectual Convergence, described, 36
International Writing Centers Association, 44, 53, 108

Introduction, Methods, Results, and Discussions (IMRaD), 220, 237
Invisible Labor: Hidden Work in the Contemporary World, 193
"'It's All Coming Together, Right Before My Eyes': On Poetry, Peace, and Creative Placemaking in Writing Centers" (Boquet), 153

Jackson, Kim, 245
Jensen, Barbara, 194
Jewell, Megan Swihart, xi, xii, 17, 204
Johnson, Brad: mentoring and, 145–46
Journal Club, 54

Kael, Harvey, 214
Key Concepts in Adult Education and Training (Tight), 34
Khan, Aisha, 119
Kiedaisch, Jean, 115
kindness, 13; framework for, 154, 158; intentional, 152, 153–56, 159, 160–63
Klauza, Matthew, 193–94
knowledge, 39, 56, 75, 77, 83, 147, 148, 188, 189, 238, 249; coaching, 210; consultant, 237; depth/quality of, 125; differential, 127; disciplinary, 128, 217, 220, 224; discrepancy in, 131–32; formal, 234; gap, 236; genre, 233, 235; incorporating, 26; insider, 61; institutional, 49, 55, 177; management, 142; principles of, 62; privileged, 135; processual, 234; production of, 165; rhetorical, 42, 114, 234; sharing, 36, 78, 140, 144, 218, 235; subject-matter, 234; tutor/student, 62
Komora, Kirsten, 200

labor, 14, 27, 88; intellectual, 4; invisible, 192–93, 195; practices, 82–83; student, 141, 195; valuing, 200–202
Lamson, Lisa, 13
Lang, Marvel, 149
Laufer, Miriam E., 8, 32, 34, 48, 51, 53, 55, 81, 99, 113, 117
Lave, Jean, 172, 218
leadership: collaboration and, 175–77; distributed, 168 (fig.); hierarchical, 167 (fig.); models, 167, 168; structure for, 166, 167, 175, 176
Leadership Team, 168, 175, 176
Learner, Neal, 157
learning, 28, 53, 55, 219, 238; collaborative, 31, 87, 166, 177; community of, 169–71; culture of, 166, 174; distance, 108; environments/creating, 162–63;

instruction and, 34–35; management systems, 22; mutual, 166, 177; on-the-job, 49; process, 250
LeCluyse, Christopher, 219, 242, 249
"legitimate peripheral participation" (LPP), 172
Lemur Center, 213
Lerner, Neal, 90, 197, 230
LGBTQIA+ Safe Space, 246
Lincoln, Abraham, 128
Linville, Cynthia, 20
literacy, 120, 181, 224
literature: review, 127–28; WC, 23, 46, 48
Locke, Lawrence, 235
logistics, 172; training, 243–46
Lu, Min-Zhan, 162
Lunsford, Andrea, 6–7, 10, 115

Mackiewicz, Jo, 118, 201
"Making the Invisible Visible" (Wulff), 152
Marquette University, 13, 142, 165, 169
McCamley, Michael, 157
McKinney, Jackie Grutsch, 4, 157, 192
Mendelsohn, Sue, 219, 242, 249
mentees, 146; mentors and, 13, 119, 145, 148–49, 187, 198; supporting, 145
mentoring, 7, 10, 139, 145–49, 166, 192, 194, 195, 201, 205, 231; achieving/maintaining, 156–60; collaboration and, 156; critical, 152, 153–56, 156–60, 162; cross-, 115, 117–20; dialogue about, 186; exploring, 13–14; graduate student, 140, 160–63; informal, 147–48, 202; models for, 161, 193; mutual, 180; observation-based, 192, 193; paying for, 195; peer, 140, 145, 146, 147, 149, 150; programs, 13–14, 195–96, 197, 200, 201; reframing, 153; relationships and, 159; source of, 196; supportive environments and, 163; teaching, 161; work of, 161, 238. *See also* co-mentoring
mentors, 146, 150, 197–98; critical, 156, 159, 160; faculty, 233; graduate student, 198; mentees and, 13, 119, 145, 148–49, 187, 198
Messuri, Kristin, 12, 183, 231
methodologies, 35, 229, 237
methods, 129–30, 229, 236
Michigan State University (MSU) Writing Center, 140, 142, 147, 148
"Minimalist Tutoring" (Brooks), 114
"Mock Tutorials: A dramatic method for training tutors" (Komora), 200
modules: creating, 41; grant-writing, 230; interactive, 108; professional, 39; pro-

grammatic nature of, 42; set of, 36–37
Moneyhun, Clyde, 79
Moore, Will, 88
Morgan, John, 86, 88
Moss, Sherry, 71, 72, 76, 79, 84; identity and, 73, 74
MSU. *See* Michigan State University
Mukavetz, Andrea, 187
multiculturalism, flattening effects of, 156
Multilingual Student Writing Support Series, 49
Munday, Nicole Kraemer, 20
Murphy, Christina, 6

Nabokov, Vladimir, 64, 65
narratives: fix-it, 157; grand, 157, 179, 192, 232; marginalized, 157; WC, 232–33
National Aeronautics and Space Administration, 239
National Alliance for Broader Impacts (NABI), 233
"National Census of Writing," 24, 44, 45
National Institutes of Health, 239
National Science Foundation Graduate Fellowship Program (GRFP), 230, 238; supporting, 233–37
National Science Foundation (NSF), 233–37; Graduate Fellowship, 11, 12; grants, 239; STEM and, 230
National University of Ireland Galway (NUIG), 58, 60, 62
networking, 11, 141, 142, 144, 145, 168
New Jersey Institute of Technology (NJIT), 113, 114, 116, 117, 118, 119, 120, 121; tutors at, 112, 115
New Jersey Institute of Technology (NJIT) Writing Center, 121
Newkirk, Thomas, 40, 41
Nicolas, Melissa, 157, 247
NJIT. *See* New Jersey Institute of Technology
Non-Directive Method, 36, 39–41
"(Non)Meeting of the Minds" (Munday), 20
Nordlof, John, 62
Norman H. Ott Memorial Writing Center, 13, 165, 166, 169, 170, 175
North, Stephen, 19, 90, 104, 179, 184
Novotny, Julia, 183, 186, 188, 189; co-mentoring and, 182; peerness and, 184
Nowacek, Rebecca, 13, 113, 116, 142, 159, 163; expert outsider and, 115; onboarding and, 234; on tutor education, 114

Nowhere near the Line: Pain and Possibility in Teaching and Writing (Boquet), 153
NSF. *See* National Science Foundation
NUIG. *See* National University of Ireland Galway

observation, 207; culture of, 193, 202; good, 196–98; high-stakes/low-stakes, 200
observation tracking sheets, 196, 199–200
Ohio State University (OSU), 140, 142, 143; mentoring at, 147; onboarding at, 144–45
Old Dominion University (ODU), 241, 242
Olson, Bobbi, 47
onboarding, 13, 38, 48, 49, 139, 140, 141–45, 149, 150, 234; accounts of, 169–71; described, 169, 176–77; first-semester, 169; presemester, 143, 144
online collaborative learning theory (OCL), 35–36
"Online Superstars," 209
Online Writing Centers Community, 109
Online Writing Conference, The (Hewett), 105
online writing lab (OWL), 44, 45, 46, 86, 87, 93, 99
opportunities: connection, 141; development, 143, 167; employment, 83; in-between-ness as site of, 109–10; leadership, 83; learning, 119, 173; part-time, 83; pedagogical, 102; professional, 102
O'Reilley, Mary Rose, 154
Oster, Sandra, 235
OSU. *See* Ohio State University
"Our Little Secret" (Boquet), 34, 40
"Our Students Can Do That" (Gardner), 41
OWL. *See* online writing lab
Oxford Guide, 21
Oxford University, 86, 88

pain, 158, 160, 162
Paré, Anthony, 225
partnerships, 171, 190, 226, 231
PCs. *See* professional consultants
Pears Casanave, Christine, 181
pedagogy, xii, 13, 53, 55, 62, 114, 130, 137, 152, 154, 160, 162–63, 172, 242, 244; directive/non-directive, 19, 105; educational, 20; research and, 76; tutoring, 17, 19–20, 48, 61, 78, 79, 86–87, 96, 134; WC, 18, 19, 48, 59, 61, 92, 98, 102, 104–6, 109, 113, 133, 134, 135, 159, 231; writing, 77, 81, 221

Pedretti, Mark, 11, 216, 221, 234–35
Peer Tutor Writing Tutor Alumni Project, 72
"Peer Tutoring: A Contradiction in Terms?" (Trimbur), 127
Peer Writing Tutor Alumni Research Project, 214
peers, 3, 6, 11, 77, 125, 126, 182–84, 189, 198; advocating by, 103; consultant, 234; staffing by, 107; support from, 68; undergraduate, 139–40, 158
Peripheral Visions for Writing Centers (McKinney), 4, 157
Perkins, G. N., 72
Peters, Ray, 141
Peterson, Nancy, 211
Pflueger, Ruth C., 118
Phillips, Talinn, 216
philosophy, WC, 54, 231, 242, 244
plural careerists, 72, 73, 79, 82, 83, 84
Poe, Mya, 230
politics, 31, 61, 155, 187
Poster, Winifred R., 193, 195
power, 243; asymmetries, 127; differences of, 127; discrepancies, 130, 131
"Power and Authority in Peer Tutoring" (Carino), 127
practice, 246; communities of, 149, 169–71, 225; hands-on, 248
Praxis: A Writing Center Journal, 37, 54
problem-solving, 5, 14, 249
professional consultants (PCs), xii, 3, 7, 8–10, 31, 32–34, 35, 36, 39, 41, 42, 46–47, 48, 49, 50, 102, 104, 107, 109, 110, 111, 116, 119, 121, 140, 217; development of, 44, 45, 52–53, 55, 56; full-time, 53; retention of, 52–53; training, 44, 45, 51–52, 56
professionalism, 18, 20, 46, 76, 109, 226
professionalization, 13, 108, 142, 145
proofreading, 59, 87, 96, 97
proposals, 229; cross-disciplinary, 233; graduate, 232–33; writing, 230, 234, 237
punctuation, 39, 63, 64
Purdue University, 3, 44–45

qualitative analysis, 129
quantitative studies, 121
Quick, Catherine, 157

Rafoth, Ben, 6, 20, 90
Raines, Helon Howell, 92
reading, 37, 38, 39, 40, 42
Reading-to-Write: Exploring a Cognitive and Social Process (Flower et al.), 89

reflection, 37, 38, 39, 41, 42, 53, 169, 205, 209, 212, 220, 244; culture of, 173; dialogic, 251; feedback and, 206–7; peer, 12; questions for, 84
Reglin, Jill, 33
relationships, 11, 155, 188; building, 148, 160–61, 166, 187, 188; collaborative, 115, 169, 170; co-mentoring, 181, 184; complex, 163; consultant/client, 188; cyclical, 80; establishing, 158, 161; graduate student, 186, 188; hierarchical, 166; interpersonal, 59, 166; mentoring, 119, 146, 159, 186, 198; peer, 171, 182–83, 183–84, 190; productive, 147; professional, 190, 226; reciprocal, 146; shifting, 186; student-teacher, 48; working, 180, 185, 186, 187, 208
research, 6, 54, 112, 128, 187, 211, 219, 221, 234, 238; agenda, 173; collaborative, 166, 173, 217; data-driven, 121; empirical, 87; financial support for, 229; pedagogy and, 76; problems, 235, 236; qualitative, 185; replicable, aggregable, and data-supported (RAD), 45; story, 236–37; undergraduate, 166; WC, 55, 98, 204, 223
resources, xii, 6, 7, 207, 208, 214, 249, 251; communal, 137; human, 48, 49; informal, 197; management of, 222; online, 211; searching for, 5; staff education, xi; writing, 107
respect, 97; definition/understanding of, 156; intentional, 156; reciprocal, 158; rhetoric of, 13, 155–56, 159, 160–63; treating with, 163; utilizing, 161
responsibilities, 3, 55, 56, 146, 174, 187, 249; leadership, 175; nontutoring, 49; tutoring, 78
retention, 9, 150; philosophical inducement for, 50; training/development and, 55–56
"Rethinking Our Work with Multilingual Writers: The Ethics and Responsibility of Language Teaching in the Writing Center," 47
rhetoric, 103, 106, 117, 118, 131, 132, 133, 135, 155, 169, 234
Rhetoric of Respect (Rousculp), 154–55, 159
Rhodes, Jacqueline, 156
Rice University, 11, 230
roles, 12, 39, 250; addressing, 10; peer, 90; redefining, 14; rhetorical, 114
Rollins, Brooke, 249
Rousculp, Tiffany, 152, 153, 154–55, 156, 159
Rowan, Karen, 174

rubrics, 13, 103, 196, 199, 200, 201, 202
Ruppo, Irina, 9
Ryan, Leigh, 6, 19, 20

St. John's College, 88
Saint Louis University, 192, 193, 194, 196
St. Martin's Sourcebook for Writing Tutors, The (Murphy and Sherwood), 6
Salomon, Gavriel, 72
Sanyal, Arundhati, 9–10, 17, 18, 23
Savini, Catherine, 218
scaffolding, 35, 36, 62, 63, 149, 182, 239
Scanlon, Anna, 13
Schaeben, Marcel, 145
Scharold, Dagmar, 207
scheduling, 16, 21, 51, 82, 148, 194, 247, 248
Schimel, Joshua, 235, 237
scholarship, 44, 54, 108–9, 217, 248; WC, xi, 98, 105, 125, 139, 169, 172, 194, 195, 220, 243, 244, 247, 251
science, 112, 113, 116, 120, 121; writing conventions for, 119
science, technology, engineering, and mathematics. *See* STEM
seeming me, 73, 80, 84
self-assessments, 223, 224
self-awareness, 98, 234
self-discovery, 78, 80
self-efficacy, 83, 120–21
self-reflection, 50, 75–76, 78, 81
sentences, 135; complex, 64; structure of, 68
set induction, 37, 38, 39, 40
Seton Hall University (SHU), 17, 23, 86, 87, 88, 93, 99, 100
Seton Hall University (SHU) Writing Center, 84, 86, 87, 99
Shakespeare, William, 65, 66
Shamoon, Linda, 115, 127
Sharkey-Smith, Matthew, 10, 59, 80
Shaughnessy, Mina, 40, 89
Shea, Kelly A., 9–10, 17, 18, 23
Sherwood, Steve, 6
Shiell, Anne, 9, 18, 22, 61, 83
SHU. *See* Seton Hall University
Sicari, Anna, 13, 171, 249
Siemann, Catherine, 10, 59
Silverman, Stephen, 235
Simpson, Steve, 230, 232
Singh-Corcoran, Nathalie, 180–81
skills, 50, 75, 83, 98, 102, 205, 210; collaboration, 226; customer, 74; presentation, 54; professional, 56, 120; reading, 65; valuation of, 202; writing, 61, 63, 65, 182

Skype, 51, 233
Slack, 208, 209, 210, 212
Smith, Louise, 33
Smith, Trixie G., 249
Snively, Helen, 233
social justice, 162, 163, 223
Socratic questioning, 80, 89, 105, 136
Spirduso, Waneen, 235
spotlight sessions, described, 54
staff meetings, 35, 39, 174
staffing, xi, 3, 5, 141, 153, 165; concerns about, 14; turnover rate and, 245
"Staffing a Writing Center with Professional Tutors" (Strang), 112
Stanislavski, Constantin, 9, 58–59, 67, 68, 69; analysis by, 65; facts/imagination and, 66; textual analysis and, 59; on unconscious, 63
Stanislavsky on the Art of the Stage (Stanislavski), 69
STEM, 10, 11, 117, 230, 235, 236; institutions, 112, 118, 119; subjects, 111, 113, 121; work, 116, 220
STEM students, 111, 113, 116, 117, 118; communication and, 120; tutors and, 120–21; WC and, 122
storytelling, 156, 189, 237
Strang, Steven, 17, 47, 51, 71, 112–13, 116, 119
strategies, 11, 18, 20, 39, 52, 89, 107, 176, 207, 208, 209, 213, 249; coaching, 212; consultation, 74; effective, 243; in-conference, 174; pedagogical, 62; problem-solving, 250; rhetorical, 131, 136; special, 37; training, 242; tutoring, 20, 53, 62, 250; visual, 236; WAC, 135
structure, 64, 83, 132, 133; institutional, 184
Studio (Illinois Central College), 31, 32, 35, 38, 41, 42
style, finding, 73–75
subject expertise, 115–17
Summers, Sarah, 128, 132, 135, 222, 235
support, xii, 124, 152; centralization of, 31; institutional, 152; services, 81, 109
surveys, 23, 50, 92–98, 245
Swales, John, 235
systems, 82, 154, 232; tutors and, 63–68

Talk about Writing: The Tutoring Strategies of Experienced Writing (Mackiewicz and Thompson), 201
Tardy, Christine, 234
TAs. *See* teaching assistants
teachers: tutors and, 79, 80–81, 91, 114. *See also* instructors

teaching, 3, 13, 47, 59, 82, 92, 97, 156, 187, 234–36, 250–51; tutoring and, 5, 18, 24, 80, 81, 87, 170
teaching assistants (TAs), 86, 152, 157, 205
Teaching to Transgress (hooks), 162
technology, 12, 45, 113, 116, 119, 210, 242, 243, 246, 247, 248, 251
Texas Tech University (TTU) GWC, 12, 217, 221–22, 226; professional development at, 222, 224–25
textual analysis, 59, 63, 66, 89
theory, 135; WC, 103, 244, 246, 247
Think-Pair-Share, 53–54
Thomas, Therese, 90
Thompson, Isabelle Kramer, 201
Thompson, Meagan, 12, 141, 171, 195, 196, 207, 211, 241, 249
Thonus, Terese, 90, 91, 93, 94, 95, 98
"Three Models of Mentorship: Feminist Leadership and Graduate WPA" (Christoph et al.), 161
Tight, Malcolm, 34
time, assumptions about, 50–53
Tinto, Vincent, 146
"Toward a Professional Consultant's Handbook: Researching Support and Training Methods" (Jewell and Cheatle), 7
training, 11–12, 37, 44, 45, 60, 96–97, 98, 99, 118–19, 128, 130, 132, 137, 140, 144, 145, 173, 204, 205, 206, 207, 211, 212, 214, 238; adequate, 246; assumptions about, 46–50; asynchronous, 244, 251; attending, 22–23; collaborative, 246; compliance, 141; consultant, 3, 8–9, 35, 126; crash course, 41; development and, 46, 50, 51–52, 53, 56; discussing, 26; education and, 34; evolution of, 251; exercises for, 9; feedback and, 18; funding, 22–23, 55; goals of, 34, 49–50; graduate, 198, 200, 202, 252; improving, 28, 242; in-depth, 214; in-person, 35, 42; informal, 202; inquiry-based approach to, 251; materials for, 6, 7, 17; modular, 31, 34–36, 41; ongoing, 22, 49, 250; online, 37, 51; organizational culture, 141; paying for, 195; pedagogical, 76; platform, 197; practices for, 51, 251–52; process, 35, 67; professional, 9, 33, 35, 37–38; programs, 143, 197, 202; relevant, 23–24; schedules/sample, 24–25, 25 (table), 27 (table); source of, 196; staff engagement/retention and, 55–56; strategic, 55, 130; students and, 52–53; synchronous, 51; time for, 51–53, 96; tutor, 17, 18–21, 22–23, 24–25, 44, 46, 47–48, 96, 242, 243–46, 247; WC, 3, 4, 214, 219
tricksters, 79, 80–81
Trimbur, John, 61, 127
TTU. *See* Texas Tech University
tutees, 88, 95, 126; concerns of, 94, 98; graduate, 99; international, 100; knowledge discrepancy and, 131–32; real audience for, 90; simulating, 97–98; tutors and, 91, 119, 130, 131, 134, 136–37
"Tutor Training Comes Full Circle: From E-mail to Practicum and Back Again" (Klauza), 193–94
tutorials, 59, 88, 94, 127; mock, 61; non-directive, 128; peer-to-peer, 115; undergraduate, 125; writing, 79, 127
tutoring, 18, 21, 23, 51, 72, 74, 76, 92, 131, 136, 149, 169, 171, 192, 196, 201, 249; approaches to, 59; authoritative affect in, 90; complexities of, 3; cross-disciplinary, 135; direct, 9, 19, 209; effective, 47; expectations of, 97–98; faculty, 87–88, 99; good, 196–98; in-person, 143; indirect, 19; insecurities with, 161; metacognition in, 89; mock, 97, 197; multidisciplinary, 135; navigating, 79; non-directive, 78; nonpeer, 17; one-on-one, 47, 89, 179; online, 80, 86, 143, 248; outtakes for, 199; paradox of, 94; peer, 91, 98, 111, 112, 125, 127, 134; practicing, 48; process, 119; professional, 81, 111, 117; resistance to, 161; strong, 47–48, 89; teaching and, 5, 18, 24, 80, 81, 87, 170; techniques for, 59; trees, 197; tutee-led, 97; writing, 7, 87
"Tutoring Style, Tutoring Ethics" (Corbett), 19
tutors, 80, 83, 116, 119, 127, 129, 130, 170, 194, 206; administrators and, 82; advice from, 63; agency and, 248–50; business, 79; comments by, 66, 131; connecting, 27, 60, 86; directors and, 165, 166; disciplinary expertise and, 115; discussions with, 29; distraction for, 198; effective, 246; empathy for, 67; expectations of, 33–34, 97; faculty, 17, 18, 19, 20, 21, 22, 23–24, 25, 26, 26 (table), 27, 28, 86–100, 102, 113, 116, 120–21; generalist, 229; graduate, 21, 22, 24, 128, 158, 160–63, 165–66, 168, 169, 170–71, 172, 173, 174, 175, 176, 177, 188, 193, 198, 201, 204, 211, 214, 241, 242, 243–46, 248–50; instructors and, 90, 91, 92, 94, 245; knowledge discrepancy and, 131–32;

meetings with, 197; online, 87; peer, 3, 6, 17, 18–21, 22, 23, 24, 26, 27, 28, 44, 61, 71, 72, 79, 84, 88, 89, 90, 92–93, 94–95, 96, 99, 102, 103, 104, 112, 113, 114, 115, 118, 119, 120, 140, 171, 204; postgraduate, 61, 63, 68; power dynamics and, 248–50; professional, 20, 23, 32, 59, 61, 63, 68, 71–72, 73, 74, 76–77, 78, 79, 81, 82, 83, 84, 111–13, 115, 116, 117, 120–21, 204; psychology, 79; qualifications of, 132–33; questions by, 66, 250; role of, 89, 90–91, 93–94, 102; skills/knowledge and, 65, 83; specialist-versus-generalist, 127; student, 113, 243, 250; supervising, 81–82; systems and, 63–68; teachers and, 79, 80–81, 91, 114; tools for, 64, 135; training, 18, 21–22, 44, 58, 61, 65, 86, 88, 96–97, 98, 99, 114, 118–19, 128, 132, 140, 166, 172, 173, 197, 204, 205, 242, 243; tutees and, 91, 119, 130, 131, 134, 136, 137; undergraduate, xi, 21, 72, 96–97, 98, 165, 166, 168, 170–71, 172, 175, 177, 204, 211; undermining, 130–31; work of, 60, 67, 71, 189, 194, 196; writers and, 63, 76–78; writing, 33–34, 63, 72, 73, 75, 78, 79, 92, 107, 113

Tutor's Guide: Helping Writers One to One, A (Rafoth), 20

Tyson, Lisa Nicole, 73–75, 103, 113, 120

University of Illinois at Chicago, 196
University of North Carolina at Chapel Hill (UNC-CH) Learning Center, 211
University of North Carolina at Chapel Hill (UNC-CH) Writing Center, 12, 142, 205, 206, 210–11, 212–14
University of Toronto, 189
University Writing Services, 195, 198

Van Cleave, Jessica, 185
violence, 174; academic, 154
Vough, Heather, 71, 72, 73, 76, 79, 84
Vygotsky, Lev, 62

WAC. *See* Writing Across the Curriculum
Walden University Writing Center (WUWC), 22, 46, 49, 50, 53, 55, 101, 102, 104–10; consultants in, 45; training at, 104, 105
Walker, Kristin, 117–18
Watt, Lorna, 237
WCenter listserv, 7, 44

WCOnline, 248
Weakley, Marcus, 11, 216, 221, 234–35
Weissbach, Robert S., 118
Wenger, Etienne, 139, 172, 218
Westbrook, Evelyn, 249
WID. *See* writing in the disciplines
WLN: A Journal of Writing Center Scholarship, 7, 37, 54, 109, 204
Wolf, John, 121
workshops, 12, 121, 144, 159, 160, 205, 234
writers: agency and, 163; graduate, 219, 225–27, 238; improving, 38, 93; multilingual, 49, 50, 216; professional, 239; proposal, 236–37; readers and, 187; tutors and, 63, 76–78
writing: academic, 67, 68, 79, 182, 206, 219, 224; assessments of, 90, 107; assignments, 33, 93; communication and, 136; conventions, 133, 223; courses, 5, 103; creative, 77; disciplinary, 224, 230, 237; groups, 190, 205, 230; process, 20, 23, 36, 39, 78, 80, 93, 152, 196, 207, 238; projects, 33, 93, 183; prompts, 223, 224; proposal, 230, 234, 237; teaching, 101, 161
Writing across Borders, 47
Writing Across the Curriculum (WAC), 3, 36, 88, 106–7, 135, 137
Writing Center Journal, 44, 54, 115, 207
Writing Center Research Project (Purdue University), 3, 44–45
Writing Centers and Disability (Babcock, Day, and Daniels), 23
Writing Centers and the New Racism (Greenfield and Rowan), 174
"Writing Centers Research Project Survey," 46
writing in the disciplines (WID), 218, 219, 223, 225, 231
Writing Lab, 44, 45, 46
Writing Lab Newsletter, xii, 44, 194
"Writing Teacher Who Writes: Creative Writing, Ancient Rhetoric, and Composition Instruction, The" (Hedengren), 77
Wulff, Alex, 13, 152, 169, 210, 246
WUWC. *See* Walden University Writing Center

Young, Vershawn, 162

Zimmerelli, Lisa, 6, 19, 20

ABOUT THE EDITORS

Megan Swihart Jewell, PhD, has served for more than twelve years as director of the Writing Resource Center at Case Western Reserve University (CWRU), where she supervised a staff of more than forty undergraduate, graduate, professional, and faculty consultants. Prior to to her work at CWRU, Jewell served as director of the Writing Center at Duquesne University, and as an undergraduate and graduate consultant at other college and university writing centers. Jewell has published articles on writing centers in such scholarly venues as *WLN: A Journal of Writing Center Scholarship, Praxis: A Writing Center Journal*, and the *Journal of Pharmacy Education*; she has published articles linking contemporary trends in writing pedagogy to avant-garde poetics in several other scholarly journals and collections. Jewell has presented her work at more than thirty national and international conferences. She currently serves on the editorial board of *WLN: A Journal of Writing Center Scholarship*.

Joseph Cheatle is the director of the Writing and Media Center at Iowa State University. He has previously worked as both a graduate consultant and a professional consultant in writing centers. He is a co-leader of the International Writing Centers Association Summer Institute and serves as an at-large representative of the International Writing Centers Association Board. Between 2017 and 2019, he was a member of the Elon University Center for Engaged Learning's Research Seminar on Residential Learning Communities as a High-Impact Practice. Last, he was part of a research team that received the International Writing Centers Association Research Grant for examining writing center documents and creating a digital repository for those documents.

ABOUT THE AUTHORS

Fallon N. Allison is the coordinator of the Academic Support Center and Studio Writing Center at Illinois Central College. Fallon's poetry has appeared in diverse publications, including the *Evansville Review* and *Spitball*. She is also a regular presenter at the International Writing Center Association (IWCA), Midwestern Writing Center Association (MWCA), and Association for the Coaching and Tutoring Profession (ACTP) conferences. Her research interests include the literary hermeneutics of Hans Robert Jauss as well as British Romantic poets' engagements with genre.

Vicki Behrens is the former assistant director of the Writing Center at the University of North Carolina at Chapel Hill and has also worked as a professional writing tutor for military-affiliated students at the University of Colorado Boulder. She has attended the International Writing Center Association Summer Institute and served on the board of the Southeastern Writing Center Association.

Elizabeth H. Boquet is a professor of English and director of the Writing Center at Fairfield University in Fairfield, Connecticut. At Fairfield, Beth has held several faculty leadership and administrative positions, including director of first-year writing, associate dean, and associate vice president for academic affairs. She is the author of *Nowhere Near the Line* and *Noise from the Writing Center* and co-author of *The Everyday Writing Center: A Community of Practice*, all published by Utah State University Press. She served two terms as co-editor of the *Writing Center Journal* and is a two-time recipient of the IWCA Outstanding Research Award.

Cassie J. Brownell is an assistant professor in curriculum, teaching, and learning at the Ontario Institute for Studies in Education within the University of Toronto located in Ontario, Canada. A former elementary educator, Cassie uses critical qualitative methods and sociocultural theories to examine issues of educational justice and equity in early childhood. She has received awards from the Writing and Literacies Special Interest Group as well as the Language and Social Processes Special Interest Group within the American Educational Research Association for her contributions to writing studies.

Matt Burchanoski is the graduate assistant director of the Ott Memorial Writing Center as well as an instructor and PhD candidate in English at Marquette University. His dissertation considers the legacies of postmodernism in twenty-first-century fiction, focusing on cosmopolitanism and humanism by investigating the works of David Mitchell, Jennifer Egan, Karen Joy Fowler, and Michael Ondaatje.

Megan Boeshart Burelle is a lecturer and Writing Center director at Old Dominion University. She teaches general education writing courses. She works with a graduate student population of tutors providing support to both undergraduate and graduate student writers. She is also the liaison between the Global Society of Online Literacy Educators (GSOLE) and the International Writing Center Association (IWCA). Her research interests include writing centers, online tutoring, and multimodal feedback. She is currently working on her PhD in English and her dissertation is about online writing tutoring and asynchronous screencasting feedback.

ABOUT THE AUTHORS

Danielle Clapham is an assistant professor of English and director of the Writing Center at the University of Jamestown. Her most recent research in rhetoric and composition focuses on spatial and disability rhetorics and academic integrity in writing centers. She also conducts pedagogical research on inclusive teaching practices and Universal Design in Learning.

Steffani Dambruch is an instructor of English at Old Dominion University and professional writing consultant at Virginia Wesleyan University. Her research focuses on the intersections between first year writing and writing center pedagogy. She is the 2018 recipient of the Joyce Neff Outstanding Affiliate Faculty Teaching Award.

Elise Dixon is an Assistant Professor of English and director of the writing center at University of North Carolina at Pembroke. Her scholarship explores how people from marginalized backgrounds compose together to develop a sense of critical agency. Her work has appeared in the *Writing Lab Newsletter*, *The Peer Review Journal*, *The Journal of Veteran Studies*, and numerous books. She is a 2020 recipient of the Conference on Composition and Communication (CCCC) Gloria Anzaldúa Rhetorician Award.

Elizabeth Festa is a Proposal Development Specialist in the Office of Research at Rice University where she supports faculty and postdocs in preparing and submitting grants. She is formerly the associate director of the Program for Writing and Communication at Rice University, where she developed the graduate student peer-coaching program for several national graduate fellowships. Her current research and pedagogical interests include best practices in training proposal editors and in facilitating proposal writing workshops.

Will Fitzsimmons is a graduate student at the University of Oregon working to complete a masters in Public Administration. He plans to work as a policy analyst specializing in affordable housing policy.

Alex Frissell is a PhD candidate in the English Department at Marquette University. He is currently completing a dissertation that uses novels written by North American authors to expand scholarship in the field of age studies. He lives in Madison, Wisconsin, with his partner, Addie, and three cats, Amelia, Jane, and Charles. In his free time he enjoys teaching guitar and listening to live jazz.

Alex Funt is the writing coach specialist at the University of North Carolina Chapel Hill Writing and Learning Center.

Genie Giaimo is assistant professor of writing and rhetoric and Writing Center director at Middlebury College. Her work has been published in *Praxis*, *Journal of Writing Analytics*, *Teaching English in the Two-Year College*, *Journal of Writing Research*, *Research in Online Literacy Education*, and *Kairos*, as well as a number of edited collections. She is the special editor, along with Yanar Hashlamon, of a recent issue of *WLN* on wellness and self-care in writing center work, and an editor of the digital monograph *Wellness and Care in Writing Center Work* (2021). Her current research utilizes quantitative and qualitative models to answer a range of questions about behaviors and practices in and around writing centers, such as tutor attitudes toward wellness and self-care practices, tutor engagement with writing center documentation, and students' perceptions of writing centers.

Amanda Gomez is a poet, instructor, and law school student. She received her MFA in poetry at Old Dominion University. She has worked as both a graduate and a professional writing tutor, and she has taught both in the high school and university settings. Her poetry can be read in print and online journals such as *Tupelo Quarterly*, *North American*

Review, and *Nimrod International Journal*, for which she was a semifinalist for their 2019 Pablo Neruda Prize for Poetry. Recently, her poetry chapbook, *Wasting Disease*, was published by Finishing Line Press.

Lisa Lamson is a PhD candidate in American history at Marquette University in Milwaukee, Wisconsin, a previous recipient of Marquette's Arthur J. Schmitt Leadership fellowship for 2019–2020, and currently works as a Lecturer in the History and Humanities department at the University of Wisconsin–Green Bay. Her dissertation examines Black Baltimorean critiques of nineteenth century educational systems to understand how girls of color were educated and for what purpose.

Miriam E. Laufer currently works as the academic support specialist for the Learning Assistance Center at Howard Community College in Columbia, Maryland. Previously, she was the manager of the Writing, Reading, and Language Center at Montgomery College in Germantown, Maryland. She is the 2019–20 president and a founding member of the Maryland College Learning Center Association. Her professional interests include supporting and training professional tutors and examining the role of learning centers in facilitating supplemental instruction.

Kristin Messuri is the associate director of the Writing Centers of Texas Tech University, where she directs the Graduate Writing Center. She is also a co-founder and co-director of Texas Tech's Women Faculty Writing Program and a recipient of the President's Excellence in Gender Equity Award. Her current research explores affect and writing initiatives, examining the workings and efficiency of writing groups, the implementation of diversity and inclusion initiatives in writing centers, and the intersection of writing center work and disciplinary research for graduate writing consultants.

Rebecca Nowacek is a professor of English at Marquette University, where she co-directs the Ott Memorial Writing Center. She is the author of *Agents of Integration: Understanding Transfer as a Rhetorical Act*, and her work has also appeared in *CCC*, *College English*, and *RTE*. Her chapter in *Naming What We Know*, co-authored with Brad Hughes, received the IWCA Outstanding Article award. Rebecca was a Carnegie Scholar with the Carnegie Academy for the Scholarship of Teaching and Learning, and the 2012 recipient of Marquette's Gettel Faculty Award for Teaching Excellence.

Kimberly Fahle Peck is the Writing Center director at York College of Pennsylvania. She is a co-author of the chapter "Research Methods: Designing Methods Instructions and Experiences That Invite Undergraduates in the Field" in *The Naylor Report on Undergraduate Research in Writing Studies*, and she served as an annotator for *The Bedford Bibliography of Research in Online Writing Instruction*. She is a co-editor of *Young Scholars in Writing*. She has presented her work at various national and regional writing and writing center conferences, and her research areas include writing centers, undergraduate research, online writing instruction, and technology mediation in writing instruction.

Mark Pedretti is an assistant professor of English and writing specialist at Providence College. Mark has recently published articles in *Composition Studies* and *Doris Lessing Studies*, along with chapters in *Bridging the Multimodal Gap: From Theory and Practice* (Utah State University Press, 2019) and *Writing Centers at the Center of Change* (Routledge, 2020). He is currently working on a book project about multimodal composition and the ideology of instrumental reason.

Irina Ruppo manages the Academic Writing Centre at the National University of Ireland Galway (NUIG), where she also teaches in the discipline of English. Irina is a graduate of Hebrew University of Jerusalem, Trinity College Dublin, and NUIG. Her publications include *Ibsen and the Irish Revival* (Palgrave, 2010) and *Ibsen and Chekhov on the Irish Stage* (Carysfort Press, 2012; with and in memory of Ros Dixon).

Arundhati Sanyal, PhD, is a senior faculty associate in the English Department at Seton Hall University and director of the Writing Center. She teaches first-year writing, nineteenth-century British literature, and philosophy and religion in the English Department and in the University Core. Her research centers on nineteenth-century and postcolonial literature and Composition/Writing Centers. Her latest publication on Tagore and Yeats appears in *Watchung Review*.

Anna Scanlon, PhD, is the director of the Writing Center at Illinois Wesleyan University. Her current publications include "Everyday Reflective Practice" in the *Writing Center Journal* and "The Anorexic Angle: Reading Popular Culture through the Lens of *Anorexia and Mimetic Desire*" in *René Girard and Pop Culture* (forthcoming from Rowman and Littlefield).

Matthew Sharkey-Smith is a senior writing instructor at Walden University. His research interests include writerly self-efficacy, writing centers, and online writing instruction. He has co-authored an article published in *WLN: A Journal of Writing Center Scholarship* and presented at various conferences including the International Writing Centers Association and the Association of Writers.

Kelly A. Shea is an associate professor of English / director of the First-Year Writing Program (and former director of the Writing Center) at Seton Hall University (SHU). She teaches undergraduate and graduate composition and literature courses; trains graduate students as composition instructors; and studies, presents, and publishes on writing, teaching, faculty development, and technology issues—and their intersections. She has published in *Writing Program Administrator, Writing Lab Newsletter,* and *Across the Disciplines*; she contributed a book chapter to *Collaborative Learning and Writing: Essays on Using Small Groups in Teaching English and Composition*; and she is a regular on the programs of the International Writing Center Association (IWCA), Conference on Composition and Communication (CCCC), and the NJ College English Association conferences. She is a co-leader of the SHU Core Curriculum reading- and writing-intensive core proficiency project and works closely with SHU's Teaching, Learning, and Technology Center on electronic portfolios, course management systems, and other pedagogy-improvement initiatives.

Anne Shiell (she/her) is a manager of writing instructional services in the Walden University Writing Center. She has presented on professional writing center staff and career paths at the International Writing Center Association (IWCA) conference, the Minnesota Writing and English conference, and the Association of Writers and Writing Programs conference. Her research interests include asynchronous writing tutoring and diversity, equity, and inclusion in writing center work.

Anna Sicari is currently an assistant professor of rhetoric and writing studies and director of the Writing Center at Oklahoma State University. She recently co-edited *Out in the Center: Public Controversies and Private Struggles,* which won the 2019 IWCA Outstanding Book Award.

Catherine Siemann is the Writing Center director at the New Jersey Institute of Technology. Her publications include chapters in *Twenty-First Century Popular Fiction, Ada's Legacy: Cultures of Computing from the Victorian to the Digital Age,* and articles in *Law and Literature* and *Nineteenth Century Gender Studies*. She is currently researching STEM students and writing center utilization, as well as writing historical fiction.

Meagan Thompson is a PhD student in American studies at William and Mary University. She earned her BA in English at Roanoke College and MA in English from Old Dominion University. She has presented at several conferences on topics related to writing center pedagogy, gender and queer theories, and cultural studies. She recently contributed an essay on the #MeToo movement to the anthology *Resistance in Pop Culture and Contemporary Culture* (2019). Her interests include trauma studies, queer theory, contemporary literature, and writing center pedagogy.

Lisa Nicole Tyson is the ePortfolio support coordinator at Old Dominion University (ODU). She has an MA in applied linguistics from ODU and has worked as both a professional writing tutor and a graduate writing tutor. Her research interests include tutoring discourse, digital literacy, and online tutoring. The main focus of her research aims to develop best practices for online tutoring, both synchronous and asynchronous.

Marcus Weakley, PhD, is the director of the Center for Writing and Rhetoric at Claremont Graduate University. His current research interests include developing heuristics for graduate-level writing center consulting and training as well as practices that integrate critical thinking and transdisciplinary concepts into writing center pedagogical approaches.

Alex Wulff is an assistant professor and the director of writing and multimodal composition at Maryville University. He teaches writing and rhetoric courses with an emphasis on writing across the disciplines. His research interests are in writing center scholarship, composition studies, and the long nineteenth century.

www.ingramcontent.com/pod-product-compliance
Lightning Source LLC
Chambersburg PA
CBHW031100080526
44587CB00011B/761